SOCIOLOGICAL REVIEW MON

Marital Violence

The Sociological Review

Managing Editors: John Eggleston, Ronald Frankenberg,
Gordon Fyfe

University of Keele

SOCIOLOGICAL REVIEW MONOGRAPH 31

Marital Violence

Edited by Norman Johnson

Routledge & Kegan Paul
London, Boston, Melbourne and Henley

First published in 1985
by Routledge & Kegan Paul plc

14 Leicester Square, London WC2H 7PH, England

9 Park Street, Boston, Mass. 02108, USA

464 St Kilda Road, Melbourne,
Victoria 3004, Australia and

Broadway House, Newtown Road,
Henley-on-Thames, Oxon RG9 1EN, England

Set in 10/12 IBM Press Roman
by Academic Typesetting, Gerrards Cross
and printed in Great Britain
by Billing & Sons Ltd, Worcester

© *The Sociological Review 1985*

Library of Congress Cataloging in Publication Data

Marital violence.

   (Sociological review monograph ; 31)
     1. Wife abuse—Great Britain—Addresses, essays,
lectures. 2. Abused wives—Services for—Great Britain
—Addresses, essays, lectures. 3. Family violence—
Great Britain—Addresses, essays, lectures.
I. Johnson, Norman, 1936-   . II. Series.
HM15.S545   no. 31   [HV6626]   301 s   [362.8'3]   84–15028

British Library CIP data also available

ISBN 0-7102-0448-5

Contents

Acknowledgments

I would like to thank Caroline Baggaley, Professor S.J. Eggleston and Professor R.J. Frankenberg for their help in the preparation of this volume.

Contributors

Mary Brailey
Housing Department, Falkirk District Council

Jenny Clifton
Social Services Department, London Borough of Camden

Anne Flitcraft
St Francis Hospital, Hartford, Connecticut

Michael D.A. Freeman
Faculty of Laws, University College London

Marjorie Homer
Cleveland Refuge and Aid for Women and Children

Norman Johnson
Department of Social Policy and Social Work, University of Keele

Anne Leonard
Cleveland Refuge and Aid for Women and Children

Susan Maidment
Department of Law, University of Keele

Patricia A. Morgan
Department of Social and Administrative Health Sciences,
University of California, Berkeley

Mildred Daley Pagelow
Department of Sociology, California State University, Long Beach and Fullerton

Evan Stark
Institute for Social and Policy Studies, Yale University

Pat Taylor
Cleveland Refuge and Aid for Women and Children

Editor's introduction

Norman Johnson

The problem of marital violence began to emerge as a significant issue in the early 1970s. The phenomenon of battered women was not, of course, by any means a new one. What was new was its recognition as a social problem requiring a political response. In Britain the response included a House of Commons Select Committee report, the formation of Women's Aid organizations in England, Scotland, Wales and Northern Ireland, considerable expansion of research interest and a corresponding increase in the number of publications. This quickening of interest was not confined to Britain. In the United States and several western European countries there was a similar development of media, academic and pressure group concern.

The intense media interest of the 1970s has now waned; the battering of women is no longer quite so newsworthy. However, as this collection of papers illustrates, academic interest has been maintained. One of the most valuable aspects of this interest is the wide span of disciplines involved: a variety which is reflected in this Monograph with contributions from Law, Medicine, Social Policy, Social Work and Sociology. A second useful feature of the study of marital violence is the opportunity it presents for making a strong link between theory and practice, and six of the contributors to the Monograph are both practitioners (in housing, medicine, refuge support and social work) and researchers.[1]

The first three papers deal with different aspects of accommodation for battered women. This is a recognition of the paramount importance of alternative accommodation if women are to escape from violent relationships. Susan Maidment examines the legal protection and remedies afforded in the Domestic Violence and Matrimonial Proceedings Act 1976, the Domestic Proceedings and Magistrates' Courts Act 1978 and the Housing (Homeless Persons) Act 1977. She argues that the legal remedies are available, but the ways in which they are used and

1

interpreted leave women without the necessary protection. Legal remedies in themselves can achieve little when faced with society's unwillingness to treat marital violence seriously.

Mary Brailey reports on research, conducted in four local authority areas in Scotland, into council house allocation following marital breakdown. She examines the assumptions and values which underlie house allocation policies and procedures, emphasizing the importance of alternative housing in helping women to break away from violent relationships. Finding alternative, permanent accommodation may be a lengthy process. In the meantime battered women will need temporary shelter. The refuges, provided chiefly by local organizations affiliated to the Women's Aid Federation England and its Scottish, Welsh and Northern Irish equivalents, meet this need.[2] Jenny Clifton's paper looks at refuge provision in the context of the ideology of the Women's Aid movement as a whole. She pays particular attention to the notions of self-help and democratic decision-making, and considers whether these principles are compatible with the practical requirements of running a refuge.

Patricia Morgan looks at the impact of state intervention on the problem of wife-battering. She considers the ways in which the state depoliticizes the issue by narrowing its definition, removing it from its class context and seeing it in terms of individual pathology rather than structure. Both the refuges and the image of the problem are transformed.

Involvement in the Cleveland Refuge prompted Marjorie Homer, Anne Leonard and Pat Taylor to carry out research into the problems of battered women in Middlesbrough. The first of the two papers based on this research examines the economic dependency of women and the patterns of control and distribution of income and expenditure within the family. The second paper considers the response of relatives, friends and neighbours to domestic violence against women. The authors identify the constraints which sometimes prevent women from seeking help from relatives and friends and which restrict the help that friends and relatives are prepared or able to offer.

It is clear from this and other research that women turn to people known to them, rather than to formal agencies, when they first seek help. Eventually, however, they may be driven to approach more formal sources of help. The paper by Norman Johnson looks at the response of the three statutory agencies most frequently approached by battered women – the police, social work and medical services.[3] Similar values and attitudes are revealed by all three agencies, and these produce similar, not particularly helpful, responses.

Marital rape, an aspect of domestic violence more frequently considered in the United States than in Britain, is the subject of Michael Freeman's paper. The relationship of rape to other forms of violence against women is examined, and Freeman argues that the immunity from prosecution in cases of marital rape should be removed.

Child abuse has always aroused much more sympathy and much greater public outrage than the battering of women. The paper by Evan Stark and Anne Flitcraft explores the relationship between these two forms of domestic violence. Evidence is produced to suggest that the battering of women may be a major precipitant of child abuse. Marital violence frequently provides the context within which child abuse occurs, either because the male batterer is also the child's assailant or because the mother abuses the child after her own battering is firmly established. The authors unequivocally reject the thesis that violence is intergenerationally transmitted.

The final paper, by Mildred Pagelow, directs our attention to the possibility of a 'battered husband syndrome'. She shows how the idea was first propounded by Steinmetz and taken up by the media in the late 1970s. Pagelow argues that marital violence is almost wholly directed against women. She does not deny that there are women who treat their male partners violently, but she does not believe that the phenomenon is sufficiently common, sustained and systematic to be termed a 'syndrome'.

In conclusion, it is worth stressing that none of the authors considers that his or her paper constitutes the last word on the particular aspect of marital violence that it addresses. Each paper is seen as a contribution to a continuing debate, and this Monograph will have served its purpose if it stimulates further discussion and research.

Notes

1 Cf. J. Hanmer and D. Leonard, 'Negotiating the problem: the DHSS and research on violence in marriage', in C. Bell and H. Roberts (eds), *Social Researching: Politics, Problems and Practice*, London, Routledge & Kegan Paul, 1984, pp. 32–53. The authors claim that in its funding of research the DHSS has systematically excluded the practitioners – Women's Aid.

2 See V. Binney, G. Harkell and J. Nixon, *Leaving Violent Men*, London, Women's Aid Federation England, 1981.

3 Housing services are covered by other authors and references to the main voluntary organizations in this field, Women's Aid Federation England and its Scottish, Welsh and Northern Irish counterparts, occur in the paper on refuges.

Domestic violence and the law: the 1976 Act and its aftermath

Susan Maidment

Abstract

This paper examines the parliamentary response to domestic violence as represented in three pieces of legislation: the Domestic Violence and Matrimonial Proceedings Act 1976, the Domestic Proceedings and Magistrates' Courts Act 1978 and the Housing (Homeless Persons) Act 1977. There is also briefer consideration of the role of criminal law, divorce and the possibility of using wardship procedures and actions in tort.

The author maintains that the most important need of battered women is the provision of alternative permanent accommodation, and that this must be the criterion by which the efficacy of the present law is judged. With this in mind, the provisions of the three major Acts are described and evaluated, with most attention going to the 1976 Act. Maidment's general conclusion is that the promises held out by the legislative reforms 'do not appear to have been fulfilled in practice'. The legal remedies are available, but the ways in which they are interpreted and implemented mean that battered women are inadequately protected. Violence against women has to be seen in the context of a patriarchal family system and the subordinate status of women. The law, on its own, cannot change deepseated public attitudes, although it may have an important symbolic and educative role to play in contributing to such a change.

The rediscovery of domestic violence as a social problem in the early 1970s elicited a substantial, and in some ways even admirable, legislative response in this country. The recommendations of the Select Committee on Violence in Marriage[1] in 1975 (the 'Select Committee') were crucial factors in the subsequent success of legislative reforms which sought to improve the legal remedies available to battered women. The Domestic Violence and Matrimonial Proceedings Act (the DVMPA), passed in 1976, and coming into force in 1977, was a private member's bill, introduced by Jo Richardson on the instigation of the National Women's Aid Federation, but it depended for its success on the government providing parliamentary time for its passage. It may therefore be appropriately treated as government supported legislation. Two years later reform of magistrates' matrimonial law, the Domestic Proceedings and Magistrates' Courts Act 1978 (the DPMCA), included new provisions giving magistrates power to issue orders for the protection of married women who had been subjected to physical violence. Between these two Acts specifically concerned with domestic violence, another piece of legislation concerned with clarifying and increasing the statutory responsibilities of local authority housing departments as regards homeless persons, the Housing (Homeless Persons) Act 1977 (the H(HP)A), had been tailored to include within its specific terms persons who had become homeless as a result of domestic violence.

These three Acts, their subsequent interpretation by the courts, and an evaluation of their effectiveness in providing legal protection for battered women form the basis of this review of the current state of the law.[2] Two major questions will, however, inform the exposition and discussion: firstly the extent to which legal remedies in and of themselves can solve the underlying social causes of domestic violence, and secondly, the extent to which the available legal remedies do provide satisfactory protection to the victims. The conclusion to the first may suggest that law reform, in itself necessary, may nevertheless be a smokescreen hiding the need for more fundamental changes in society; and the conclusion to the second may suggest that the ultimate powerlessness of the law could perhaps be mitigated somewhat if it were to be administered in the utmost good faith. In other words, while the law will never be enough to solve the social problem, it could perhaps do better.

A third issue concerns the current parameters of the debate. The practical resolution of the problems of domestic violence is now seen to be squarely based on the question of accommodation. The Select Committee had recognized the importance of refuges in providing an immediate place of safety for women who needed to leave home because of violence. Although no governmental response to this was forthcoming, local voluntary groups, often under the umbrella of the Women's Aid Federation, did substantially increase the amount of refuge provision in the late 1970s. What the empirical research and the cases coming to court now show is that the provision of alternative permanent accommodation for battered women is their most difficult and most practical need. It is against this current understanding that the efficiency of the present law must be measured.

The criminal law

The legislative response after 1975 was concerned essentially with improving the civil law remedies available to battered women. In some ways therefore this response was a statement about the virtues of decriminalization in this area.[3] As a result, developments since 1976 have left largely untouched the use of the criminal law in the protection of the victims and punishment of the perpetrators of domestic violence. Empirical evidence both before, after and to the Select Committee had testified to the general unwillingness of the police to prosecute in cases of domestic violence. All forms of physical domestic violence, and even some forms of emotional violence (e.g. threats of physical injury) do constitute criminal offences for which the perpetrator may be prosecuted. There is, however, no legally enforceable duty on the police to prosecute in any particular case, and their discretion in this seems in law to be absolute. There would be a ground of challenge to a police policy not to prosecute generally for domestic violence, but this is not in fact their policy, nor would it be easy to prove. The police practice, when called to a domestic violence incident, to suggest that the victim bring charges herself for a common assault, is clearly inadequate, since private prosecutions, though possible in England and Wales, require a certain amount of expertise and emotional courage. Since legal aid is not available for them, without expensive legal assistance, battered women are therefore unlikely in practice to take up this procedure.

The Select Committee was of the view that the police should prosecute more often, and in cases other than the most serious, which was then their practice. Pahl,[4] however, conducting her research between 1976 and 1980, found that the police were still being 'unhelpful', unless the couple were not married but living together, or married but not living in the same house.[5]

One of the explanations given by the police for their inaction has been challenged. Claims that women become 'reluctant victims', and refuse to proceed with police prosecutions which they have instigated, are not borne out. The Bedfordshire Police found that this occurred in only eighteen out of 104 cases (17 per cent),[6] and in the Stoke study[7] in only eight out of ninety-six cases (8 per cent). Both of these studies were conducted at a time when the woman was actually a compellable witness in law, i.e. she could have been *compelled* to give evidence against her husband. In 1978, however, the House of Lords decided that a wife should *not* be 'treated as a compellable witness against her husband in a case of violence on her by him' (*Hoskyn v Metropolitan Police Commissioner*[8]). The argument was based on a repugnance at forcing the wife against her will, and the discord and even perjury which might result. The dissenting judge suggested that law enforcement was too important in cases of serious injury to be left to depend on the wife's choice whether to give evidence, but also that some wives might be reluctant for reasons other than those of protecting their marriages or their husbands. The fear of, or threats from, her husband might equally be reasons for her reluctance.

The Police and Criminal Evidence Bill before Parliament at the time of writing intends to change the rule back, so that a spouse will be a compellable witness for the prosecution where the charge is one of violence against her or a child. The needs of law enforcement have therefore predominated. But the battered wife *need* not be compelled to give evidence; she *may* be compelled. The police as prosecutors could therefore recognize the reasons for her reluctance, and attempt to understand the ambivalence that many victims of domestic violence feel about their past treatment, and their fears of 'total upheaval and loss of security' which official and legal action incurs. [9] Where the wife's reluctance is due solely to fear of her husband, then compelling her to give evidence may help her; where she is confused as to whether she wants the prosecution to proceed, then compelling her *may* be detrimental to her real interests.

Some police forces did respond to the Select Committee's invitation. It has been widely reported[10] that when the Bedfordshire police did tighten up their prosecution policy, they were disappointed by the reluctance of the judiciary to impose anything other than a derisory sentence. Out of 288 calls to the police in a six month period, 81 per cent of the complaints were not pursued to trial, but out of the seventy-nine cases disposed of by the courts, only three resulted in immediate custodial sentences (i.e. less than 4 per cent). Nearly 26 per cent resulted only in the man being bound over to keep the peace.

One development which might have increased the use of the criminal law in domestic violence cases was the revised Criminal Injuries Compensation Scheme, which from 1 October 1979, allowed members of the same family who were living together to claim financial compensation under the government's *ex gratia* scheme. The conditions attached to such claims are 'normally' that the injuries are worth more than £500 (as judged by damages in a tort action), thus implying that only 'serious' injuries are included; that the offender will not benefit from the award; and that the offender has been prosecuted. It is not known whether the number of prosecutions has increased, or whether police attitudes have changed in consequence. What has emerged is the low take-up by this new eligible group, not surprising according to Wasik,[11] since normally prosecution is a condition precedent to the claiming of compensation. At one level therefore the Scheme 'reasserts the central role of the police and the criminal process in the provision of remedies for the victims of family violence'[12] while at the same time ignoring the reality.

The arguments over whether the use of the criminal law is a more appropriate societal response to domestic violence than the civil law[13] have not changed or abated. The unwillingness of the police, backed by the judiciary, and reflecting perhaps a wider societal perspective, to treat domestic disputes as crimes of violence is still opposed by those campaigning on behalf of the women victims. The educative function and social statement conveyed in the use of the criminal law that violent behaviour is unacceptable is often emphasized; so also is the appropriateness of the criminal law in identifying that 'the primary issue is the husband's conception of his rightful authority' rather than his personal pathology.[14]

The civil law: injunctions under the Domestic Violence Act 1976

The three main changes in the law as a result of the DVMPA were that injunctions were no longer available only as ancillary to other matrimonial proceedings, e.g. divorce; that cohabitees were entitled to injunctions on the same terms as married persons; and that the enforcement of injunctions could now directly involve the police whenever the judge had attached a power of arrest to the injunction.

The DVMPA did not affect the power of the courts to continue to issue injunctions in the course of matrimonial proceedings, and a substantial number of these are still ordered. In 1982, 1,673 matrimonial injunctions with a power of arrest were ordered, suggesting that the total number of matrimonial injunctions would have been nearly 7,000.[15] Nor did the DVMPA alter in any way the types of injunctions (non-molestation and exclusion/ouster), nor the grounds as developed by the judges in the cases on which they could be ordered. Non-molestation injunctions continue to be available for both physical and emotional violence. In 1982 a husband who was harassing his wife by sending threatening postcards and making frequent telephone calls to her place of work was ordered not to molest her (*Horner v Horner*[16]). In general there are few reported difficulties in persuading judges to make non-molestation injunctions; they are also available in emergencies, on an *ex parte* application (without notice to the other side). According to the Women's Aid Federation England (WAFE) survey,[17] however, ouster injunctions are 'not so easy, and the violence has to be proved severe'.

The initial willingness of the judiciary to take a sympathetic view of applications for injunctions was evident. The House of Lords in *Davis v Johnson* (1978)[18] ruled that the purpose of the new Act had been protection and that this must override any question of rights to property which may arise on a claim to exclude a property owner or tenant from his own home. The case also established beyond doubt that cohabitees were entitled to exactly the same protection as if they were married; and even if the cohabitation had actually ended by the time of the court hearing (*Maclean v Nugent*[19]). (Unmarried persons who do not live together 'as husband and wife' must still resort to the legal action for damages in tort with an ancillary injunction attached; divorced ex spouses may claim matrimonial injunctions from the divorce courts, but probably only where there is some outstanding issue arising from the divorce or it is necessary for the protection of the children, otherwise they too must seek an injunction in tort.)

The judges also developed the principle that ouster injunctions, though available in domestic violence cases, were not limited to those circumstances. In *Spindlow v Spindlow* (1970),[20] not a case of domestic violence, the court ruled that ouster injunctions under the DVMPA could be a means of resolving disputes over accommodation, i.e. who should stay in the home when the relationship or marriage had broken down and it was impossible for both parties to stay in peace. This principle is now well established, that the DVMPA, despite its title, does not only apply in domestic violence cases.

According to the *Judicial Statistics*, the success rate of applications for injunctions under the DVMPA is high. The most recent figures[21] confirm that the refusal rate has dropped from 8.4 per cent in 1977 to 2.8 per cent in 1982. In general then the rate of refusals is low, but the decreasing rate is probably explained by a more stringent vetting by solicitors before making an application to court in the light of comments made by senior judges about 'unmeritorious' applications. There have also been enormous variations in success rate over the country, depending presumably on the attitudes of particular judges: in 1979 this varied from 2.9 per cent refusals in the North Eastern Circuit to

12.3 per cent in the Western Circuit,[22] although by 1982 such vast differences had disappeared. The WAFE study[23] of women in refuges also found a much higher refusal rate, of as much as 55 per cent, although this may have been the very reason why the woman was in the refuge rather than at home.

Until 1983 the senior judges had also developed a considerably liberal view of the grounds on which ouster injunctions would be granted. Although they insisted on asking such questions as 'does either party *have* to leave?' (*Elsworth v Elsworth* (1979)[24]) and if yes, which one should it be (*Walker v Walker* (1978)[25]) by balancing the hardship that would be caused to each (*Bassett v Bassett* (1975)[26]), ultimately they saw the overriding issue as protecting the welfare of the children (*Samson v Samson* (1982)[27]). So the parent who would have care of the children would thus inevitably get the right to stay in the home. Since in most cases, in practice, the mother has custody by consent of the father, the injunction would require him to leave, and this would in many ways prejudge any custody issue which might arise in subsequent divorce proceedings. The criterion might also have the effect of benefiting indirectly one parent, who apart from the children's welfare, might be considered to be unmeritorious. It was this possibility of the mother staying in the home on her children's 'coat tails' which ultimately led to a major change in the law by the House of Lords in 1983 (*Richards v Richards*).[28]

Despite some positive developments, therefore, there was also a considerable and growing backlash. There is a widely held belief among the legal profession that injunctions are sought without justification. This, it is said, explains why women discontinue the proceedings. According to some Bristol solicitors,[29] this occurs in about a third of their cases; and Law Society estimates of emergency legal aid certificates discharged or revoked on proceedings being discontinued are similar.[30] The Booth Committee on Matrimonial Causes Procedure (1983),[31] made up of representatives from all those professionally involved, from a judge to a probation officer, reports similar conclusions:

> Injunctions and orders are frequently sought without any, or any
> sufficient, prior effort to seek the cooperation of the respondent
> spouse. In our experience it is too often the case that the first
> intimation of such proceedings comes to a husband when he is
> served with an application for an order that he should leave the
> matrimonial home. . . . There is no effective sanction against an
> applicant who seeks this form of relief without proper cause. It is
> sometimes the case that ouster orders are sought in order to give

one party an apparent tactical advantage over the other in securing the occupation of the matrimonial home for an indefinite period.[32]

It is not possible to substantiate or deny these claims empirically in the absence of further research. One fruitful source of enquiry might, however, be to study the relationship between the 7,691 applications for injunctions under the DVMPA in 1982 and the 72,320 petitions for divorce on the grounds of unreasonable behaviour, many of which will contain allegations of violence. One might hypothesize at this stage a surprise that there are not more injunction applications.

The judicial backlash has been evident for some years now. This has been so particularly in the context of limiting the availability of ouster injunctions. *Elsworth v Elsworth* (1979)[33] was considered to be a timely reminder from the Court of Appeal that the initial and fundamental question always had to be whether it was really necessary for either party to leave, rather than assuming that this was the case, and then asking which party it should be. By 1977 concerns at unnecessary *ex parte* injunctions had been voiced; according to the President of the Family Division, as many as 50 per cent were unmeritorious, i.e. they were made 'days or even weeks after the last incident of which complaint was made'. He thought that they wasted time, caused expense to the legal aid fund, were unjust to husbands, and ruled that they should only be allowed in cases of 'real immediate danger of serious injury or irreparable damage'.[34] Ouster injunctions in particular will never be made *ex parte*, unless the case is really exceptional (*Masich v Masich* (1977)[35]). According to the Booth Committee (1983), ouster injunctions are now never granted *ex parte*.[36]

The unavailability of *ex parte* ouster injunctions creates serious practical difficulties for women. The effect is that an alleged victim must either suffer the threat of further violence, or leave home pending an opportunity to put her case in court. The alternative would merely be that the man would have to leave home for a short period before an early court hearing. The present practice may explain why ouster injunctions are not seen as a particularly helpful remedy to women.

Powers of arrest are also only attached in exceptional circumstances. The Select Committee had argued very strongly that injunctions would not be able to be enforced unless the police were given this responsibility, and WAFE continues to hold this view.[37] The DVMPA section 2 nevertheless limited the circumstances in which the power of arrest could be attached: there must already have been actual physical violence and the judge must be satisfied that it is likely to occur again. Even so, the judges have said that powers of arrest are not to be attached as a routine matter (*Lewis v Lewis* (1978)[38]). In practice, powers of arrest are only attached to ouster injunctions;[39] according to WAFE the violence had to be even more severe and persistent for the judge to attach them, and a power of arrest had little effect upon police willingness to arrest and prosecute;[40] and Migdal[41] reported that the police still prefer, if they do anything, to arrest for breach of the peace or breaking and entering rather than for breach of the injunction, because in this way they are not bound by the terms of the DVMPA to bring the offender before a judge within 24 hours (excluding Sundays).

The *Judicial Statistics* show that nationally only about 25 per cent of injunctions under the DVMPA have a power of arrest attached. Again, however, there have been sharp regional variations: in 1982 from 13 per cent in the North Eastern Circuit to 34 per cent in the South Eastern Circuit (including outer London). Where a power of arrest is not attached, the ordinary law enforcement machinery of the civil courts must be used to enforce injunctions which are being broken. The evidence to the Select Committee of the inadequacy of the bailiffs and tipstaffs, and the recommendations that the police should arrest more often for criminal offences which occur as a result of a breach of an injunction are still as pertinent as they were then.

The major change in the law on the granting of ouster injunctions came with *Richards v Richards* in 1983.[42] The House of Lords ruled that the welfare of the child was not the 'first and paramount consideration', but that other considerations such as the 'conduct of the spouses' were also relevant. There was no precedent for this surprising decision, and it is alleged[43] that the court was influenced by Lord Chancellor Hailsham's view that 'conduct' ought to be reintroduced into matrimonial disputes, especially in questions of maintenance. The significance of the decision is particularly important where the DVMPA is being used to get an ouster injunction in cases where there has been no violence. Mrs Richards wanted her husband out, on the claim that she would be caring for the children, although it was she who had had the affairs which may have caused the breakdown of the marriage. In cases of domestic violence, with which this paper is dealing, the victim should still be able to get an injunction, since it will be the man's conduct which will be in issue. The reintroduction of conduct as a consideration does, however, mean that the man may make counter-allegations about the woman's own conduct, and at the least the court will have to allow evidence on this and make some judgment about it. In other words, the door has been opened to a full scale 'washing of the dirty linen in public' even if the woman is eventually granted an injunction on the particular facts of the case.

The final development of note concerns the judicial interpretation[44] that injunctions are only a first aid or short term remedy, rather than a long term solution, and that normally they will not be granted in the first instance for more than three months (though they are renewable). The same ruling has been made about powers of arrest.[45] The origin of this three months' rule is the problem that while ouster injunctions do not alter the property rights of the parties they clearly do interfere with them. The judges are therefore encouraging the parties to use the injunction period to take further legal or even practical steps to arrange a long term solution to their accommodation. For the married woman, there are at least legal procedures whereby she can seek permanent orders, and this is regardless of the type of property, whether owned, privately or council rented. She may apply under the Matrimonial Homes Act 1967/1983 for an ouster order to protect her right of occupation, on the same grounds as under the DVMPA, and these orders may be more permanent than injunctions. She may also petition for divorce, and apply for an order protecting her right of occupation in the matrimonial home. As yet divorce law has not reintroduced 'conduct' into this decision, and the practice has been to ensure above all else that the home is secured for the children's accommodation, and by implication their caretaker's too (*Mesher v Mesher* (1980)[46]). (Whether this will change under the influence of the new Matrimonial and Family Proceedings Act 1984 which elevates 'conduct' to a new significance in all financial and property questions following divorce is impossible to predict.)

For the cohabitee, there are no special procedures for longer term orders. In the case of owned property, she may be able to prove in court that she owns a share of it by virtue of financial contributions that she may have made to its purchase, and if so, she may be able to persuade the court to protect her and her children's occupation of their home until they are grown up (in the same way that the divorce courts do) (*Re Evers* (1980)[47]). Even if she cannot prove any share of the ownership, she may be able to show that she has a contractual licence to live in the home until the children are grown up (*Tanner v Tanner* (1975)[48]). In the case of property rented by the man either solely or jointly with her, the problem is that he is in law a secure tenant, both in private rented property and also now in council property (Housing Act 1980). In the private sector a request to a landlord to assign a tenancy (unless it contains a covenant against assignment) should be granted if it is reasonable, and the evidence of an ouster injunction should be sufficient proof. In the public sector, the Housing Act 1980, which gave legal security to council tenants for the first time, indirectly created great difficulties in cases of violence. The man's secure tenancy cannot be assigned, unless he has lost his right of security, for example by non payment of rent, or causing a nuisance etc. So whereas prior to 1980 some local authorities willingly transferred tenancies to former cohabitees who had an injunction, this is no longer legally possible except by consent of the tenant. All attempts by WAFE to amend the law to include domestic violence as a ground for removing security of tenure have so far failed.

In the light of the above legal developments it is useful to compare the experiences of battered women in using the DVMPA. The WAFE study investigated the housing problems of women in refuges:

> Few women in the survey wanted to go back to their previous homes, but some were being forced by the housing authority to pursue this route to permanent accommodation. While 30% of women in the survey were trying this route to housing, only 8% were successful and a year later, only 4% were still living in their former homes. It was clear from this research that without much more effective protection, this was not a viable housing option for most women.[49]

For these women, injunctions under the DVMPA are one method of returning home. Sometimes, however, it was forced on them by the local authority; and indeed the DVMPA was used as a ground for refusing to treat battered women as homeless. Thirty-two women had obtained exclusion orders but were still living in refuges because they were afraid to go back home or the man had not moved out. Although one third of the women were trying to get rights to go back home, only 16 per cent actually wanted to return. They feared for their safety, had bad memories, or feared the response of neighbours.

These findings cannot be extrapolated to women who do not go to refuges, but raise serious questions about the policy underpinning ouster injunctions. For some women, going back home is not a desirable solution, even on a short term basis. No conclusions are possible without fuller information on which women seek injunctions and why, and how far staying at home represents a permanent solution. According to a SHAC study,[50] battered women from owner occupied homes tended to have their partners legally excluded, while women from local authority tenancies did not. For many lower class women refuges in the short term and local authority rehousing in the longer term are clearly more viable outcomes. For many women as well, divorce and the discretionary powers of the court to deal with the matrimonial home (*infra*) will present a long term solution.

The magistrates' courts: family protection orders

The DPMCA 1978 introduced for the first time coercive orders in the magistrates' courts against domestic violence: personal protection orders, akin to non-molestation injunctions, and exclusion orders, akin to ouster injunctions. The magistrates may issue *ex parte* protection orders, but not exclusion orders without notice to the other side. Their powers are therefore limited even more than the county court, and equally problematic in this respect. They may also attach powers of arrest on the same terms as the county court. The fundamental differences between the DVMPA and the DPMCA are of three kinds: the magistrates can only grant orders to married persons, they cannot deal with anything other than *physical* violence, and they are bound by very strict statutory criteria. There may therefore be cases where an application may be appropriately made to either court; there may also be cases, such as those involving cohabitees or emotional violence, where only the county courts have jurisdiction. Since no magistrates' court matrimonial statistics have been published for some years, it is not known how applications to the two different courts compare nor how this varies regionally. What is likely, however, is that the choice of court, if it is available, has been determined by solicitors' practices and traditions and confidence in the quality of decision-making rather than by the intrinsic nature of the case. The government has also now put pressure on the Legal Aid fund to require that solicitors normally commence proceedings in the magistrates' court where there is an alternative.[51]

Divorce

The major achievement of the DVMPA was to make injunctions available to married women without having to commence divorce proceedings. The principle remains appropriate, for the purpose of the injunction is to gain immediate legal protection without having to make decisions about the long term future of the relationship. The irony, however, is that divorce for battered women is now seen as 'a most suitable solution ... rather than an unfortunate alternative'.[52] Dobash and Dobash[53] report that divorce is not lightly entered into, and that

15

all the factors which operate against women leaving home in the first place also militate against the breaking of the relationship through divorce. Borkowski *et al.*[54] also reported that going to a solicitor for legal advice was an ultimate rather than early response in these cases.

Once the decision to divorce is taken, English law makes it unlikely that a woman will not succeed. Her petition will be based on irretrievable breakdown of marriage as evidenced by her husband's behaviour, such that she cannot reasonably be expected to live with him (Matrimonial Causes Act 1973, s.1(2)(b)). 'Unreasonable behaviour' is the most common ground of divorce, used in 40 per cent of all petitions. Over 99 per cent of petitions are in practice undefended, and go through under the Special Procedure without a court hearing. Even if the husband does want to defend, it is unlikely that he will pursue this through to trial, and even if he did, his violent behaviour will satisfy the judge that there are grounds for divorce. As ancillary to the divorce decree, the woman will be able to claim custody of any children, financial support for herself and the children, and ownership, or at the least, occupation of the matrimonial home.

Where the couple have been married for less than three years, under the present law a divorce petition can only be presented if the petitioner is suffering exceptional hardship, or the respondent has been exceptionally depraved. In these cases, prior leave to present the petition has to be given by a judge. In 1982, 1,906 applications were made for leave, and it is estimated that only about 5 per cent are refused. This merely indicates that lawyers are very careful before allowing applications to go forward. In principle, however, cases of serious violence ought to attract the permission to petition for divorce within the first three years of marriage.

The Matrimonial and Family Proceedings Act 1984 has removed the three-year discretionary bar and replaced it with a one year absolute bar. In future no divorce petition will be possible until one year after marriage, although the evidence for the divorce may have arisen within the first year. The purpose of the new rule is to show due respect for the institution of marriage and prevent impetuous petitions too early. One need only add that Scotland has never had any time bar to divorce.

It is predictable therefore than in cases of serious violence occurring soon after the marriage, the new rule will cause some distress. Continuing violence after divorce is also a problem.[55] The DVMPA cannot be used since the parties are no longer married or cohabiting. The only possibility is an injunction ancillary to the divorce proceedings, but it is still an open question whether the divorce court can issue an injunction when there are no further issues outstanding arising out of the divorce, e.g. financial matters. There is, however, authority for the view that the divorce court will always intervene at any stage to protect the welfare of the children of the marriage (*Stewart v Stewart* (1973)[56]).

Other legal procedures

There are other ways in which a battered woman *with a child* might be able to get an injunction, and this would be so either as an alternative to existing procedures, or even in circumstances where other procedures are unavailable, e.g. in the case of the divorced woman, or of the 'guilty' woman against whom the *Richards v Richards* (*supra*) rule operates. Wardship is a legal procedure designed solely and centrally to protect children. Anyone with a genuine interest in the child's welfare can ward the child and seek the court's directions on any matters relevant to the child's welfare. Wardship is particularly useful as an emergency measure, since an *ex parte* application itself makes the child a ward of court for twenty-one days (with a further *application* for a hearing of the case necessary to continue the wardship beyond that period), and the court then has jurisdiction to issue ancillary injunctions. Judges have therefore granted a battered mother non-molestation and ouster injunctions against the father in order to protect the ward.

The action in tort (for assault and battery or trespass) for damages has already been mentioned as a possible method of getting an ancillary injunction, and of particular use to non-cohabitees (e.g. boyfriend and girlfriend) or even divorcees. There is no reason, however, why a wife should not sue her husband in tort with the aim of getting financial compensation for injuries suffered. A case has been reported[57] in which a wife, who had already petitioned for divorce, sued her husband, and received £9,605 damages and her costs for a broken nose and cheekbone which resulted in double vision and an ENT problem. These damages were separate from any financial provision on divorce that she might claim although they would be taken into account as part of her resources in calculating how much financial provision she would be ordered.

Rehousing

The H(HP)A 1977 remains the most viable solution to finding alternative long term housing for non-owner occupier women, and for women in refuges, the majority of whom, as WAFE found, do not want to return home, even with an injunction. The H(HP)A 1977, while providing for homeless persons in general and homeless persons with dependent children in particular, did have battered women specifically in mind as a category who might make use of its provisions. Thus a person is defined as homeless in section 1(2) if he has accommodation but 'it is probable that occupation of it will lead to violence from some other person residing in it or to threats of violence from some other person residing in it and likely to carry out the threats'. Homeless persons with dependent children or who are pregnant are deemed to have a priority need for accommodation (s.2). A woman who leaves her husband and home may, however, be held to be intentionally homeless 'if it would have been reasonable for [her] to occupy . . . accommodation which is available for [her] occupation' (s.17). The Code of Guidance issued with the Act (but not a definitive legal interpretation) says that 'a battered woman who has fled the marital home should *never* be regarded as having become homeless intentionally because it would clearly not be reasonable for her to remain'.

The local authority duty to rehouse only applies, therefore, where the battered woman is pregnant or has a dependent child, is homeless, and is not intentionally homeless. But the battered woman must first satisfy the housing department that she is homeless, i.e. that violence is *probable* if she goes back home, and that it is not *reasonable* to expect her to go back. Both of these criteria raise difficult questions of evidence for the woman to prove in the face of local authority disbelief. According to the WAFE study,[58] 32 per cent of women in the survey applying for rehousing were refused on the grounds that they were not homeless; in some cases because they could not show visible bruising or produce evidence of assault. In some cases they were said not to be homeless because they had accommodation in a refuge. In *R v Ealing Borough Council ex p. Sidhu* (1982)[59] the court held that this argument was 'totally unjustified' and 'deeply regrettable'; it was important that refuges be seen as temporary crisis accommodation, and women in refuges were 'homeless'. In 8 per cent of cases women were refused housing on the grounds of intentional homelessness; either because they had left home voluntarily, or had turned down the first offer of accommodation. Nine per cent were refused as not being in priority need, even though they were pregnant (see s.2(2)) or had no dependent children (but according to the Code of Guidance, single battered women should qualify as having a priority need, as being 'vulnerable' (s.2(1)(c)).

In *R v Ealing Borough Council ex p. Sidhu* (1982)[60] the court also rejected the local authority practice of requiring a final custody order before accepting that the applicant had a priority need for housing because of dependent children. The question of dependence was a question of fact, not conditional on a prior court order. According to WAFE[61] 20 per cent of women reported that the local authority had insisted on a divorce or custody order before accepting their duty. This is no longer lawful, and in any case was contrary to the Code of Guidance. In some cases local authorities were insisting that women have the tenancy of the previous home transferred to them (though there could be legal complications in this, as described earlier); or that they pay off rent arrears (although in *Williams v Cynon Valley District Council* (1980)[62] the court confirmed that a non-tenant wife is not responsible for her husband's rent arrears).

The *Ealing* case[63] is important because by extrapolation it suggests that any precondition, such as a divorce petition, custody order or injunction (e.g. ouster injunction[64]) or any other precondition which has to be met before the local authority accepts its duty to rehouse, is unlawful. In all cases the local authority must satisfy itself *on the facts* whether the applicant qualifies under the Act. As the Code of Guidance says 'the fact that violence has not yet occurred does not, on its own, suggest that it is not likely to occur'. And in any case non-molestation orders or injunctions are clearly no guarantee that further violence may not be feared or even occur.

Another major problem for battered women applying under the H(HP)A is the question of 'local connection', i.e. which local authority is responsible for them. According to section 5, the local authority to which the application is made has no duty if the applicant has no local connection, and has a local connection in another area, *and* there is no *'risk'* of domestic violence' (compare section 1 which talks of 'prob-ability') in that other area. Again the woman must be able to satisfy the housing department of the risk of domestic violence if she goes back home and there are the same problems of proof as already described, although the Code of Guidance says that the 'fears of those concerned' are a relevant consideration. Seventy-five per cent of women in the WAFE survey who applied for rehousing had applied to the 'refuge local authority', and the question of local connection was therefore a frequent one. Section 18 defines a local connection as being normally resident by choice, employed, or having family associations, or other special circumstances. The *Agreement on Procedures for Referrals of the Homeless* (1979), entered into by local authorities to interpret their duties with respect to each other (but not legally binding), says that a refuge does not qualify as a 'residence of choice'. Nor is it 'normal' if it is 'temporary welfare accommodation', and the *Agreement* suggests as a working definition of 'normal residence' six months out of the past twelve months and/or three out of the past five years (and *R v East-leigh Borough Council ex p. Betts* (1983)[65] upheld the reasonableness of this definition). 'Family associations' are defined as parents, adult children, brothers or sisters residing in the area.

R v Bristol City Council ex p. Browne (1979)[66] suggests that local authority rejection of an application on the grounds that there is no risk of domestic violence in the area where the applicant from a refuge has a local connection, will not be easy to challenge. Mrs Browne and her seven children had escaped from her violent husband in the Republic of Ireland to a Bristol refuge. The Bristol City Council rejected her application for rehousing on the grounds that, contrary to her claim, she would not run a risk of further violence if she went back to her home in Ireland, since the local welfare officer had arranged new accommodation for her. According to the judge, the local authority had considered the application properly, and was entitled to conclude that the fact that she had suffered violence in the past 'does not mean that she would necessarily suffer any risk of violence if she goes back'.

The duty to rehouse if the woman qualifies is to 'secure that accommodation becomes available for [her] occupation' (s.4(5)). According to section 6 this duty can be fulfilled by making accommodation available, securing that accommodation is obtained from some other person, or giving such advice and assistance as will secure that accommodation is obtained from some other person. According to the Code of Guidance, permanent accommodation should be provided as soon as possible. Mobile homes are not regarded as suitable for children. If permanent accommodation is unavailable, interim accommodation must be used, such as hostels, refuges, bed and breakfast 'but only as a last resort'. According to WAFE women could remain for six months to one year in a refuge awaiting local authority accommodation; according to the DOE Homelessness Statistics 1978 (unpublished), compared to the homeless generally, fewer battered women were rehoused directly, and excluding those referred to a hostel or a refuge, more were put into bed and breakfast accommodation.

Mrs Browne in the Bristol refuge was offered advice and assistance by the Bristol City Council in order to secure the offer of accommodation from her Irish welfare officer. The court held that the Council's offer of her travel arrangements and paid tickets back to Ireland fulfilled its duty under section 6.

The final difficulty of the H(HP)A concerns the procedure for challenging local authority decisions considered wrong. The local authority is required to give reasons for its decisions (s.8), but no right of appeal against the decision is given by the Act, nor is there any specific enforcement machinery to ensure that the local authority carries out its duties properly.

There is, however, a general legal procedure that can be used to challenge local authority statutory decisions: this is the application for judicial review in the High Court. It is nevertheless a limited remedy in a number of ways. Firstly, the ordinary person is not aware of its existence; lawyers are not usually familiar with it, certainly not as an emergency (interim) measure; and legal aid may be difficult to get for such proceedings. Secondly, the grounds for the application are restrictive: it is not an appeal, and therefore a challenge to the *merits* of the decision cannot be made. The grounds for review must be that the local authority did not exercise its discretion properly, either by wrongly interpreting the law, by following incorrect procedures or by abusing its discretion, e.g. by having an improper purpose, by taking into account irrelevant considerations, by taking an unreasonable decision, by acting in bad faith, or by having an inflexible blanket policy. It may also be that the rules of natural justice must be followed so that the local authority must give the applicant an opportunity to fairly state his case so that it is informed of all the arguments before taking its decision.

The application for judicial review is now the only legal procedure for challenging local authority statutory decisions. Earlier examples of bringing actions in tort in the county court for breach of statutory duty have now been overruled (*Cocks v Thanet District Council* (1982)[67]). The application for judicial review does, however, allow the applicant to claim damages, as well as an injunction (to prevent the local authority continuing to operate its unlawful decision), or for an order of certiorari (to quash the decision) or mandamus (to order the local authority to take a fresh decision).

There are also non-judicial remedies which may be useful.[68] In particular, a complaint to the Local Commissioner for Administration (local 'Ombudsman') of 'maladministration' by the local authority may be made. This is again not a challenge to the merits of the decision but to the way in which the decision was taken. It might be, for example, failure to follow the Code of Guidance.[69] Several successful claims of maladministration under the H(HP)A have in fact been made.[70]

For those battered women in refuges most likely to seek rehousing in council accommodation, the H(HP)A, despite its particular applicability in domestic violence cases, has not it seems been interpreted altogether in their favour. In the WAFE survey 'less than half the

Women's Aid groups thought that the housing prospects of women in their refuge had improved since the Act came into effect'.[71] Some felt that local authorities had tightened up their criteria in order to limit their responsibilities towards the homeless, and any initial gains had been eroded by spending cuts. The problems that remain are local authority attitudes towards battered women, as well as the lack of appropriate accommodation for them.

Conclusions

Both lawyers (e.g. Freeman;[72] Maidment[73]) and sociologists (e.g. Dobash and Dobash;[74] Wilson[75]) agree that the problem of violence against women is a deep societal one, arising out of a patriarchal family system' in which husbands' 'authority over their wives' creates a particular 'marriage power relationship' and a 'subordinate status to wives and mothers'.[76]

That premise is important in recognizing the limitations of legal procedures in relieving the needs of battered women. The law itself and the availability of legal protection cannot alone change social attitudes, although they may play an important symbolic and educative role conducing to such change. The operation of the law, however, as has been seen particularly in the areas of police response, ouster injunctions and rehousing duties, is vulnerable to official interpretations which derive from the basic premise.

The current state of English law on domestic violence is therefore of a legal system which provides *all* the necessary remedies, but which in its operation fails to protect women as fully as it should. As Freeman says, recognition 'that the lawyer has a limited role in combating domestic violence should nevertheless not underestimate what a good lawyer can do to help women who have been battered'.[77]

The challenge to the legal system rests on the evidence that women do not resort lightly to legal action. The breakdown of a relationship, whether for reasons of violence or otherwise, is a long process, in which resort to a lawyer is a carefully considered and ultimate resolution.[78] That is not to say that the man's side of the case has no validity (the 'his' and 'hers' versions of marriage breakdown are well documented)[79] and judicial resolution of disputes will remain an unenviable necessity. But the woman's claim for a legal response deserves full sympathy and consideration.[80]

At present the promises of legal protection for battered women held out by the legislative reforms of the late 1970s do not appear to have been fulfilled in practice. One suspects they are an improvement, although the absence of better empirical information makes this assessment difficult. What has emerged is that the two major issues in the protection of women are a need for greater use of criminal penalties, including imprisonment, and the provision of separate accommodation. Ouster injunctions have become increasingly difficult to get, and are not available as an emergency interim arrangement. They may become even more difficult following the reintroduction of 'conduct' as a legal consideration. While to owner occupier women injunctions to return home are an appropriate remedy, to women in rented property, rehousing by the local authority in the long run (and short term use of refuges) appears to be the desired solution.

If housing provision is the real issue, the future provision of legal remedies needs to be informed by fuller and better information on the effectiveness of injunctions (and divorce court property orders) in securing safe accommodation for women. (For example, recent evidence that most divorced women who remarry go to live in accommodation provided by their new husbands is an important consideration.[81]) It may be that the DVMPA was a pyrrhic victory. If it was, and public housing, temporary, and permanent, is the only practical solution, then the law will be powerless in the absence of fuller housing stock and public spending.

Ultimately the effectiveness of the legal remedies is limited by society's unwillingness to cope with the problem of domestic violence. The widespread scepticism of the efficacy of legal remedies is therefore not the fault of the law; it is the problem of the people who operate the law in the way they assume society approves.

Notes

1 House of Commons Select Committee on Violence in Marriage, Report HC 553 (1974/75), London, HMSO.
2 A general review of domestic violence law is not provided here. It is assumed that readers are familiar with the general outlines. For a statement of the law in the late 1970s, see M.D.A. Freeman, *Violence in the Home*, London, Saxon House, 1979; S. Maidment, 'The law's response to marital violence' in J. Eekelaar and S. Katz (eds), *Family Violence: An International and Interdisciplinary Study*, Canada, Butterworths, 1978, pp. 110–40; S. Maidment, 'Civil v criminal: the use of legal remedies in response to domestic violence in England and Wales', *Victimology*, 1983, vol. 8, pp. 172–87.
3 Maidment, op. cit., 1983.
4 J. Pahl, 'Police response to battered women', *Journal of Social Welfare Law*, 1982, pp. 337–43.

5 Ibid., p. 340.
6 Cited in Freeman, op. cit., p. 190.
7 B. Dawson and T. Faragher, *Battered Women's Project: Interim Report*, University of Keele, 1979.
8 [1978] 2 All E.R. 136.
9 M. Borkowski, M. Murch and V. Walker, *Marital Violence*, London, Tavistock, 1983.
10 Freeman, op. cit., p. 190.
11 M. Wasik, 'Criminal injuries compensation and family violence', *Journal of Social Welfare Law*, 1983, pp. 100–8.
12 Ibid., p. 104.
13 Maidment, op. cit., 1983.
14 R.E. Dobash and R. Dobash, *Violence Against Wives*, London, Open Books, 1980.
15 *Judicial Statistics* (1982), 1983, London, HMSO. Since *Richards v Richards* [1983] 3 WLR 173, however, all injunctions in the course of matrimonial proceedings have to be commenced by an application for an order under the Matrimonial Homes Act 1983, Section 1.
16 [1982] 2 All E.R. 495.
17 V. Binney, G. Harkell and J. Nixon, *Leaving Violent Men: A Study of Refuges and Housing for Battered Women*, London, Women's Aid Federation England, 1981, p. 85.
18 [1978] 1 All E.R. 1132.
19 [1979] 9 *Family Law* 163.
20 [1979] 1 All E.R. 169.
21 *Judicial Statistics* (1982), op. cit.
22 This was also noted by S. Migdal between different courts in the West Midlands area: S. Migdal, 'Domestic violence: has the act beaten it?' *Family Law*, 1979, vol. 9, pp. 136–9.
23 Binney, Harkell and Nixon, op. cit.
24 (1979) 9 *Family Law* 21.
25 [1978] 3 All E.R. 141.
26 [1975] 1 All E.R. 513.
27 [1982] 1 WLR 252.
28 [1983] 3 WLR 173.
29 Borkowski, Murch and Walker, op. cit.
30 Lord Chancellor's Office, *29th Legal Aid Annual Report*, 1979, London, HMSO.
31 Lord Chancellor's Department, Matrimonial Cause Procedure Committee (Chairman, The Hon. Mrs J. Booth), *Consultation Paper*, 1983.
32 Ibid., pp. 38–9.
33 (1979) 9 *Family Law* 21.
34 *Practice Note* [1978] 2 All E.R. 919.
35 (1977) 7 *Family Law* 245.
36 Lord Chancellor's Department, op. cit., p. 37.
37 Binney, Harkell and Nixon, op. cit., p. 85.
38 [1978] 1 All E.R. 729.
39 *Practice Note* [1981] 1 All E.R. 224.
40 Binney, Harkell and Nixon, op. cit., p. 85.
41 Migdal, op. cit.

42 [1983] 1 WLR 173.
43 *Legal Action Group Bulletin*, November 1983, pp. 1–2.
44 *Practice Note* [1978] 2 All E.R. 1056.
45 *Practice Note* [1981] 1 All E.R. 224.
46 *Mesher v Mesher* (1973) [1980] 1 All E.R. 126.
47 [1980] 1 WLR 1327.
48 [1975] 3 All E.R. 776.
49 Binney, Harkell and Nixon, op. cit., p. xv.
50 SHAC, *Violence in Marriage*, from SHAC, 189A Old Brompton Road, London S.W.5.
51 Legal Aid Handbook 1983, pp. 198–202 (in *New Law Journal*, 9 March 1984, p. 216).
52 Dobash and Dobash, op. cit., p. 239.
53 Ibid.
54 Borkowski, Murch and Walker, op. cit.
55 Dobash and Dobash, op. cit., p. 240.
56 [1973] 1 All E.R. 31.
57 *New Law Journal*, 9 April 1983, p. 317.
58 Binney, Harkell and Nixon, op. cit.
59 (1982) 80 LGR 534.
60 Ibid.
61 Binney, Harkell and Nixon, op. cit.
62 (1980) *Legal Action Group Bulletin* 16.
63 (1982) 80 LGR 534.
64 It was reported in *Roof*, November 1980, p. 159, January 1981, p. 4, that some local authorities view the gaining of an injunction as removing the need for rehousing.
65 (1983) *The Times*, July 30.
66 [1979] 3 All E.R. 344.
67 [1982] 3 All E.R. 1135.
68 D. Hoath, *Homelessness*, London, Sweet and Maxwell, 1983, ch. 6.
69 D.J. Hughes, *Public Sector Housing Law*, Butterworths, 1981.
70 Hoath, op. cit., p. 211.
71 Binney, Harkell and Nixon, op. cit., p. 84.
72 Freeman, op. cit.
73 Maidment, op. cit., 1983.
74 Dobash and Dobash, op. cit.
75 E. Wilson, *What is to be done about Violence against Women?*, Harmondsworth, Penguin, 1983.
76 Dobash and Dobash, op. cit., passim.
77 M.D.A. Freeman, 'Dealing with domestic violence', *Family Law*, 1979, vol. 9, p. 111.
78 Borkowski, Murch and Walker, op. cit.
79 J. Bernard, *The Future of Marriage*, Harmondsworth, Penguin, 1976.
80 Pahl, op. cit.; Maidment, op. cit., 1978.
81 M. Mclean and J. Eeekelaar, *Children and Divorce: Economic Factors*, Oxford, SSRC Centre for Socio Legal Studies, 1983.

Making the break

Mary Brailey

Abstract

Mary Brailey's paper reports on research into the rehousing of
women after marital breakdown in four local authority areas in
Scotland. The four areas represented a range of allocation and homelessness policies. The paper identifies the underlying assumptions of
rehousing policies in cases of marital breakdown. One such assumption is that people fabricate stories of breakdown, manipulating the
housing system in order to secure a house, move to a better house
or evade rent arrears. The research uncovered no evidence of such
abuse; most women did not have a sufficiently sophisticated knowledge of the housing system to manipulate it in the manner suggested.
Another assumption is that marital breakdown is a 'bad thing'
and that reconciliation is to be preferred. This leads to procedures
designed to give the parties time for reconsideration, minimum
separation periods being stipulated by some authorities.

In the four areas studied the proportion of battered women
whose applications for rehousing were successful varied from 19 per
cent to 52 per cent; they were usually denied access to the better
housing. The author argues that if the underlying assumptions were
changed, there would be scope for effective change within the
existing framework of law and local government operations.

Introduction

Increasing numbers of women are taking the step of leaving violent or
abusive men. Nonetheless, it takes a great deal of courage to leave an
established relationship and home and launch out into the unknown.
Many women, grossly disadvantaged in terms of access to decent private

housing, are dependent on their local authority as a source of housing.[1] Research recently carried out in Scotland concluded that housing department policies and procedures rest on an essentially negative view of marital breakdown. Yet this view was contradicted by the women who had managed to make the break to independent housing and who were extremely positive about their new lives and about the decision to separate.

This paper examines how the negative view of marital breakdown determines the housing department approach and how that approach could change with the recognition that the phenomenon of women leaving violent men is essentially a positive one.

The research

First, a few words should be said about the study itself. The aim of the research, which was funded by the Equal Opportunities Commission and carried out during 1981-2, was to look at problems faced by women in gaining access to council housing. It concentrated particularly on women applying for housing as a result of the breakdown of a relationship.

It was not intended to focus specifically on those relationships characterized by domestic violence, since it was felt that this had already received more attention in the housing field than non-violent relationships.[2] But a startling proportion of 'marital breakdown' applicants were experiencing domestic violence - between 40 per cent and 65 per cent.

Four local authority areas in Scotland were selected for the study, and these represented a range of allocation and homelessness policy. In each area, senior officials were interviewed, committee minutes and policy reports were examined, details of people applying for housing and receiving housing offers were collected and analysed; and a total of thirty-five women were interviewed who had been rehoused following marital breakdown. Of these, twenty had come from violent relationships.

Housing department policy

Women seeking council housing in order to escape from violence at home are affected by the council's general approach to housing needs arising from marital breakdown. Many councils do not have a comprehensive formal policy on 'marital breakdown' but tend to adopt a network of practices and procedures erected on a base of subconscious assumptions and values. This statement by the director of a housing department illustrates a range of such values:

> 'First of all you're getting more than one tenancy for the one family. . . . That's affecting your normal allocations, where people on the list are getting houses deprived to them. . . . And you might have been making housing that easy that a straightforward argument could develop into a serious marital problem. . . . Transfer applicants who couldn't get a transfer, they were saying "it's easier if we say we've been separated; you can get another house and I'll move in there", and that's what was happening. There's no flies on these people: if there's a loophole or way round it, they're in there!'

Let us consider some of these assumptions in detail, to see whether they are substantiated by the facts, and to look at the effects they have on women applying for housing as a result of marital breakdown, particularly where violence is involved.

The household

Council housing has traditionally been provided for families. Moreover it is allocated on the basis of a conventional household model – the man and his family. In 1979, eighteen Scottish local authorities out of a total of fifty-six did not create joint tenancies between husbands and wives.[3] Small wonder that 85 per cent of council tenancies where the household was headed by a couple were in the man's sole name.[4]

This was at a time when a woman without her name on the rent book was totally unprotected in law against arbitrary eviction by her husband or cohabitee. Women were only too well aware of the vulnerable position this placed them in. One woman interviewed during the study compared the security of her new home to her powerlessness in her husband's house: 'I ken it's all mine. See, he used to say, "you do what you're told, and it's *my* house". And I hated that, when you've nowhere to go.'

The relationship between lack of rights in the home and exposure to the risk of violence and eviction is well argued by the Scottish Law Commission in the report which eventually led to the introduction of occupancy rights.[5]

A legal system which denies, as Scots law presently denies, any right of occupancy to a spouse as such, may indirectly encourage toleration by one spouse of violence by the other spouse. A wife who may only occupy the family home while her husband permits it, may tolerate violent conduct by that husband as the necessary price of maintaining that occupancy for herself and her children.[6]

Despite the introduction of legal protection for non-tenants, there are still strong arguments in favour of joint tenancies, although a major problem is that they imply liabilities for rent payments which many women have no resources to meet. But the psychological benefits should not be underrated. A man is less likely to play king of the castle if his wife shares the tenancy. The woman will feel more secure, particularly if she knows nothing of her legal rights – unfortunately the rule rather than the exception. And a joint tenancy recognizes both partners as equals, even if this is not matched by equal access to resources.

The question of who stays in the marital home when a relationship breaks up is directly affected by the current tenure position. The woman is unlikely to secure a transfer of a sole tenancy to herself if she has no children. Where there are children, housing officials are torn between the conflicting principles of 'the house was allocated for the benefit of the whole family' and 'it's the man's tenancy'. The tenant himself often feels that it is indeed his house, typified by one man who accused his wife and children of 'trying to steal his home off him'. And many women share this view, as this statement illustrates: 'I wouldn't consider trying for the tenancy. I understand now that I could have. But it would have been on my conscience, putting him out.'

One housing department in the study offered the option of joint tenancies very positively, explaining clearly in a written statement the advantages and disadvantages of joint tenancies so that tenants can make a fully-informed choice.

Two houses for one family

Council housing is in short supply. At the end of 1980 there were over 157,000 applicants on Scottish housing lists.[7] Meeting the housing demands arising from marital breakdown is generally perceived within the bureaucracy – and by many tenants and would-be tenants too – as giving two houses to one family while other families have no housing at all. Policies are therefore devised around the question of *which* partner should be housed.

This view is based on a perception of marital breakdown as a process or event which effectively splits one household into two. We could, alternatively, view a family or a couple as two (or more) individuals or households which are currently – and not necessarily permanently – sharing one house. In this light, it appears problematic to deny either individual the right to housing just because they have been sharing with somebody else in the meantime. It would generally be considered unreasonable to make the rehousing of a young couple staying with their in-laws conditional upon the in-laws giving up their own tenancy. It is equally inappropriate to apply such an approach in the case of marital breakdown.

Furthermore, housing demands do not increase in direct relation to the rising incidence of marital breakdown. People who separate and divorce frequently remarry; almost a quarter of women separating in 1974–75, for instance, had remarried three years later.[8] And many start to live with a new partner even sooner than that.

Policies designed to allocate housing to only one partner, if possible, exacerbate conflict between the parties: an undesirable result under any circumstances but still more so in the case of a relationship which is violent. Now that local authorities can no longer evict a tenant in order to secure the tenancy for his wife, the onus is on women to take their own legal proceedings against their husbands to obtain a transfer of tenancy. The process is long-winded and frustrating and there is no guarantee of success. The end result – a transfer of tenancy against the wishes of the tenant – is frequently unsatisfactory. The study encountered several women who had abandoned their tenancies or were about to do so due to perpetual harassment from their former husbands.

Once again, however, there are examples of good local authority practice as well as bad. The result of Glasgow's policies is that in most cases both parties are housed. A woman applying for housing so that she can leave a violent relationship will generally be rehoused regardless of whether or not she has children, and the man will remain in the marital home. Alternatively, the tenancy will be transferred to the woman, usually with the acquiescence of the man, since he is provided with housing elsewhere. The accommodation offered to whichever partner leaves the marital home is of an 'equivalent' standard to the marital home itself.

Marital breakdown is 'a bad thing'

Councillors and housing officials inevitably share the apprehension felt by perhaps the majority of the population at rising divorce rates. So much in our society is structured around the institutions of marriage and the family that it is hard to visualize where we would be without them. Since the lack of alternative accommodation can very effectively inhibit the break-up of a marriage, housing policy-makers quite accurately perceive that they can play a part in upholding the institution of marriage.

This is compounded by the genuinely held belief that for the individuals concerned a reconciliation would generally be preferable to a permanent separation. Accordingly, procedures are evolved with the objective of guarding against hasty decisions being taken in the heat of the moment and later regretted. Minimum separation periods are stipulated before any application will be actively considered, and many authorities still require legal proceedings to have been started or even completed in relation to separation, divorce or custody.

Such conditions and delays can result in real hardship, and there is no doubt that, if they are designed to discourage women from leaving home, they achieve their objective. As one woman who had stayed in bed and breakfast accommodation said:

'It's not surprising people go back to their husbands if that's the best temporary accommodation they have. You've no choice, especially if your family aren't helping. It's terrible when there's nowhere for a woman to turn to and that's really what's happening now.'

Given the effectiveness of these procedures, it is important that the assumptions underlying them are sound, yet those assumptions are highly questionable.

In fact, the fabric of society is not being threatened by marital breakdown. The institution of marriage is still thriving, to the extent that over 90 per cent of the population have been married by the age of forty. Increasing divorce has been paralleled by an increase in the rate of remarriage.[9] And the idealized image of the 'normal' family – accurate or not – still dominates our minds 'like an eternal freeze frame from the video of life!'[10]

The decision to leave a marriage is rarely taken lightly. People stay for years in the most appalling marriages for a wide spectrum of reasons, which have been documented elsewhere.[11] Even having decided to leave, the decision to approach the council for help with housing often takes still longer. Almost a fifth of our sample of women applying as homeless because of marital breakdown had already been away from the marital home for over three months, and had used this time as a 'breathing space' in which they had reached the decision to separate finally. It is not surprising, therefore, that the imposition of minimum separation periods after application to the housing department was bitterly resented by many women.

Finally, the very notion that marital breakdown is 'a bad thing' does not square with the experience of many of the women who have split up from their men. Even in violent relationships, the process of splitting up is inevitably distressing and emotionally painful. But time and again the study found women who had no doubt whatsoever that the benefits of a tension-free and self-fulfilled life made all the deprivations worthwhile. Here are some examples:

'I've been brainwashed for years into thinking I couldn't make decisions. I've always had someone to depend on. I've never had the courage before. I'm surprised at being able to do it.'

'Sometimes it's hard to believe. To have lived the life we did, scared and frightened. It's great to know you can go to bed and know you're going to sleep through the night.'

'I'm happier here with very little than I was with my husband with all that pressure all the time. I think the rough times really are over now. I've got over the worst of it and survived, and that's the important thing.'

Abusing the system

Because council housing is in short supply it is rationed by arranging applicants into queues, generally in accordance with relative degrees of housing need. Most elements of housing needs can be verified by housing officials but this is not true of the breakdown of a relationship. There is therefore a widespread belief that people fabricate splitting up in order to manipulate the system to secure housing, or a move to a better house, or to evade rent arrears on an existing tenancy. Prevention of such potential abuse is the rationale for much 'marital breakdown' policy, and for a generally inquisitorial approach.

This view grossly overestimates the level of knowledge and understanding of the system among its users. A small section of any community becomes very familiar with the intricacies of the welfare state and learns how to use it to its advantage. But many women seeking housing to escape from domestic violence have had no previous contact with local authority services at all. In fact, ignorance of the process was a significant problem for many and was exacerbated by the suspicious reception of officials:

> 'It's hard to walk out of a place when you don't know what to do or where you're going, and you've got a wee baby and everything.
> I'll never forget that night. . . . They said "I'm going to check up" as though they don't believe you. They've no respect for you.'

Nor is there any evidence of widespread abuse of the system to secure a transfer to other accommodation. It is of course true that some couples – even those with a violent relationship – are reconciled after the woman and children have been rehoused. Given the financial, emotional and social pressures to do so, it would be amazing if this never happened. But among the samples examined by the study, the majority of husbands of those rehoused were still living in the marital home, either on their own or with new partners. And many of those husbands who had left the marital home were known to have moved in with new partners or with relatives. This suggests moreover that there is less under-occupation of the marital home than might be feared as a result of rehousing the woman and children elsewhere.

It is ironical, within the context of policies designed to support and maintain marriage and family life, that in order to prevent abuse, many authorities take steps to discourage reconciliation once rehousing has taken place. In Glasgow, for instance, many women were only granted temporary tenancies initially on condition that their husbands would not join them in their new home. One woman in another area found the situation ridiculous:

> 'They wanted me to sign a paper to say that my ex-husband wouldn't come and live with me, even though my divorce was nearly through. Imagine thinking I'd go to the trouble of getting divorced just to get a house'.

Some policies can, however, benefit applicants at the same time as minimizing abuse of the system. Glasgow has adopted a policy of offering to people leaving a relationship accommodation of an equivalent standard and location to the marital home. This is partly to avoid 'up-market' moves to more popular housing, but it also has the effect of preventing 'down-market', unpopular housing being offered to people in no position to refuse it.

Housing staff sometimes resent the way in which services are used. Temporary accommodation, for example, should provide not only a place to stay until permanent housing is available, but also temporary refuge for those people who may only wish to stay until the heat has gone out of the situation at home. But successive uses of temporary accommodation as a short-term refuge are often seen as illegitimate. One woman, who was a constant visitor to a homeless unit after assaults by her cohabitee, elicited this note from a member of staff: 'Warned applicant against misuse of District Council Bed and Breakfast *every* time she has a fight with her spouse.'

It is considered that those who use temporary accommodation without moving in to permanent housing did not have a genuine need in the first place. People are encouraged to assert an intention to separate permanently, and are then assumed to have changed their minds if they subsequently reconcile. This has implications for all 'marital breakdown' applicants since it legitimizes 'cooling-off periods' which can be very harsh on those who have already reached firm decisions before approaching the department.

In fact it was the housing authority with the least liberal approach to marital breakdown which showed the most understanding of the need for temporary refuge for those who might not yet wish to leave their relationships. As the Director of Housing put it:

'That's where the homeless unit gets most of its use, as a wee kind of retreat most of the time. . . . And you can tell the nights when they're going to present themselves and how long it's going to last for, and after the weekend they're back again.'

The bureaucracy which defines behaviour as fickle or manipulative misunderstands the complexity of the separation process. The purpose of intervention should be to provide a favourable context for well-considered decisions and to make temporary and permanent housing available as and when the applicant requires it.

Leaving violent relationships

So far we have discussed policies and practices related to marital breakdown in general. In some ways, things are somewhat easier for someone who can prove that her relationship is violent. One of our study areas was typical of many housing departments in that marital breakdown was not seen as a legitimate reason for rehousing unless it involved domestic violence. Other women would be refused help and told to return home if their husbands stated that they were prepared to take them back.

But on the other hand, women leaving violent relationships face particular difficulties. The burden of proving violence, wide-ranging variations in the interpretation of what constitutes violent behaviour, requirements to exhaust legal remedies, and the need to involve other people and agencies to provide corroborating evidence are discussed elsewhere in this Monograph.[12] As a result, many women are deterred from pursuing their housing applications and, more surprisingly, a large number are refused help outright despite the risk of violence.[13]

What is more, if domestic violence is a condition of receiving any help at all in order to leave a relationship, women are forced into the invidious position of having to define themselves – both to themselves and to the outside world – as 'battered women'. This label reinforces the negative self-image already engendered by the stigma attached to the status of divorcee or single parent, and saps the confidence so important for building a new life: 'You're labelled if you're in these places [bad estates]. Being a battered wife is a label too. People think you're disreputable.'

Rehousing

Different housing department approaches to marital breakdown and to domestic violence have a marked effect upon the outcome of housing applications. Among the four areas covered by the study, the proportion of battered women applying, who were rehoused, ranged from 19 per cent in an authority with very restrictive policies to 37 per cent in Glasgow and 52 per cent in another area. Similarly, the proportion of battered women turned away without any help was negligible in three of our areas but as high as 42 per cent in the unsympathetic authority.

Almost as important as the chances of being housed at all is the quality and location of housing offered. Here again, positive policies can have really beneficial effects, although 'marital breakdown' applicants – in common with other homeless people – are still denied access to the best housing.

Generally there is a desire among housing officials to help those they perceive as 'genuine' to move away from the risk of further violence. This sometimes conflicts with the woman's own wish to be rehoused in the same area as her former husband for other reasons, as this view from an official illustrates:

'Quite a few come along and say there's been violence and they still want to stay in the same town. To me it seems a bit silly just to put them in the next street, and we try to put them away as far as possible. But their mother's probably in the same town to look after the kids. . . . There's all sorts of excuses you have to try to bear in mind, although really you should be trying to get them as far away as possible. We try to do what we can to help the actual applicant'.

Glasgow shares the concern of many authorities that concentrations of people on low incomes and high child densities can create management problems as well as a poor environment for the people themselves. In an effort to avoid such concentrations, it introduced a procedure to boost the applicants' position on the housing list so that they qualify for housing in different, more popular areas. This procedure is used extensively for single parents, most of whom are being rehoused following marital breakdown, in order to house them close to sources of emotional and practical support, nurseries and schools and away from their former partner. It was hoped that the policy of equivalent accommodation referred to previously would avoid concentrations of single parents in particular areas, but this has been less successful, partly because a high proportion of the people who are forced to turn to the council for help with housing after marital breakdown tend to live in relatively deprived areas initially.[14]

A positive approach

The study confirmed the existence of a framework of policies and practices based upon a negative view of marital breakdown and a positive desire to maintain the institutions of marriage and the family. Accordingly, there is no attempt to accept the applicant's definition of her housing needs and to deal with them on her own terms.

Let us take an alternative view. Let us look at the breakdown of a relationship as the end of an increasingly unhappy period and the start of a new life, bearing in mind the self-realization and self-fulfilment which follows the end of a relationship characterized by physical abuse, oppression and self-effacement. Let us recognize that increasing marital breakdown does not threaten the fabric of society but merely leads to a more dynamic pattern of household formation and dissolution.

How then would we wish housing policy to respond?

Most importantly, marital breakdown should be recognized as a legitimate reason for independent housing, regardless of whether domestic violence is involved. The state of marital breakdown should be defined by the applicant herself and accepted on her terms. There should be no requirements for proof of intent to separate, nor proof of violence having taken place. If marital breakdown results in homelessness so that it is impossible to wait for housing through the waiting list, no more conditions should be imposed than on any other homeless applicant.

If temporary accommodation were being provided within a supportive rather than deterrent context, it could be of good quality and pleasant to live in. Information about rights to housing, and the procedures and processes to be gone through would be positively disseminated. Glasgow has already taken a very welcome step in this direction by appointing a team of welfare workers to help people staying in temporary accommodation, and it is introducing measures to eliminate its reliance on commercial bed and breakfast establishments.

The standard 'cooling-off period' or minimum separation period would no longer be required if the applicant's own assessment of the situation were to be respected. It would be acceptable to seek housing assistance before having reached any final decision about the future, or to have a change of heart subsequently. Non-directive counselling should be available if requested, and applicants should have the chance to talk to their partner and others without fear of prejudicing their housing prospects.

Different forms of housing should be provided to cater for the particular needs of single parents and single people. Shared arrangements should be encouraged as should furnished accommodation. A demand for these has been established by two recent surveys of women living in hostels,[15] and this study too provided examples of women who had given up individual accommodation as a result of vandalism, break-ins and harassment.

In the longer term it is important - as and when central government housing expenditure allocations permit - to experiment with new forms of housing design which facilitate more social contact between households while still maintaining scope for the privacy and independence which women have fought so hard to achieve. Specialist housing associations and co-operatives are in a particularly good position to do this, and several innovative schemes already exist.

The study revealed substantial potential for mutual support among women living independently. Single parenthood in particular can be a very isolated lifestyle, and many women felt lonely and tied down by children and low income. Yet many had found others they could turn to - particularly through staying in Women's Aid refuges - and some had themselves acted as a source of support to others. Most felt a sense of solidarity with other women despite the immediate reality of their own isolation. Women who agreed to take part in the study often did so feeling that they could share their experiences and thereby help others to achieve what they had done. Many had learnt new skills around the house and could share these with others.

This solidarity could be harnessed by the encouragement of self-help women's groups within local communities, for the mutual support not only of women setting up home without men, but also of those within marriages. The State could make a meaningful commitment to such groups through the provision of premises and funding. It could also aim towards financing self-help Women's Aid groups to the extent that they could provide refuge space for a far higher proportion of women than is currently the case. At present, for instance, Glasgow Women's Aid provides refuge space for fewer than 3 per cent of the women becoming homeless in the city as a result of domestic violence, despite widespread acknowledgment of the additional support afforded by staying in such a refuge in preference to other forms of temporary accommodation.

Conclusion

A woman who has left a violent marriage and established an independent life for herself concludes this paper with her message of encouragement to others:

'Material things used to bother me. Other women stay because they're too frightened to go out and start again in the world. A lot of women feel they're too old to start again. People keep kidding themselves their men are getting better. I say, don't take it, because he'll never change. You're better off leaving. It's hard, but it's worth it!'

Notes

1 R. Madigan, 'Women and housing', in Glasgow Women's Studies Group, *Uncharted Lives: Extracts from Scottish Women's Experiences, 1850-1982*,

Glasgow, Pressgang, 1983; M. Brian and A. Tinker, *Women in Housing: Access and Influence*, London, Housing Centre Trust, 1980; H. Austerberry and S. Watson, 'A woman's place: a feminist approach to housing in Britain', *Feminist Review*, No. 8, 1981.

2 V. Binney, G. Harkell and J. Nixon, *Leaving Violent Men*, London, Women's Aid Federation England, 1981; R. E. Dobash and R. Dobash, *Violence against Wives*, London, Open Books, 1980.

3 Institute of Housing (Scottish Branch), *Housing Problems resulting from Matrimonial Breakdown*, Institute of Housing, 1981.

4 A.J. Manners and I. Rauta, *Family Property in Scotland*, HMSO, 1981.

5 These rights and others were introduced in Scotland by the Matrimonial Homes (Family Protection) (Scotland) Act 1981. The provisions of this legislation are clearly explained in F. Wasoff, *A Guide to the Matrimonial Homes (Family Protection) (Scotland) Act 1981*, Scottish Women's Aid and Shelter, 1981.

6 Scottish Law Commission Memorandum No. 60, *Report on Occupancy Rights in the Home and Domestic Violence*, HMSO, 1980.

7 Shelter (Scotland), *Dead End Street*, Edinburgh, Shelter (Scotland) 1981.

8 Office of Population Censuses and Surveys (OPCS), *General Household Survey 1979*, HMSO, 1981.

9 Study Commission on the Family, *Happy Families*, London, Study Commission on the Family, 1980; E. Craven, L. Rimmer and M. Wicks, *Family Issues and Public Policy*, London, Study Commission on the Family, 1982.

10 L. Segal (ed.) *What is to be done about the family?* Harmondsworth, Penguin, 1983.

11 V. Binney, G. Harkell and J. Nixon, op. cit.

12 See paper by Maidment.

13 Figures supplied by the Scottish Development Department on the basis of local authority homelessness returns reveal that over a twenty-one month period, 38 per cent of people applying to Scottish local authorities for housing as a result of a violent marital dispute were provided with neither temporary nor permanent accommodation. Almost a fifth of these did not lose contact with the department but were denied help because they failed one of the tests of eligibility under the Housing (Homeless Persons) Act 1977.

14 For example, during two sample months in 1980 and 1981, one district which contains a large number of 'deprived' areas and accounts for 10 per cent of Glasgow's lettings accounted for 13½ per cent of women applying because of domestic violence and 21 per cent of those housed as a result of domestic violence.

15 H. Austerberry and S. Watson, *Women on the Margins: A Study of Single Women's Housing Problems*, London, City University, 1983; Glasgow Council for Single Homeless, *Homeless Women in Glasgow*, Glasgow, Glasgow Council for Single Homeless, 1983.

Refuges and self-help

Jenny Clifton

Abstract

Jenny Clifton's paper begins by pointing out that refuges are not only providing a useful service, a place of sanctuary for battered women, but are also a practical expression of the women's movement. The internal organization of refuges reflects the ideology of Women's Aid, notably the principles of self-help and democratic decision-making, and the paper asks if these principles are compatible with the practical requirements of running a refuge.

Questions are raised about the most appropriate roles for paid refuge workers and support groups given the ideological commitment to self-help and democratic control. Workers in a particular group of refuges performed four main roles: liaison and negotiation with outside funding agencies; helping the women with complex legal, housing and welfare matters; general emotional and practical support of the women; work with children. It is clear that some of the women wanted workers to assume a more directive approach, but this was pressure which workers felt bound to resist in the interests of encouraging self-help.

Self-help was very much more than an empty ideal. Five distinct areas of self-help could be identified and the principle worked in the sense that the women did become more self-reliant and confident. The refuges also managed to interest some women in the broader concerns of the women's movement and to help them towards a broader conception of the roots of marital violence.

The development of refuges for battered women began in the early 1970s and in the following years extensive media coverage, governmental enquiries, legislation and national campaigns served to confront the public with the unwelcome issue of violence to women. However, a decade later it seems that the plight of such women and their children is not so visible. The work of refuges continues but in a climate of government cuts it may be endangered. The research on which this paper is based was undertaken several years ago but its continued relevance lies in the indications it provides of the importance of refuge provision in offering a secure escape from violent men and a stepping-stone to independence. In their book, Borkowski, Murch and Walker point to the continuing ignorance of professionals about refuges and the lack of recognition or understanding of their work. There remains, therefore, a need to explore the experience of those who live and work in refuges.[1]

The rapid spread of refuges can be perceived as one of the major developments in voluntary effort in recent years. It can also be seen as one of the most obvious and practical expressions of the women's movement.[2] What are the implications of these different perceptions? Are those involved in running refuges solely providers of services, or are they part of a radical movement? How are refuges perceived by the women who live in them, and what impact do the intentions and ideologies of Women's Aid groups have upon them? A major principle upon which most refuges are founded, and on the basis of which traditional views on violence to women are challenged, is that of self-help of a collective nature - women together creating their own solution to the problem of violence from men. Is there a contradiction between adherence to the principle and the practical requirements of running a refuge? What exactly is the role of workers and support groups and are the former really necessary?

Some aspects of these questions will be explored here through a discussion of the work of one group of refuges, in order to illustrate the process of negotiation involved in offering practical support while attempting to promote improvements in the position of women. The discussion is also intended to clarify the request for state assistance in funding refuges. This paper thus has both an internal and an external focus on refuges, through which it is hoped to further an understanding of their role. In writing it, experience gained from working in refuges and in conducting some small-scale studies was heavily relied upon. One such study focussed on the perceptions of the refuge of a group of women who had left.[3] Before approaching this study and discussing the refuge it concerns, it is important to explore further the context of refuge provision.

Jenny Clifton

The growth of refuges

The opening of every refuge has demonstrated such a level of desperate need that it became increasingly difficult for local authorities to deny the existence of the problem in their areas. Some authorities, influenced by widespread public concern, readily available funds through the urban programme and arguments concerning the cost-effectiveness of the voluntary provision of refuges, approved the establishment of refuges and provided financial aid. Requests for funding gained initial support from studies suggesting that the refuges seemed more relevant to the needs of the families concerned than either the relative isolation of homeless family accommodation or the drastic course of children coming into care.[4] To grant-making bodies, refuges were likely to be seen as further sources of care for the less fortunate, innovatory extensions of welfare provision. The internal organization of refuges was probably perceived as being of little relevance except that the funders' preference for refuges to be run on hierarchical lines with clear rules of admission will often have been demonstrated to Women's Aid groups by the irritation of public officials when having to deal with several different women, not all or any of whom may be workers, and over problems of accountability for rehousing.[5]

As far as those who have campaigned for refuges are concerned, many have seen themselves as responding to deficiencies in welfare provision: whatever their individual motives they perceived refuges as a means of alleviating a neglected social problem. Many have come from social work and allied backgrounds and had come face to face with difficulties in helping battered women. As their concern was not only to create provision but also to find new, non-stigmatizing ways of working, self-help was frequently an important objective for refuge operation.[6]

Undoubtedly the commitment of a large proportion, if not the majority, of those who work in and for refuges is founded in involvement in the women's movement. Wife-battering is seen by them as an extreme representation of structural and ideological forces maintaining the subjugation of women within the family, and, consequently, the basic task is to challenge and change existing social norms and values. Refuges challenge narrow definitions of violence to women by demonstrating the scale of need and the prevalence of violence in 'normal' households.[7] They can also be said to demonstrate the discrimination suffered by women, both generally and in the application of social policy, can act as organizational bases for the dissemination of feminist ideas and can be the practical implementation of a personal ideology.[8]

Many refuges grew out of women's centres and difficulties have arisen from women attempting to balance time-consuming refuge work with commitments to wider objectives.[9] Nonetheless, the support of the wider movement has undoubtedly provided the will to create and ensure the growth of refuge provision.

The Women's Aid Movement and self-help

In their guidelines for running a refuge, the National Women's Aid Federation, to which the majority of refuges are affiliated, made explicit the connection between refuges and the women's movement, and emphasized self-help as a fundamental principle of refuge organization: 'The self-help principle should be stressed and refuges run democratically with decisions being taken by women in conjunction with women in support groups.'[10] Why should self-help and democratic control be basic to a refuge?

For women to involve themselves in providing a solution to their plight and to take control of their own lives is a fundamental reversal of their previous situation – powerlessness in the face of male violence. Self-help can therefore be a means of building self-confidence and personal strength, which will stand the women in good stead when they begin a life alone.[11] It may also help prevent a return to a violent relationship. This connects with Women's Aid's analysis of violence to wives as a direct result of women's subservience to men.[12] As Elizabeth Wilson has written: 'Women's Aid recognised that the violence in marriages expresses a power relationship of which one part is the violence and another the economic dependence of women on men.'[13]

The view of the battered woman's situation as a normal outcome, or the extreme representation of the position of all women, leads to a desire to remove distinctions between helpers and helped: women working in and for refuges need them as much, if in a different way, as do the women who live there.[14] Finally, many of those involved in Women's Aid's groups are involved in other women's groups and have come to value non-hierarchical forms of organization.[15] The capability of the vast majority of women who use refuges is evidenced in follow-up studies of residents and their success in managing life alone, and supports Women's Aid's desire to avoid creating a 'client' or dependent status for women in refuges.[16]

The aim of self-help precludes refuges being run by wardens, house-mothers or whatever – there can be no formalized hierarchy. Also, there should be no concentration of power and as information is power, a concentration of information is considered contrary to self-help. In response to the kind of difficulties to be discussed below, many refuges have employed paid workers. Such workers are in an ambiguous position and their very presence can be seen as a threat to self-help. Refuge support groups share such difficulties: both groups usually being the main repositories of information about the refuge and bearing a continued responsibility for it which places them in a different position from most of the women who live there. Can the differences be handled without recourse to hierarchical forms of organization and by agreeing ways in which responsibilities can be shared?

The group associated with the refuges to be discussed here believed in the value of self-help but also found that there was much work to be done which necessitated the employment of paid workers. A major purpose of the study referred to here was to examine the operation of self-help and the constant negotiation involved between workers, support group, and women in the refuge. The experience often seemed one of juggling beliefs and actual experience. The dilemmas arising from this juggling act concerned ways of ensuring reasonable physical standards – sometimes a dispiriting task in the absence of generally accepted rules of hygiene combined with poor housing conditions, means of securing continued funding and good relations with relevant outside agencies, and ways of handling clashes between women in the house.[17] It also seemed that workers were engaged in a subtle intervention process of attempting to persuade women to a different view of their capacities, not least because the experience of the women was so often one of being controlled and dependent.

The refuges and the study

The refuges to be discussed here resulted from the initiative of a group comprised of social workers, community workers, doctors and other interested individuals, all of whom had in the course of their daily work encountered difficulties in offering an appropriate response to battered women seeking help in their locality. The group also shared an allegiance to feminist perspectives on women's position in society.[18] The lack of accommodation, a safe place of escape to which any woman defining herself as in need could turn, seemed the first and most obvious requirement, so that the group saw as its first task the acquisition of property for use as a refuge. At the discussion stage, several months before such property was available for use, it was also felt that financial aid was essential in order to furnish and maintain the short-life accommodation promised by a housing association, and to employ workers who could manage it and who could assist the women who came. Thus, before the first refuge was opened, an approach was made to the local authority for finance from the Urban Programme. At this stage it was envisaged that a refuge for sixteen families would be the objective and that this would require two full-time workers, together with the active participation of members of a support group. Beyond a few obvious considerations about the liaison required with local agencies, there was a notable lack of understanding of what was entailed in running a refuge. It was clear that the eventual rehousing of women from the refuge was of crucial concern and negotiations on this issue were successfully conducted with the local housing departments, as were meetings with the local Department of Health and Social Security, given the necessity of a prompt response from them to women's requests for financial support.

The workers' role, in so far as it was defined at all at this stage, was to be the continuation of the work of liaison with relevant agencies and to respond to the women's individual problems. Although there was little clear conception as to what these problems might be, it was believed to be both desirable and necessary that the women play a major part in helping themselves and each other. Through helping themselves they might gain more confidence in their own abilities and acquire expertise in matters of future importance to them, so countering their accustomed social and economic dependence. It was anticipated too that the burden of stigma facing each woman would be reduced through being in close proximity to others in the same situation and that, on the basis of their shared experience, they could offer each other empathy and understanding beyond that which workers could give.

Thus the refuge opened with the relatively vague notion that communal life would have therapeutic value and that worker and volunteer involvement would be minimized. The group was anxious to avoid a 'warden' image for the workers, which might result in an alienating and institutional environment, and wanted rather to develop a facilitating role which would involve the women in practical and supportive tasks wherever possible and blur customary client-worker divisions.

In the years following the opening of the first refuge in 1975 the realities of the difficult and demanding work involved in running a refuge became abundantly clear. In attempting to fulfil the twin aims of providing an effective service of accommodation and advice to as many women as possible and of promoting self-help in the refuge, workers met with many dilemmas. The amount and complexity of the work required in simply ensuring the continued existence of the refuge – its funding, accommodation and credibility in the eyes of important supporting agencies – and in assisting individual women with negotiations on housing and legal matters proved enormous. The importance of this service aim was confirmed by the desire to make the refuge stay as brief as possible, given the demands on space, poor physical conditions and the tangible achievement represented by a woman's departure to a new home. Over this period numerous short-life properties had been occupied as refuges, entailing constant struggles against decay, and up to sixty women had been accommodated at any one time. While there had been little time to devote to a concentration on the relationships within the refuge, there was evidence of considerable involvement of the women in the growth of the refuge. Two women had begun to work for the refuge on leaving, and playgroups, funding efforts and 'public relations' exercises were all areas of participation. With secure funding and permanent premises – the refuges comprised nine houses at the time of this study – came a more explicit examination of the workers' role. The follow-up study of women who had used the refuge, which attempted to gain their perspective on the experience, was an important part of this appraisal. The workers had discovered that mobilizing the refuges' potential to build on the women's initial step in asserting the right to a life free of violent oppression required much encouragement in the face of the women's long held assumption that the subjugation they had experienced at the hands of men was inevitable. There was much which the women lacked the expertise to handle, yet workers retained the desire to be non-directive and indeed their motivation stemmed from the desire to negotiate a suitably supportive role.

The workers' role appeared to require intervention at two levels: in the interlinked problems both of individuals and of communal organization. While the refuge community has the potential to be supportive to individuals, this potential varies. It depends on the personalities and abilities of the women resident at any one time and the extent to which workers intervene to enhance an atmosphere conducive to mutual support. In this sense, refuge organization is a fluctuating process.[19] Rarely was it found that each woman's problems could be met wholly by others in the refuge, but the objective of self-help made it desirable that individual needs were met in ways which were helpful in developing mutual support. This might mean, for example, explaining the process of negotiating on finances with the Department of Health and Social Security so that a woman could do it herself and then help others to do so.

In the context of these brief reflections on the workers' role, how far had the women participated and how had they perceived the running of the refuge? The follow-up study gives some indication of their views.

Self-help in the refuges

Refuge workers identified five areas for self-help within the refuge in which women were involved to a varying extent depending on their own wishes. Information from the study is available on each.

(a) *Individual problems:* Women in the refuge faced a range of problems and decisions concerning their future. Usually these concerned financial support, obtaining custody of the children, legal remedies against the husband, rehousing and settling children into new schools. Most women in the study confirmed that they had been involved in negotiations with a number of officials, few of whom they had encountered previously, and many felt that learning to handle these contributed to their increased confidence upon leaving the refuge. Each house had an office from which telephone calls could be made and letters sent, while guidance was always available when queries arose. There were other difficulties, relating rather to life in the refuge, which women in the study said that they had preferred to deal with themselves rather than involving workers or the whole group. Among these were problems with the other women in the refuge, times when the refuge itself got them down and difficulties with their children. It seemed that to share some difficulties meant crossing personal boundaries of privacy or vulnerability which might have increased stress rather than relieved it.

(b) *Mutual support:* The workers were aware that many problems hardly became identified as ones with which their help might be required, due to the extensive sharing of experiences among the women. One woman in the study described the value of this: 'You are all in the same position and so you can talk about it. It's a great help because they understand what you're going through.' Another said: 'When I was pretty queer the women took over the kids. They fed and bathed and dressed them.' There were, however, problems which women had preferred to talk over with workers and these tended to concern financial, legal, or child care issues where detailed information might be required. There seemed to be a distinction between support required with these kind of worries, where workers' expertise was particularly valued, and that gained from general discussion which could arise from 'being in the same boat'. While appreciating the workers' attempts to empathize, many women commented on the importance of shared experience: 'I don't think anyone can ever understand until they've been through it themselves.'

That women turned to workers for information may reflect the importance attached by workers to ensuring that basic information was available to each woman concerning the decisions open to her and to assisting in the negotiations which arose from such decisions, in addition to the value attached to the tangible help which they did, in fact, offer. Meanwhile, much of the immediate support on arrival, introductions to the local Social Security office, and preparation of rooms for new families would be undertaken by the women and sharing of opinions about the merits of various courses of action occurred among the women all the time. The comments on the relief obtained from sharing experiences underlines the importance of specific provision for battered women.

(c) *Running the refuge:* The forum for the involvement of women in the domestic management of each refuge was the weekly house meeting which workers also attended. This arena for communal decision-making has always held great significance for the workers. Yet for the women in the study it was a source of considerable dissatisfaction and highlighted their ambivalence over the notion of self-help. The roots of their reaction seemed to lie in the workers' reluctance to impose direction when set against the women's struggle to live harmoniously together, given contrasting standards of hygiene and child care. Having many rules pertaining to refuge life had always been considered inimical to the involvement of a changing population of women in the running of the refuge, and indeed the only rule which most women in the study could recall was the one disallowing men entry to the refuge. This rule was acknowledged to be appropriate in ensuring the security of the refuge although it required periodic reaffirmation in the face of impending breakdown in relationships between women in the houses.

Much of the daily life in the refuges was governed by implicit norms of behaviour rather than by rules – women usually paid rent and cared for children without the need for enforcement, although this could depend on the composition of families in the house. Typically, it was only when norms were not adhered to or when new forms of unacceptable behaviour arose that the question of making rules was raised. Many women in the study had wanted more rules and yet had not felt free to introduce them, which suggests that they may not have grasped the principles on which the refuge was run, or had had difficulty in operating them. The majority of women suggested that changes should be made in the way the refuge was run which would impose more structure and make communal life more manageable, but the implication was that someone 'in charge' would need to enforce them. In reflecting upon how they would run a refuge differently, more than one woman made a comment such as this: 'I'd make sure it was really comfortable and I'd make sure they kept it like it, if they didn't they could go back home.' Topics of discussion and disagreement in house meetings had most frequently concerned the level of cleanliness, problems with children and conflicts between women. The dissatisfaction and confusion over the origin and enforcement of rules is evident in the comments made in this context, typical of which was: 'The ideas were good but people needed to take more notice of what was said, but it was useful getting the women together to decide what should be done.'

It was evident that any particular woman's experience of the refuge had depended in large measure on the group of women among whom she found herself, but in general the attempts to cooperate with a large group of other women and their children had proved quite stressful at times. The physical state of the houses acted as a kind of barometer of the state of well-being within them, and it was around such a basic issue as cleaning that the realities of attempts to achieve a self-help community were perhaps most clearly expressed.[20] The significance of this extends to women's first impressions of the refuge. It seemed from many women's comments that even the best refuge, in terms of facilities and physical conditions, fell far short of their accepted living standards, and that this might be a cause of discouragement to women leaving a violent home is suggested by several comments: 'I wanted to run home. I thought what have I come down to.' 'I nearly never came. Absolute disgust. I thought how could human beings actually have lived there?' Only their desperation and the immediate relief obtained from the company of the other women overcame such feelings.[21] Of course it was not simply problems of cleanliness which elicited such comments but the lack of furnishings and the overcrowding, together with the state of repair of some houses, due to dependence on short-life property and multi-occupation.[22] However, the comments do highlight the need to ensure minimum standards in the attempt to reduce the stress of communal life which is endemic to refuges.

In general, the considerations arising from these comments relate to the delicate balance of worker and women involvement in suggesting and imposing limits, and it seems from these women's comments that a reluctance on the part of workers to take a lead in guiding the women's involvement might have compounded the problems, rather than assisted the process, by making it hard for the women to learn their own potential role.

(d) *Involvement in the organization:* The women's involvement in the broader work of the refuge's survival, as distinct from the domestic management of their particular house, proved limited. To many women the constant efforts required to raise and administer funds, maintain houses and liaise with statutory authorities could seem irrelevant when compared with their own pressing concerns. However, some women had become full-time workers and others had participated in radio appeals, given talks at meetings and taken an active role in the Women's Aid Federation. These activities provided a valuable external focus to counterbalance the personal difficulties the women had faced.

(e) *Women's issues:* This final aspect of self-help is one around which much discussion takes place among workers and women. The refuge is affiliated to the Federation and committed both to its campaigns and to linking Women's Aid with other issues concerning the position of women in society. Apart from directly expressing the strength of women's collective efforts, the refuge hopes to interest women in the broader concerns of the women's movement. There was evidence of a change in perception towards women's position on the part of many women in the study, as will be shown, and those who attended meetings of the Federation were able to perceive the collective power of the organization of which they were a part.

Women and workers

How did the women in the study see the workers' role given the tasks they set themselves in enhancing the opportunities for women to make their own way forward, without being directive? Their attempt to be on equal terms with the women while acknowledging their helping role was clearly valued as was their expertise, and most women saw the workers' tasks as comprising a combination of practical and emotional support. Some comments illustrate these points:

'They were friends – they weren't like anyone official. I had a taste of social workers when I was a kid. They weren't like that – more like hippies.'

'They were answering phone calls all day, put women in contact with other agencies, making appeals, talking to women about problems, taking children out.'

'They were good friends. Social workers. I mean, people who helped other people. I've never been helped or looked after like it before.'

Clearly the workers had succeeded in playing an important part in the support available in the refuge and were not perceived as 'in charge'.

The impact of the refuge

The women in the study were asked what they had liked least and valued most about refuge life and what they thought it was trying to achieve. The refuge was experienced not simply as a building but as a community: attitudes to the physical conditions could not be separated from attitudes to living with a large number of other people. Arguments, the lack of privacy, problems arising from the sheer presence of so many children and the sharing of facilities were all sources of complaint. However, paradoxically, it was the company of other women which was most highly valued. The support of other women who 'knew what it was like' could break down feelings of isolation and stigma and provide security as these comments show:

'The company [was the best thing]. You were never on your own and then you start talking and you think "There was somebody else nearby who was getting beaten up".'

'Company. It was just a feeling of knowing nothing could happen to me while I was there – there was always someone to talk to.'

'The assurance that it wasn't just me because you tend to blame yourself but I wasn't the only one and there were others worse off than me.'

Although all the women had experienced marked changes in their circumstances and now faced life alone with the children, when asked what differences the refuge had made to their lives, their comments chiefly concerned perceived improvements in self-image and capabilities. Many women said they felt more confident: 'It's made me stronger in myself, given me more courage.' 'You feel more independent. You feel you're your own self.' 'I feel as though I can talk to people a lot better.' Others stressed the importance to them of learning about other women's problems or the acquisition of practical skills. For many it had marked a significant turning point: 'I think it's made me more aware of my rights. I know there's always somewhere to go if the same thing happened again.'

The women had also gained new perspectives on their experience of violence and its causes. Prior to their arrival at the refuge, almost half the women had attributed their husband's violence to his individual characteristics – in particular, mental illness or excessive drinking. Five spoke of their husband's assumption of the right to dominate them; four women had blamed themselves for the eruption of violence and a few others mentioned external stress or marital interaction. Asked to explain their present perspectives, eighteen women said that their views had altered – almost entirely away from individualized explanation. Only three maintained that the blame lay with their husband's personality, while ten blamed stress such as financial difficulties, unemployment, and family difficulties generally. Several more women now felt that such stress had affected both partners, putting forward more complex explanations in terms of family interaction, and an increased number felt that the root cause lay in women's status in the family and in society. What is important about these changed views is the part they play in the women's perceptions of themselves and of their subsequent plans. The women's broader conception of the roots of marital violence helped to release them from the burden of guilt and the stigma which so often weigh upon women trapped within violent marriages, and it appeared that the opportunity to share experiences with others had played a crucial part in this change.[23]

Asked what they thought the refuge was trying to achieve, the comments of eighteen women out of the twenty-nine related to the provision of emotional and practical help and sanctuary – the service aim of the group. A typical comment was:

'It's to help women I should say – to help them every way they could. There were some women in an awful state. I think living in a refuge, it was like a haven, a place where they couldn't be hurt.'

Sixteen women emphasized the refuge's attempts to effect changes in the women's abilities or perceptions of themselves, giving them time to think and to learn independence: 'It was to get me to stand on my own two feet instead of relying on other people.' For seven women the refuge represented a wider challenge concerning the position of women:

'For most women it was to rehabilitate them – so that they could run their own lives. Whereas before they thought of themselves as useless bits around the house, they became human beings.'

'It was about the rights of women. To show women that they shouldn't be battered by their husbands and to help them get away.'

'You were trying to get a better position for women who live in bad conditions with their husbands and show them that things should be better than that.'

It can be seen from these diverse comments that the refuge had offered far more than accommodation in a crisis: it had given a new perspective through sharing experiences with other women – to them the most crucial advantage of a refuge.

The limits to self-help

At a time when the notion of self-help is promoted both by those seeking a democratized form of welfare provision and by those intent on reducing state welfare, it seems essential to clarify the role of funded workers in refuges. The attempt so far in this paper has been to offer an inside view of refuge operation: the next step is to link this to the external issue of the claim for proper funding and state support of refuges.

That self-help in refuges is not simply an empty ideal has, it is hoped, been demonstrated here. However, the need is also evident for workers of a particular kind – workers who will ensure the enhancement of opportunities for self-reliance and confidence building, relieve some of the pressures arising from ensuring the refuge's continued existence, be available for a range of advice and information and, not discussed here but of considerable importance, work with children in the refuge.[24] There is much for workers to do and a secure source of funding is essential for this. The impact of funding is amply shown in the Women's Aid Federation England report as are the struggles many refuges have had as their sources of funding have expired. That report found that funded groups housed twice as many women in better conditions than was possible for the unfunded ones.[25] In their conclusions, the writers stress the burdens placed on voluntary helpers, as do Jan Pahl and more than one contributor to the DHSS conference held in 1981.[26]

What then are the main tasks of workers in a refuge? One major concern is to reduce the strains of communal life. Even under the most favourable of circumstances, living communally presents enormous problems.[27] Communal living on the basis of democracy and self-help may present even more. Success presupposes a strong commitment to the exercise and battered women may well not start out with such a commitment: their choice was to leave a violent relationship rather than to enter a refuge. Their focus will tend to be outside the refuge, in the search for permanent accommodation, finding schools for their children, the pursuit of divorce, and their efforts are often geared to leaving the refuge as soon as possible. The refuge is frequently viewed instrumentally, at least initially, and not only may there be little commitment to living communally, but also a diversity of purposes. While some will want protection and security above all, others will want to explore new relationships and experiences; while some will be negotiating reconciliations, others will be seeking to establish their independence. These aims will alter during a woman's stay.

The turnover of women in a refuge is high and the constantly changing population makes stable relationships within the house hard to maintain, although they may well continue when women have left. Add to this the poor physical conditions which result from being housed in short-life property and from multi-occupation, high occupancy rates, sharing bedrooms between families and the activities of large numbers of children and the scope for strain is evident. The impact is not always one of reinforcing solidarity, and communal discussion may often centre on poor conditions and interpersonal conflicts. Success in negotiating the intricacies of communal living may require a personal strength not immediately available to women who may more often experience confusion, uncertainty, distress and insecurity upon arrival at the refuge.[28] Women are largely assisted in overcoming these feelings by finding other women who have shared them, but those living in a refuge may not always be able to take on the entire responsibility for the quality of communal life. The support offered by workers can ease some of the difficulties. Just as important is proper funding to provide the type of facilities most wanted by women in refuges – a combination of communal and private space which would enhance the chances of successful communal life.[29]

A refuge is not simply concerned with the management of domestic routine. Drawing on the experience of the refuge described here, there seem to be several areas of expertise, the availability of which is essential to the interests of the women and the continuation of the refuge. The morale of the women is partly dependent upon the efficiency with which their specific problems are being resolved. The identification of tangible goals, perhaps obtaining custody or an additional social security payment, and especially the offer of new permanent accommodation, which may mark the end of dependence on the refuge, is of considerable psychological significance. Success in the pursuit of such goals is only secured through the application of detailed knowledge and negotiating skills and when there is a constructive relationship between the refuge and those agencies controlling the resources the women require. Such a relationship is dependent on the agency, for example the housing department, local Social Security office or firm of solicitors, understanding and sympathizing with the needs of the refuge and being confident that the means exist to resolve problems should they arise.

Often the need is simply for good personal relationships between key personnel in the various agencies and those in the refuge. At other times it is a matter of negotiating, often at a senior level, for policy and practice statements and guidelines governing the relationship between refuge and agency and agency and battered women generally. This may be a matter of appealing to good sense, public image, basic humanity, or to duty and responsibility, and sometimes it is a matter of bargaining. This occurs most frequently with social services departments, where responsibility for family welfare overlaps, and housing departments, where the bargain concerns responsibility for homelessness. Careful structuring of the context within which the day-to-day relationship between refuge and agency occurs, may usefully commence before the refuge opens. In any event, it requires skills and understanding which it takes time to accumulate, and consistency which the women in the refuge, as a transient population, are unable to provide.

Understanding, let alone obtaining one's entitlement to the various welfare benefits, is complex enough. Ensuring that discretion is exercised favourably, that a housing authority accepts its responsibility, that the best possible arrangements are made over access to children, are examples where considerable skill may be required. The desired response is not always achieved simply through requesting it, demanding it, or even fighting for it. Women staying in a refuge need to have the chance to learn these skills and gain confidence in using them. Offering assistance with this is a major task of workers.

Similar difficulties arise when considering the refuge's management and development needs: problematic financial management cannot be afforded any more than maintenance and repair to property can be neglected. Securing adequate resources and planning their deployment for expansion or extension of refuge activities is unlikely to be the primary concern of women living in the refuge for perhaps an average of three months.

Children in refuges can benefit greatly from organized play activities and workers with time to give them additional attention. There is usually a large number of children at any one time in a refuge and some will be in a distressed state due to experiences in their recent past. While their mothers need time to recover, the children too need considerable help and support in the major changes which are happening in their lives. As their stay in the refuge continues, children need planned activities to improve their experience of communal life.

The perceptions of women living in a refuge can sometimes seriously conflict with the values and practices upheld by workers and support group members. Such conflict can bring into sharp relief the dilemmas concerning the purposes and ideologies of a Women's Aid organization and refuges handle such situations in a variety of ways. Issues have arisen in the refuges described here in connection with racial tension or hostility on other grounds between some of the women, which have led workers to intervene in the interests of maintaining tolerant attitudes. Some women who seek refuge have long-standing problems which are manifested in an inability to fit in with the needs of other women in the house or to care adequately for their children.[30] Workers have felt that ways must be found of supporting them while ensuring the survival of the refuge for the benefit of the wider group. They have felt that the refuge would be betraying its aims by rejecting such women, thereby excluding them from the support of fellow women. Failure to live with such dilemmas could lead to a refuge becoming geared to those who need it least in terms of learning to cope alone, and when workers and support group have encountered conflict over such matters they have felt it their responsibility to offer the necessary support.

The issues outlined above illustrate some of the potential tasks of refuge workers and support groups and show too the need for a constant process of negotiation between such groups and the women living in the refuge. A refuge is pursuing complex and diverse objectives and the women who live there have complex and diverse problems to resolve. It seems desirable for women to determine for themselves the extent of responsibility they want for the refuge and to have opportunities to learn to manage their own lives while not being overburdened with the weight of all the problems involved in running a refuge.

Conclusion

This paper has attempted to illustrate the value and appropriateness of refuge provision as a response to violence to women, and has focussed on the central importance of self-help in assisting women to make real choices about their future. This may mean making a permanent break from a violent relationship or returning to a relationship with new-found strength to challenge the violence or leave should it recur. A refuge may offer both a service and the opportunity to participate in a movement for social change: to dichotomize the two may not capture adequately the intentions either of those working with the refuges or the women who live in them. Yet while potential funders may dislike the campaigning aspect of Women's Aid, refuge groups are offering more than a simple service of advice and accommodation. It is hard to escape the implications of refuge provision – by their very existence refuges demonstrate the nature and level of incidence of domestic violence and urge it as a logical concern of the state rather than simply as a problem to individuals.[31] Self-help cannot be used as a justification for leaving refuges unfunded: there is a clear need for well-equipped and comfortable accommodation and for workers who will join in offering support and shared management. What is needed is a partnership in which state aid is given to underpin a provision which can remain under the management of local groups. Such co-operation at the local level has proved possible. Research studies indicate the need for policies to be developed in response to violence within the family, which include the provision of stable finance for refuges, in recognition of the valuable part they play in offering women and children real alternatives to a violent home.

Notes

1 The National Women's Aid Federation has produced several papers, many of which represent campaigns on policy issues. Examples are: *And Still You've Done Nothing*, 1976; *Battered women, Refuges and Women's Aid*, 1977. There is now a separate Federation for England which produces its own leaflets. A valuable source of opinion on the problems of battered women is the report of the proceedings of the Select Committee on Violence in Marriage, 1975. See also E. Pizzey, *Scream Quietly or the Neighbours Will Hear*, Harmondsworth, Penguin Books, 1974; E. Wilson, *What is to be Done About Violence Against Women?*, Harmondsworth, Penguin Books, 1983; M. Borkowski, M. Murch and V. Walker, *Marital Violence – The Community Response*, London, Tavistock Publications, 1983.

2 The association between Women's Aid and the women's movement is explained by Hanmer in two papers: J. Hanmer, 'Women's Aid and the women's liberation movement in Britain', paper presented at the British Association for the Advancement of Science, September 1976; J. Hanmer, 'Community action, Women's Aid and the women's liberation movement', in M. Mayo (ed.), *Women in the Community*, London, Routledge & Kegan Paul, 1977. The potential conceptions of Women's Aid as 'philanthropic venture' or 'social movement' have been pinpointed by H. Rose, 'In practice supported, in theory denied: an account of an invisible urban movement', *International Journal of Urban and Regional Research*, vol. 2(3), 1978. A similar discussion is to be found in J. Pahl, 'Refuges for battered women: social provision or social movement?', *Journal of Voluntary Action Research*, vol. 8, Nos. 1-2, pp. 25-35, 1979.

3 This material was obtained from a small-scale, follow-up study of women who had stayed in the refuges discussed in this paper, which are located in London. Twenty-nine women were interviewed during 1978-9. The writer had been involved in these refuges from their beginning. The actual interviews with the women in this study were undertaken by a research worker, Jane Temple, whose work is gratefully acknowledged. It must be stressed that the views expressed in this paper are those of the author and not necessarily of others involved in refuge work. It is also the case that since this research work was undertaken there have been several changes among the workers in the refuges and the refuges themselves have changed in some respects. Nonetheless, it is felt that the views of the women have continuing relevance. The author would like to thank the workers at the refuge for all their advice and help during the course of this research and above all the women who were generously prepared to talk of their experiences. I would like to thank too the Equal Opportunities Commission for their financial assistance with the research. Finally, I would like to thank Roger Sherrott for his work in co-writing a previous version of this paper.

4 See the report from the London Boroughs' Association Officers' Working Party on violence in Marriage: 'Refuges for battered women in London', Social Services Committee, 1976. Also relevant is N.A. Barr and J.W. Carrier, 'Women's Aid Groups: the economic case for state assistance to battered wives', *Policy and Politics*, vol. 6, No. 6, 1978.

5 The London Boroughs' Association, however, did discuss self-help as a basis for refuge organization.

6 See, for example, the pamphlet by Colchester Women's Aid: 'Colchester's battered women need refuge', 1976. See also, A. Weir, 'Battered women: some perspectives and problems', in M. Mayo (ed.), *Women in the Community*, London, Routledge & Kegan Paul, 1977, and R. Daniels, 'Battered women: the role of women's aid refuges', *Social Work Today*, vol. 9, No. 12, p. 10, 1977.

7 Wilson, op. cit., pp. 194-202.

8 See Weir, op. cit. See also N. Timms, 'Battered women: a study in social problem definition', *Yearbook of Social Policy*, 1974, and R.P. Dobash and R.E. Dobash, 'Community response to violence against wives: charivari, abstract justice and patriarchy', *Social Problems*, vol. 28, No. 5, June 1981.

9 J. Pahl, *A Refuge for Battered Women: A Study of the Role of a Women's Centre*, London, HMSO, 1978, discusses such issues in relation to the Canter-

bury Women's Centre.

10 Quote from National Women's Aid Federation, *Battered Women, Refuges and Women's Aid*, 1977.

11 J. Pahl, 'A bridge over troubled waters: a longitudinal study of women who went to a refuge', unpublished report presented to the Department of Health and Social security, 1981, ch. 11, p. 113.

12 R.E. Dobash and R.P. Dobash, *Violence Against Wives: A Case against the Patriarchy*, Shepton Mallett, Open Books, 1980, Chs 2 and 12.

13 E. Wilson, op. cit., p. 196.

14 See J. Pahl, 1978, op. cit., pp. 9–10, and J. Hanmer, 'Community action, Women's Aid and the women's liberation movement', in M. Mayo (ed.), *Women in the Community*, London, Routledge & Kegan Paul, 1977, pp. 96–7.

15 See Weir, op. cit., 1977.

16 For example, see J. Pahl, op. cit., 1981, and J.R. Clifton, 'It's lonely but we're coping', workshop paper presented to the Department of Health and Social Security seminar on Violence in the Family, University of Kent at Canterbury, 1981.

17 J. Pahl, op. cit., 1978 and op. cit., 1981.

18 For a discussion of a feminist analysis of the family and its application to family violence, see D. Marsden, 'Sociological perspectives on family violence', in J.P. Martin (ed.), *Violence and the Family*, Chichester, John Wiley and Sons, 1978 and R.E. Dobash and R.P. Dobash, 'Wives: the appropriate victims of marital violence', *Victimology: an International Journal*, vol. 2, 1978; also R.E. Dobash and R.P. Dobash 1980, op. cit. See also J. Hanmer, 'Women's Aid and the women's liberation movement in Britain', paper presented at the British Association for the Advancement of Science, September 1976.

19 Hilary Rose notes this aspect of refuge life: 'Developing successful non–hierarchical forms of self-management is an intractable task needing continuous self-appraisal by the group. Refuges constantly fluctuate, engaging in a continuous dialogue.' Rose, op. cit., 1978, p. 35.

20 Some interesting reflections from their study of communes, which seem relevant to this issue, can be found in P. Abrams and A. McCulloch *Communes, Sociology and Society*, Cambridge University Press, 1976.

21 See J. Pahl, op. cit., 1981.

22 See V. Binney, G. Harkell and J. Nixon, *Leaving Violent Men*, London, Women's Aid Federation England, 1981.

23 J.R. Clifton, op. cit., 1981.

24 Binney, Harkell and Nixon, op. cit., 1981, ch. 7.

25 Ibid., p. 47.

26 Pahl, op. cit., 1981, p. 100. Department of Health and Social Security seminar on violence in the family held at the University of Kent 1981.

27 See Abrams and McCulloch, op. cit., 1976.

28 Here again, Abrams and McCulloch, ibid., was felt to be relevant when communal life in the refuge was considered.

29 Binney, Harkell and Nixon, op. cit., 1981, p. 42.

30 See Pahl, op. cit., 1981, p. 112.

31 Borkowski, Murch and Walker, op. cit., 1983, p. 206.

Constructing images of deviance: a look at state intervention into the problem of wife-battery*

Patricia A. Morgan

Abstract

Patricia Morgan's paper describes what happens when the state intervenes in the social problem of wife-battering. Her analysis refers to the United States, but there are clear implications for other countries, including Britain. The author argues that the state, through its social problem apparatus, manages the image of the problem by a process of bureaucratization, professionalization and individualization. This serves to narrow the definition of the problem, and to depoliticize it by removing it from its class context and viewing it in terms of individual pathology rather than structure.

Thus refuges were initially run by small feminist collectives which had a dual objective of providing a service and promoting among the women an understanding of their structural position in society. The need for funds forced the groups to turn to the state for financial aid. This was given, but at the cost to the refuges of losing their political aims. Many refuges became larger, much more service-orientated and more diversified in providing therapy for the batterers and dealing with other problems such as alcoholism and drug abuse. This transformed not only the refuges but also the image of the problem of wife-battering.

Social problems are shadowy phenomena. Certain behaviors or conditions may exist in a society for decades and never blossom into problematic public issues. The images of particular social ills can be transformed, can shift from one dimension to another with surprising speed. Witness, for instance, the issues of abortion, drug use, family violence

---

*An earlier version of this paper was prepared for the American Sociology Association Meeting, Toronto, August 1981.

and homosexuality in the past few decades. These issues indicate that what we understand as social problem phenomena are not necessarily 'natural' outcomes of societal processes, but can also be seen as political images: ideological constructs which are organized, managed and perpetuated, often, by the state. The shifts in public awareness of particular issues, and the transformation of the problem's images, import and consequences can be charted within a general process of state intervention.

One useful method of looking at this process would be to utilize O'Connor's formulation of the state, as simultaneously promoting accumulation and legitimation.[1] This would mean that often state intervention policies involving social problems incorporate a wide and sometimes conflicting range of interests. The state's overall need to promote capital accumulation in the long run necessitates constant attempts to regulate the reproduction of labor power. In the last several decades this has included an expanded intervention, through a welfare service system, to manage social relations, and particularly the more problematic aspects of social relations in contemporary society such as family disorders, mental illness and violence. However, the state does not simply 'manage' these problems but intervenes in such a way as to maintain, in the long run, the delicate balance between legitimation and accumulation. This represents not so much a conscious state policy, but rather a process of state intervention which acts to promote narrow individualistic definitions of problems, of their causes and their 'cures'. In this light it can be argued that the state manages not just the problem itself, but also the image of the problem; that is, an image of social problems which supports the state's legitimacy and guards against definitions which may threaten social order.

A more concrete understanding of how the state constructs images of deviance requires a systematic look at the process of state intervention. It is important to understand the state as the embodiment of a particular set of social relations which can be identified as bourgeois or capitalist. This set of social relations can be broken up into various aspects which, when working in concert, act to impede other, more structural definitions of social disorder. Thus, when the state recognizes social problems, their management becomes bureaucratized and professionalized, and the conceptualization of the problem itself is individualized. The critical process here involves the fragmentation of class issues at the hands of the state.

The fragmentation of class issues through a bureaucratic process also acts to shift political demands into social ones. In general, bureaucratization promotes the stratification of society not in terms of one's relation to production but rather interest groups, electoral constituents, and tax-paying citizens, identifying the social order as a 'mass of individuals'. Through this abstraction from class relations, problematic social relations lose their class character, become individualized, and segment into an expanding state bureaucracy.[2] Social relations become artificially constituted as bureaucratic structures expand to absorb increasing demands from below.

Consequently, structural issues become isolated and segmented through a process of individualization. Bureaucratized state services operate most efficiently (and thus almost 'naturally') when 'social' problems are identified as stemming from individual pathologies rather than from structural relationships within society. It is the individual who is seen as both the victim and the cause of the problem. Moreover, the individualization of problems, handled through the state bureaucracy, is shaped by a process of professionalization. Through the use (or the misuse) of science, the state creates criteria for the handling of social problems. The ability to determine one's own health, safety and welfare - the fulfillment of social needs - becomes the property of a professional elite, promoted and legitimized by the state instead of being an integral part of the community. In this way the definitions of problems (or of special needs) and the methods used to address them correspond to, rather than threaten, capitalist social relations.

These factors represent distinct features of the process of social problem intervention within the modern state. This process became fully developed in the United States with the rise of social welfare spending during the long wave of economic expansion after World War II. The state management of these problematic social relations also involved the criminal justice system as a legitimate alternative to the handling of problematic populations. Recently, much of what has been defined as 'deviance' increasingly represents a nexus of interests involving both criminal justice and social welfare: represents what we may call a social problem apparatus, which keeps those conflicts and contradictions that arise out of maintaining order separate from the relations of production, and thus depoliticized. This is done by labelling as 'social' problems which in fact are political and economic - hence the growth of 'social problems' and most recently the growth of an apparatus designed to manage them, especially among the more marginal sectors of the working class - women, minorities and youth.

In the United States the social problem apparatus grew partly out of the waves of civil unrest and demands on the state which characterized the 1960s. On the one hand, the anti-war movement, demands for racial and sexual equality, growing drug use and other such issues all resulted in a more sophisticated, expanded and expensive criminal justice system. On the other hand, many of these demands pressured the state to provide more resources for social needs, resulting in an expanded official recognition for service intervention in the areas of health care and welfare.

The expansion of the social welfare state was made possible by the general expansion of the economy in this period. The western industrialized nations witnessed rapid economic growth both in terms of industry and in the wealth of their citizens. Not only was per capita disposable income increasing, but so was the tax base upon which to build an expanded social service sector.[3] Thus the social welfare apparatus expanded and began providing treatment for those with drug, alcohol, and mental health problems, nutritional and health needs for children, welfare and food for the poor and elderly.

The criminal justice system in the United States was undergoing similar shifts. In the post-war period, especially after 1960, an increase in street crimes, widespread civil unrest, the anti-war movement, and demands for racial and sexual equality, all contributed to a more unwieldy, expanded, and expensive criminal justice system. Historically decentralized under local and state level control, the increase in the state's own need for public order brought a growing centralization in an attempt to rationalize social control. The creation of the Law Enforcement Assistance Administration (LEAA) under the U.S. Department of Justice in 1968, and the expansion of other programs within the Department, oversaw the handling of the increasingly widespread offenses coming through the system and the various demands for 'due process' within the system itself. By the end of the 1970s the expansion of both the social welfare and criminal justice systems was adding to a fiscal crisis within the state itself. Demands were straining the supply of state resources.

This contributed to the development of overlapping functions in the social welfare and the criminal justice parts of the state. Social welfare-type programs were incorporated into the criminal justice system in an effort to lessen the economic costs of maintaining the system and to re-establish its legitimacy. Social service agencies began promoting the social control aspects of treatment and counseling for problematic populations as an inexpensive alternative to a coercive approach, but also as a way to defuse criticisms of the 'giveaway' nature of social programs more generally. In the process, the two functions - social welfare services and repressive social control - partially merged and lost certain distinctions. The result is the beginning of a social problem apparatus which continues to establish new methods of social control.

For example, Weisner has recently described the process whereby alcoholism treatment institutions have mortgaged themselves to the criminal justice system.[4] Treatment agencies are able to maintain clientele and thus funding, by receiving clients through local criminal justice diversion programs. Although most of these clients are not 'alcoholics' this helps lessen an overloaded court system while helping to control specific segments of the population. For many, no cure is intended; the purpose of alcohol treatment in these situations has moved from medicalized services to social problem management.

Thus, social problem management is a process which expands the basis for social control while it depoliticizes political questions. It incorporates demands through quasi-medical models, individualizes and personalizes structural problems, and obscures any class interests inherent in them. The structural and political contexts to 'social problems' are hidden under the processes outlined above. According to Gusfield, these policies are essentially masked under the mantle of science:

> Science is the idiom of our age. It is the language in which command is cast as the compulsion of external nature. Authoritative law that rests its claim to legitimacy and acceptance on the technical reasoning of the realm of science denies any moral status. It denies that a moral decision has been taken, that a political choice among alternatives has been made. The ownership and responsibility for social problems and their solution are given as a matter of fact and not of values.[5]

Consequently, mainstream social science acts to legitimize the state's ownership of social problems through narrow explorations of problematic populations, or symbolic meanings of societal responses, instead of the larger structural issues. What mainstream social science has characterized as social problems, and thus generalized out of class context, may represent conflicts and contradictions endemic to the system itself. Social scientists thus generally neglect to analyze fully the process of state intervention and the impact it has on constructing and maintaining particular (and narrow) images of problems. State intervention into social problems has been viewed as either basically inherent in the state's repressive apparatus, or as undifferentiated activities within the social welfare system.

The reality remains quite different. The social problems image, when incorporated into state welfare and criminal justice systems, often masks political ends by defining problems in terms of a view of society as a mass of individuals empty of class context. With the state's broadened intervention subsuming more political issues under social problem programs and policies, social problem management is no longer simply a matter of repressive or service institutions. Further, contemporary welfare policies cannot simply be superficially characterized as programs designed to deflect real political threats or as concessions to grassroots demands.

The social problem apparatus can thus be viewed as the child of both the criminal justice system and social welfare systems. It incorporates the models of professionalism and science, bureaucratizes them, and maintains a definition of 'problems' directed toward individual pathologies. It is the way in which the social problem apparatus incorporates service and service agendas which makes it unique. Within the past decade tangible boundaries have begun to emerge around particular sets of agendas. As these boundaries coalesce into institutionalized forms, established professionalized bureaucracies are undergoing subtle shifts in goals. No longer purely social welfare or criminal justice, social control and social needs are being shaped into a single entity – social problem management.

Wife-battering and the refuge movement

The enfranchising of different social problems within the state goes through similar processes, shifts and changes in image. The example of the problem of wife beating is used because the period from its recent identification as a social problem to its incorporation within the state has been very rapid. It has just been within the past ten years that the problem of wife-battering has been 'discovered'. From the ten to twenty shelters for battered women in the U.S. and Britain of ten years ago, there are now hundreds of shelters in the U.S. alone, along with numerous other services (counseling, referral, legal) found in countries all over the world.[6] What was once a private individual family problem has become public, thanks largely to the women's movement and the public dissemination of women's problems and needs.

The problem was first identified by feminists as a manifestation of gender domination. In a society which allowed for a pervasive discrimination of women, both in the home and in the workplace, women could be seen by their husbands and cohabitants to be 'appropriate' victims of violence in the home.[7] The aim of the feminists was to battle this historical discrimination by providing immediate help and sheltering for battered women, revealing the pervasiveness of gender domination in the home, and in some cases by making the links between the maintenance of gender-dominated social relations and the contradictions found in contemporary industrial or capitalist societies.[8]

Set up as specific crisis intervention resources for battered women, the first refuge organizations were structured similarly to other feminist community groups. The primary aim was to provide a safe haven for abused women and to promote public awareness of the problem. They included gay and straight women, were organized collectively, and were grounded in the belief that violence against women generally was a pervasive manifestation of gender domination in contemporary society.

Education, for both refuge workers and their constituents, was seen as a necessary part of the organization's work. The aim of the refuge was generally to make these women aware of their structural position in society and to help them lead independent and safe lives. Although many of these intentions were put aside in the day-to-day struggles of the organization, nonetheless, they formed implicitly the image of the problem at hand.[9]

Soon, however, this began to change. Public discourse, scholarly research, and government intervention produced a plethora of treatment and service models which have acted to bureaucratize, individualize, and professionalize the handling of the problem. Refuges, formerly run by small collectives of feminist activists, often with a strong community base, were replaced by larger 'service' centers administered by boards of directors and staffed by professionals, which additionally provided services for batterers, legal assistance, drug and/or alcohol treatment, and psychiatric counseling.[10] Whereas once the aim was to educate women to live independent lives, it shifted toward family reunification. Where once the impact of gender domination was raised as a way of understanding violent abuse of women, now the focus is on individual pathology, the 'illness' of the batterer and the psychological profile of the victim.

This rapid change within the past half dozen years has also generated immediate help for thousands of women worldwide and millions of dollars in local, federal, state, and private funds aimed at the problem. Although some of these changes can be seen as a victory, especially by those who have fought for the rights of women in the home, this victory is only partial and carries a potentially dangerous price tag. The image of wife-battery, when first brought to public attention by feminists, contained both political and humanist elements. The step-by-step process by which this image has been narrowed is important to the understanding of how state intervention serves to transform and narrow definitions and explanations of problems.

Constructing the image:
bureaucratization and professionalization

Awareness of the problem in the feminist community and the rapid growth of the refuge movement soon produced a plethora of books and articles about wife-battering, attempting both to generate public awareness and find theoretical explanations. Two major theoretical strains soon developed. One, grounded in mainstream sociological and psychological disciplines, was essentially a causal model. That is, research was based in propositional assumptions attempting to link together event or conditional phenomena to the problem of wife-battering. This line of research tended to view violent actions against women within the context of individual and family psychology, neglecting gender domination and the condition of women in society as particularly relevant.[11] Attention instead focused on individual character disorders (of both wife and husband), on the psychological results of a violent culture, on theories of alienation, and on the association between domestic violence and other 'deviant' characteristics such as drug abuse, alcohol abuse, history of criminal behavior and family background.

The second theoretical model was grounded in an historical structural analysis. Research charted the condition of women outside, as well as in, the home through various stages of pre-capitalist and capitalist development. These studies tended to see some combination of patriarchy and capitalism as forming the environment which supported and legitimized violence against women in general and particularly in the home.[12] It was particularly important to create a critical understanding of these violent situations. Thus, the task was to go beyond psychosocial causal definitions and to understand those definitions themselves as ideological constructs grounded in the political economic reality of contemporary industrial society. Thus, a structural analysis saw battered women's refuges as primarily crisis intervention/education centers, while causal theories implicitly promoted refuges as service delivery centers.

During the first few years of the refuge movement, the immediate task of providing help and education for battered women was accompanied by two other equally important tasks: creating public awareness and fundraising, both of which, while an essential aspect of the refuge movement in the U.S., in turn resulted in its transformation. Public awareness drives were aimed at reaching those who were in need of help and in legitimating the problem itself. Based on increased awareness, shelters sought funds from a variety of private progressive foundations, community and religious groups. However, because the money from private foundations tended to be small, necessitating a constant effort, an overwhelming amount of organizational resources was spent in fund-raising. Also, the refuge movement grew so rapidly that small private, community or church funding sources were soon overwhelmed with demands for funds.

Soon organizations began petitioning for local, state, and federal funds, and found a great response on the federal level.[13] To be success-ful, grant applications were required to conform to a model most amen-able to state interests. Practically, refuges, in order to meet funding agency guidelines, have had to modify, in some cases transform, the character of response to their constituents, as well as the character of their own organizations. Collectives became bureaucratized, appointed boards of directors, and incorporated professional counselors and treatment staff into their organization in order to abide by the condi-tions of their service grants and contracts, or to put themselves in a better position to obtain funding successfully. In addition, these requests began pouring into these agencies at a time when the existing functions of many government bureaucracies were being questioned. Both mental health and criminal justice agencies, which had grown so rapidly in the 1960s and early 1970s, were open to responding to a 'new' social problem which would buttress their overall position within the state in the 1980s. Soon a competitive process developed among the various agencies, each vying for responsibility and control – and thus more funds – over the problem of domestic violence.[14] Consequently, there has been a two-fold requirement for wife-battery refuge organiza-tions: the promotion of treatment/service models and the promotion of research in the causal model. The results have been far-reaching.

Significantly, this process was accomplished through state interven-tion in criminal justice as well as social welfare agencies. In the mid-1970s, when the first refuges opened in the U.S., official intervention into the problem was limited to local police departments. In fact, over 60 per cent of police responses in a given community were in answer to domestic disturbance calls.[15] Generally, the dispositions ended with the initial call, because the police tended to consider wife-battering as a private family matter rather than a criminal offense.[16] The reluctance of the police to arrest the assaulter or assist the victim, coupled with the almost impenetrable red tape of the court system, provided con-tinual humiliation and increased danger for assaulted women.

Consequently, early goals of the feminist refuge movement were demands for legal changes, and for police cooperation in assisting vic-tims and arresting assaulters. However, because local criminal justice systems were generally unwilling or unable to respond adequately, the federal criminal justice apparatus stepped in to set up guidelines and policies able to defuse the potential political impact of the problem while developing a rationalized system capable of relieving pressures on local courts and police, probation and prosecuting offices.

The federal Law Enforcement Assistance Administration (LEAA) led the attempt to rationalize police response to the problem of battered women. Between 1974 and 1979, over thirty-five direct service programs for battered women were funded: refuges, technical assistance projects, information dissemination networks, police crisis intervention training, and court diversion programs.[17] The stated rationale was to improve police response to domestic disturbance calls and promote services for both 'victims and perpetrators'. The actual purpose, however, was a bit more complex.

As a viable and political public issue, the potential criminalization of wife assaulters threatened to put too many strains on a criminal justice system already burdened by high crime rates and limited resources. However, although the police and court system could not afford regularly to process the wife abuser, the general repressive apparatus remained committed to a social control mandate. The solution, then, was to provide service models for local police departments to divert offenders, that is, to 'manage' more efficiently the offense through social service networks.

Thus, the reforms instituted by the criminal justice system seem to have been quite responsive. New local and state regulations throughout the country did mandate police to arrest battering husbands. Public defender and district attorney offices did set up programs to deal more directly with the problem. These programs were generally set up from models developed by LEAA and were often funded from LEAA resources. Although most of these new programs provided needed help for battered wives, their overriding purpose was to minimize costs to local criminal justice systems, to expedite the handling of family dispute cases, and, importantly, to capture control of the problem in such a way that its radical political implications would be minimized.

Consequently, the police arrested more violators but then diverted them from the court process through probation department programs which generally involved minimum counseling requirements. Wife-battery became subsumed under the general rubric of 'domestic violence' in these agencies, which tended to treat all violence in the family as the same problem. Domestic violence service centers opened up under probation or district attorney departments with LEAA funds. These service centers did little to distinguish among 'clients' – whether beaten women or batterers. Often they utilized the record-keeping requirements of the various sponsoring agencies to ferret out 'welfare cheaters', probation violators, or others normally caught up in the criminal justice system. Those 'offenders' with money were generally allowed to be diverted to private treatment facilities, e.g., alcoholism clinics or private psychiatrists where records of attendance are rarely kept. Conversely, lower class batterers were either sent to jail or routed into state-run services designed chiefly for the more repressive forms of social control.

In sum, the early feminist orientation of the refuges for battered women has given way to pre-existing social control and welfare service goals. The community base has been replaced largely by middle class, white, straight professionals whose main interest in the organization is one of service delivery.[18] Requests for state funding were based on the psycho-social causal models, for these were the theoretical models which already framed existing state social welfare programs. Refuges themselves, many initially working from a feminist-collective perspective, soon became mired in conflicts between the two models. These conflicts were based in the organization's own environment and the resources they needed in order to keep operating. Thus, many refuges were transformed into service centers aimed at family reunification, including drug and alcohol treatment, psychological counseling and a range of other activities which in some cases allows for full participation by the batterers. Finally, the newest refuges often no longer stem from grassroots feminist community orientations, but rather start out as state-sponsored service delivery organizations connected to existing religious, service, or welfare-type state organizations.

Constructing the image: individualization

A common way to individualize a social problem is to have the problem associated with another, already narrowly defined problem. Thus, once recognized by the state, programs and policies are incorporated into existing problem frameworks. It becomes important, then, to study historically the narrowing of problem definitions, and the process whereby different social problems become aggregated while under the management of the state.

In the arena of attributions of domestic violence, for instance, the problem of alcoholism was an early contender. Some pilot studies reported some alcohol involvement in the battering event. A body of literature linking alcohol to disinhibition from everyday normative constraints found receptive audiences in both sociological and popular publications covering battered women.[19] And, importantly, within the past few years both the alcoholism movement within the U.S. and local, state and federal alcohol abuse agencies have begun to include violence against women in the home as part of the 'alcoholism' problem.

The statistics that do exist linking the two problems raise more questions than they answer. Despite this, there are increasing numbers of recommendations to include alcoholism therapy in domestic violence counseling services, for refuge workers to recognize that 'drinking and domestic violence go together', that 'as long as drinking continues nothing else will improve', and for every refuge worker to understand the disease of alcoholism and its relationship to the violence problem. Thus alcohol-specific service delivery models are currently being incorporated into domestic violence community organizations. This process is changing the structure of these organizations, the image of the problem presented to constituents, the characterization of new refuges and service centers, and, ultimately, the public definition of the wife-battering problem in this country. Significantly, the fault is not within the ascription to alcohol abuse itself, but in the treatment/service ideology which frames the alcohol problem in the United States and which threatens to subsume any structural grassroots inquiry into the question of violence against women.

A brief examination of the historical shifts in the image of alcohol problems and its incorporation into the state will give a better understanding of the present changes in the image of the problem of wife beating. Until the post-World War II period, alcohol drinking problems were generally defined as problems of intemperance. The properties of alcoholic substances themselves were said to lead to a loss of self-control, decreased work performance, broken families, corruption of the nation's youth, and generally profound damage to the fabric of society. State intervention was principally aimed at controlling the substance alcohol, at making its obtainment difficult and eventually its consumption illegal. Alcohol prohibition was thus based on the notion that the state had a responsibility to promote self-control, job performance, family life and so on, over its responsibility to promote and protect the alcohol beverage industries.

With the demise of prohibition in 1933, the state was vested with a new and somewhat contradictory responsibility of continuing to promote alcohol control along with a competing demand to promote the economic expansion of the alcohol beverage industry and corresponding state revenues. This was done primarily by decentralizing alcohol control to the state or local level, which became largely responsible for alcohol sales, distribution and production. The image of the alcohol problem remained the same; it was based on the evils of the substance itself. At the end of World War II, when consumption began a sharp increase, these contradictions sharpened, leading to new policies which transformed the image of the problem from one of intemperance to one of illness.

The alcohol disease model was wholeheartedly supported by the alcohol beverage industries, which recognized that transferring the onus of the problem 'from the bottle to the man' could ultimately threaten temperance ideology. In the 1950s, industry associations formed scientific task groups, gave funding support to alcoholism researchers, lobbied in state legislatures for a 'public health' commitment to alcohol problems, and devised public campaigns supportive of the disease approach.[20] Moreover, the development of the disease model as it became incorporated by government treatment and research policies represented a growing reliance on scientific management, professionalism, and 'expert' planning as a way of structuring the social welfare state apparatus. In general, the psycho-medical model offered a new and more rational way to order the state's legitimizing apparatus: supplying 'services' to the disadvantaged, instead of relying upon a coercive social order. It neutralized potentially problematic populations through a service model which appeared to give equal success to the state's resources while it personalized and individualized formerly social and structural explanations to problems.

This ideology was institutionalized into the social welfare system during the late 1960s. The National Institute of Mental Health (NIMH), as well as the National Institute of Drug Abuse (NIDA), the National Institute of Alcohol Abuse and Alcoholism (NIAAA), the National Institutes of Health (NIH), the Alcohol and Drug Abuse Mental Health Administration (ADAMHA), and others were all formed within the framework.

This overall expansion in federal service programs and funds resulted in a fundamental shift in the images of several related social problem definitions. In the mid-1970s a former director of NIDA acknowledged that the previous decade had seen an 8,000 per cent increase in federal mental health expenditures, funds which were rationalized by this service/treatment model.[21] This development, at least in the case of alcohol, eased the conflict of a state attempting to control an alcohol problem and promote an industry simultaneously. Federal alcohol problem policies have become more centralized and greatly separated from state and local alcohol control programs. A wide gap exists between alcohol rehabilitation programs and the overall place of alcohol beverages in society.

The purpose of this discussion has been to account for an important historical shift in the image of a social problem: from one with structural dimensions to a limited individualized framework.[22] The parallel between what once happened to the alcohol problem and what is happening now to the image of wife-battering is, unfortunately, not only striking but predictable.

Conclusion

In constructing a non-threatening image of the problem of wife-battering, the state has eliminated the need for inquiries into the condition of women in contemporary society – the political, economic and cultural environment of women in late capitalism. The growth of the medical approach, and professionalized treatment organized through public and mental health services, has not only provided an environment supportive of the individualization of wife-battery, but has essentially guaranteed that battery be subsumed under this rubric.

Transformations in the handling and image of battered women have had the strongest impact in the area of social control and in the re-imposition of class domination. The newer organizations now 'treating' the problem bear little resemblance to the early refuge movement which first opened the way for many women to escape their victimization. Often, refuges and service agencies created under (or funded through) the state, at the least, compromise the safety of these women.[23] Under the officially sponsored refuges, 'the requirements for evaluation and reporting can seriously compromise client confidentiality and clients themselves can be trapped for welfare fraud, drug problems, or parole violations'.[24] Yet, those requirements are part of many agencies' funding criteria. The worst consequence for battered women, however, is that they are increasingly open to further victimization through a slightly more sophisticated process of victim-blaming than was present before the refuge movement began. Many refuges screen for psychological defects, for drug or alcohol 'addiction', and for other 'indicators' of unfitness for help or sheltering. Often professional psychiatrists in these agencies prescribe tranquilizers to help these women 'cope' with their problem.

These social control devices are masked under the cloak of modern professionalized services. The professionalization of responses to wife abuse is also an example of how the state captures legitimacy of the problem's identification and handling under the name of science.[25]

By channeling everything into professionalized medical or service categories capable of handling a wide range of problems, the continued atomization of problematic behaviors is guaranteed.

The trend toward the rationalization of the criminal justice system provides further evidence. Professionalized social services, coupled with discretionary treatment at the hands of police or courts, segment problem behaviors into separate professional scientific responses. Thus, batterers get channeled into particular treatment or service alternatives, or are incarcerated, on the basis of medical scientific frameworks. In reality, as before, class categories remain invisibly at work as specified segments of the working class are subject to punitive sanctions.

Finally, the inevitable consequence of the state's fiscal limitations in the era of political and economic austerity and conservatism has not bypassed the refuge movement. Bolstered by right-wing attacks against programs which 'interfere' with the contemporary family and against policies designed to service the marginal sectors of the working class, the state has begun to withdraw some support for 'family violence' services. In 1980 a proposed Domestic Violence Prevention Program bill never made it through Congress, blocked by the ultra-conservatives who felt threatened by the programs that would be funded. Many existing service programs were being phased out of Reagan's new budget at the time of writing, and LEAA has been essentially dismantled. Although a great many refuge groups are supported almost totally by state-level or local funds, other refuges (both feminist and 'professional') are in danger of closing as well.

The state may be withdrawing its financial support, but the restructuring and identification of the problem has, in effect, been established. Service delivery systems, previously established by the federal LEAA and incorporated into local criminal justice systems, will probably survive. These are the systems which have wide discretionary powers to 'divert', 'treat', or jail the batterer according to the state's own criteria. Service delivery programs and refuges, on the other hand, will become almost buried within established mental health, substance abuse, or other counseling agencies. The problem will be addressed minimally, or not distinguished much from other professionalized services within the social problem apparatus.

The purpose of this paper has not been to judge the success or failure of the refuge movement, but rather to steer the analysis in somewhat new directions. Theoretically, we should acknowledge the importance of systematically examining these movements in order to understand more fully the state as a set of relationships committed to the constant task of re-establishing non-threatening social relations.[26]

State apparatuses are inherently designed to address political problems through capitalist forms – as 'social problems'. The state, in the last analysis, embodies a set of capitalist social relations which utilize the mantle of science and technology to manage social issues. The growth of the interventionist state has essentially meant the growth of bureaucratic and professionalized forms penetrating everyday life, shaping social problem images as narrow associations. Problematic behaviors are addressed in a linear fashion, according to prevailing 'scientific' models. Consequently, progressive movements, which come to depend on professionalized institutions, may eventually become dependant on these 'causal' models for their very existence. Thus, organizations such as refuge shelters, which begin with a commitment to radical social change, become transformed into progressive adjuncts of the state apparatus, in the process transforming the image of the problem as well.

Notes

1 J. O.Connor, *The Fiscal Crisis of the State*, New York, St Martin's Press, 1973.
2. Cf. J. Holloway, J. Macdonald, R. Paine and O. Stassinopoulau-Holloway, 'The crisis of the state and the struggle against bourgeois forms', presented at the Conference of Socialist Economists, State Expenditure and Cuts Group, Loncon, May 1978.
3 I. Gough, *The Political Economy of the Welfare State*, London, Macmillan, 1979.
4 C. Weisner, 'Treatment as social control: the political economy of alcohol problem management', *Journal of Drug Issues*, vol. 13, no. 1, 1981.
5 J. Gusfield, *The Culture of Public Problems*, Chicago, University of Chicago Press, 1981, p. 94.
6 B. Warrior, *Working on Wife Abuse*, Cambridge, 46 Pleasant Street, 1978 (first edn., 1976).
7 R.E. Dobash and R. Dobash, *Violence Against Wives: The Case Against the Patriarchy*, New York, The Free Press, 1979.
8 M.D. Pagelow, 'Battered women: a new perspective', presented at the International Sociological Association Seminar on Sex Roles, Deviance and Agents of Social Control, Dublin, August 1977; B. Warrior, op. cit.
9 See paper by Clifton in this Monograph.
10 P. Morgan and L. Wermuth, 'Alcohol and family violence: an overview of information and resources', paper prepared for the National Institute on Alcohol Abuse and Alcoholism, March 1980.
11 M. Straus, R. Gelles and S. Steinmetz, *Behind Closed Doors: Violence in the American Family*, New York, Doubleday, 1979.
12 Cf. Dobash and Dobash, op. cit.
13 In Britain only 10 per cent of Women's Aid groups received money from housing departments in 1978, although two-thirds of the groups received grants for paid workers. The chief sources of funding have been the Manpower Services Commission and the Urban Programme. See V. Binney, G. Harkell

and J. Nixon, *Leaving Violent Men*, London, Women's Aid Federation England, 1981.

14 Cf. Weisner, op. cit. 1981; R. Spiegleman, 'Beyond nothing works: the politics and ideology of alcohol treatment in diversion', paper prepared for the American Sociological Association Meetings, Toronto, 1981.

15 J. Bannon, 'Presentation of police difficulties with female battering cases', prepared for the U.S. Civil Rights Commission, Connecticut Advisory Committee, September 1977.

16 E. Eisenberg and L. Micklow, 'The assaulted wife: "catch 22" revisited', *Women's Rights Law Reporter*, June 1976.

17 Morgan and Wermuth, op. cit., 1980.

18 L. Ahrens, 'Battered women's refuges: feminist cooperatives vs social service institutions', *Radical America*, Summer 1980, pp. 41–9.

19 R. Langley and R. Levy, *Wife Beating: The Silent Crisis*, New York, Pocket Books, 1977.

20 P. Morgan, 'The state as mediator: alcohol problem management in the post-war period', *Contemporary Drug Problems*, Spring 1980.

21 Ibid.

22 Cf. P. Morgan, 'Alcohol, disinhibition, and domination: a conceptual analysis', paper presented at the Alcohol and Disinhibition Conference, Social Research Group, Berkeley, California, February 1981.

23 C. McGrath, 'The crisis of domestic order', *Socialist Review*, vol. 43, 1979, pp. 11–30.

24 Ibid., p. 27.

25 R. Crawford, 'You are dangerous to your health: the ideology and politics of victim blaming', *International Journal of Health Services*, vol. 7, no. 4, 1977, pp. 663–80.

26 Holloway *et al.*, op. cit., 1978.

The burden of dependency

Marjorie Homer, Anne Leonard and Pat Taylor

Abstract

The control of financial resources is an important indicator of the distribution of power within families. This may be particularly significant when economic power is accompanied by physical violence. This paper considers economic dependency among a group of women using a refuge. It examines family income levels, the control and distribution of this money and of responsibility for paying bills, together with evidence on living standards. Using 140 per cent of the supplementary benefit standard as a poverty line, it was found that 63 per cent of the families lived in poverty.

Much more significant, however, were the patterns of control of resources. Five allocation systems were identified, but the overall picture which emerged was that overwhelmingly it was men who controlled family finances. Women were kept chronically short of money, and some even had to hand over their child benefits. The women therefore suffered severe deprivation and had to go without basic household items and sometimes food. Control of the purse was even more complete when husbands were unemployed. The long-term solution requires a change in public and personal attitudes which must include giving women more equal access to economic and social resources in their own right.

The economic dependency of women continues to be a fundamental feature of our society. Attempts by women to leave violent relationships, or to find viable alternatives to them, continue therefore to be constrained by this basic inequality. A further outcome of women's material dependency may be their primary poverty irrespective of the family income level. Refuge residents have often experienced considerable deprivation although their household may not be officially

77

'in poverty'. Of course, women and children coming to the Refuge are chiefly from low-income families. One aim of the enquiry was, therefore, to examine the extent, the experience and the significance of poverty for women and children leaving domestic violence; and especially to explore the connection between their financial circumstances and their economic dependency.

The material in this paper is part of a much larger study of the experiences of eighty women who had stayed in the Cleveland Refuge between 1977 and 1982. The aim was to build up as complete a picture as possible of the women's lives and the problems they faced.

Context

All except three of the eighty women in the study had lived in Cleveland prior to coming to the Refuge. The economic base of the county is in steel, heavy engineering and oil refining, despite 60 per cent of Cleveland being rural. The area's dependence on capital intensive industries meant that unemployment remained consistently higher than the national average throughout the 1970s. In the current recession the county's unemployment rate has remained the highest in the UK outside Northern Ireland (18.4 per cent in April 1982).[1] Male unemployment has particularly affected the county's higher than average population of unskilled manual workers, there being a residual core of long-term unemployed in this category.[2] There is no tradition of employment for women outside the home,[3] and opportunities created in the

Table 1: Socio-economic status of husbands

Category	Research		Cleveland[4]	England & Wales[4]
	No.	%	%	%
Employers, managers and professionals	7	9	15.2	23.0
Other non-manual	2	2.6	16.5	20.1
Skilled manual	29	37.2	41.2	37.5
Semi-skilled manual	11	14.0	18.0	14.9
Unskilled manual	20	25.6	9.1	4.5
Unclassifiable	9	11.6		
Total	78*	100.0	100.0	100.0

* The financial study excludes two women already single parents when they came to the Refuge.

early 1970s have been largely eroded by recent closure and contraction.[5]

There was a wider spread of socio economic groupings than was expected, given the poverty of the majority of the women who use the Refuge. However, nearly 90 per cent of husbands were manual workers, or unclassifiable long-term unemployed.

Before coming to the Refuge half of the women in the sample had husbands who had been out of work for periods of at least three months and up to ten years.

Table 2: Male employment position

Category	Research group		1981 OCPS Knight[+]
	No.	%	%
Employed	39	50.0	60.0
Unemployed:			
Short-term*	15	19.2	27.0
Long-term**	22	28.2	
Long-term sick	2	2.6	6.0
Other	—	—	7.0
Total	78	100.0	100.0

  * More than three months, less than twelve
 ** At least twelve months.
 + A study of low-income families in Scotland.[6]

Cleveland's structural unemployment is reflected in the circumstances of these families. Some wives could not remember a time when their husbands had worked, and rejected the notion of a 'usual occupation'; for example, 'he's never worked since I knew him'. For these families unemployment and desperate poverty is a consistent part of their lives, while for the majority of those experiencing short-term unemployment the meanness of their present living standard follows on from lean years of low pay.

Family incomes

Examination of family income levels, the control and distribution of this money, and of responsibility for paying bills, together with the evidence on living standards, reveals the starkness of the women's experience.

In this connection the term 'family' is used for the base economic unit of either a couple, or parents and children under seventeen years. Where older children were at home we assumed that any contribution to the family income was offset by costs. Income has been assessed on 'normal' net weekly wages for the three month period immediately before a woman came to the Refuge. The usual practice has been followed of accepting the short-term supplementary benefit rate (expressed as 100) as the 'poverty line'. Family income is then shown as a percentage of this. Since supplementary benefit rates are intended to cover all basic household expenses, social security payments for housing and heating allowances are included in the calculations. The 'Townsend line' of 140 per cent of the supplementary benefit rate has also been considered. This was suggested in 1965 to be a more realistic standard by which to measure poverty since it allowed for extra needs payments to those on supplementary benefit, disregarded earnings and gifts.[7]

Table 3 shows thirty-five families (45 per cent) with income which was on, or below, the state poverty line; this figure is increased to forty-nine families (63 per cent) when the Townsend standard is applied.

Table 3: Family income level

Income as % of S.B. standard	Families	
	No.	%
Below 90	3	3.9
91–100	32	41.0
101–120	6	7.7
121–140	8	10.3
141–200	15	19.2
Over 200	9	11.5
Not known	5	6.4
Total	78	100.0

Four out of the five families whose income was unknown may be assumed to have been above the 140 per cent level since their occupations put them in socio-economic groups II and III (M). Thus there were twenty-eight families who were not in poverty when treated as a unit. This view of the situation changed remarkably during our examination of the distribution of income and financial responsibilities within each family; among wives as individuals poverty was both more widespread and more severe.

Distribution of income within the family

All official investigations into levels of income and expenditure are based on either the household or family unit though it has been increasingly recognized that the poverty of individuals within an 'out of poverty' unit can, and does, exist. Examination of financial arrangements within the family has made little progress in official studies. However, there has been a flowering of interest in patterns of control and distribution of income within the family among researchers engaged in community and feminist studies. Conversations with women leaving domestic violence reveal the urgent need for such studies and provide a rare opportunity to extend this work. We have, therefore, both examined the control and distribution of income which existed prior to women coming to the Refuge, and attempted to measure women's incomes in relation to their financial responsibilities. The result has been to show the extent of the poverty which women experienced and its connection to the distribution of power within the family.

A considerable body of work now exists on the control, distribution and management of income within the family. The following four types of allocative system have been suggested by, among others, Jan Pahl,[8] whose interest in this subject arose out of her own research among women at the Canterbury Refuge:[9]

(a) *the whole wage system* in which the husband hands over the whole of his wage packet and the wife manages their financial affairs, giving him a certain amount for his own spending money;

(b) *the allowance system* in which the husband gives his wife a sum of money for her housekeeping responsibilities;

(c) *the pooling system*, i.e. the 'share and share alike' method; this usually reflects a more egalitarian relationship and it is thought to be found when both partners are working; the joint bank account is usually a feature of this system;

(d) *the independent management system* which is marked by the feature of quite separate flows of money for husband and wife.

We found, however, that Pahl's classification was inadequate to understand what occurred for a substantial number of women in our sample and we have made appropriate modifications. A *whole wage (his)* category was added to the system Pahl describes, and the traditional whole wage system was redesignated *whole wage (hers)*. Table 4 shows the number of families using each of the five patterns identified.

Where there was a *whole wage (his)* pattern of management seventeen women in our study received no money whatsoever from their partners. Of these, nine also had to hand over all their Child Benefit,

Table 4: Patterns of income distribution and management

Pattern	Families	
	No.	%
Whole wage (his)	17	21.8
Whole wage (hers)	16	20.5
Allowance	38	48.7
Pooled	4	5.1
Independent	3	3.9
Total	78	100.0

while there was a partial loss of this among the other eight. In the vast majority of these cases, the men were unemployed and the daily control of both money and women was indeed grim. Living standards were very low. Louise, who had two babies, reported that she had had no heat without permission to switch on the electric fire, no hot water, no washer and no soap powder. Thus she washed nappies in the sink in cold water only. Louise identified her husband's priorities as 'going out with his mates' and his own entertainment, a common complaint.

Four men had apparently abandoned any responsibility for maintaining their wives and children who were on the verge of destitution when they came to the Refuge. Other women probably fared little better except that they were not so urgently in need of food from family and friends.

In sixteen cases the *whole wage (hers)* system operated but for the majority of women in this group there was a departure from the ideal type in that 'pocket money' for husbands was neither set nor could it be restricted. For all but three women it was money on demand, and wives felt unable to withstand this pressure. Dissatisfaction here was particularly high among the wives of the long-term unemployed, with the wives of the men in work expressing much less bitterness. This underlines the point that distribution is more of an issue when money is short. Generally, however, these sixteen women had responsibility for all household bills with no means of restricting access to their purses, and they were not even sure of getting the money in the first place: 'I got the money to meet everything and to give him money. Some weeks there wasn't any for him to go drinking but he used to take it anyway'.

The largest number of women in our sample, thirty-eight (49 per cent), described an *allowance* system of distribution. Here again their difficulty in keeping the money they received made nonsense of any attempt by five of these women to meet their budgets. Three women complained of being given an allowance and having it taken off them within twenty-four hours and of losing their Child Benefit also, for example, 'He gave me £15 on Wednesday and took it back on Thursday'.

The remaining thirty-three women receiving an allowance did not mention this problem, although they reported unreliability in receiving that allowance and the amount given was fixed by the man. Seventeen women expressed dissatisfaction with the arrangements, with thirteen experiencing considerable difficulty in the task of meeting heavy household responsibilities with a disproportionately small share of the household income. Problems existed not only where men were out of work - wives of the employed men in this group (30 per cent) were also very short of money, though generally where men earned the highest wages fewer difficulties were reported. There was one frequently expressed complaint: sixteen wives (42 per cent) in the allowance group did not know how much their partners earned, or received in state benefit, compared to twenty-six (33 per cent) in the total sample.

Four women described a *pooled system* of distribution and management of income, i.e. 'everything was put on the table and money put away for commitments and the rest for food'. However, two women did not know how much money was coming into the home and took the arrangement on trust. Equality broke down at the point of pocket money: three out of the four women concerned had none, although their husbands did, a feature that was common to the majority of families in our study. The remaining three women kept their money separate from their husband's in an *independent management system.*

In the circumstances we investigated, patterns of income control, distribution and management lose some of their relevance. Out of the seventy-eight families represented in our study at least sixty-seven men controlled family incomes through a variety of distribution patterns. The pooled and independent management systems entail a greater degree of equality in the control of family income, but very few families in this study (9 per cent) adopted these less autocratic forms of budgeting. Usually the *whole wage (hers)* system still left the overall control of income in the hands of the man. In three cases the system operated to give the women some control of family finance. In a fourth case it was not certain where control lay.

The unemployment and low paid, sometimes part-time, employment of women seems to be crucial in facilitating the control patterns we have described. For instance, where men exercised total management of the income no women went out to work, a factor which apparently both aided and grew out of their husbands' dominance. On the other hand, where women in our study were employed this seems to have had the effect of the man then reducing the money which he allowed his wife, or expecting her to take on further financial responsibilities.

Responsibility for family expenditure

When the inequitable distribution of family income is taken in conjunction with the allocation of financial responsibilities then the primary poverty of women is seen to be more extensive than even the above evidence suggests. An exploratory measurement of the responsibility which each woman had for basic items of weekly household expenditure in relation to her money was made for the sixty-two women in the *whole wage (hers)* and *allowance* patterns of distribution and management, and where women's only source of income was their child benefit under a *whole wage (his)* system. (Elsewhere women either had no responsibilities, or there was an equal management system.) There were forty-four women and their children out of this group (71 per cent) who appeared to have actually lived on, and indeed sometimes well below, the supplementary benefit standard when income was examined in relation to their financial responsibilities. Almost half of the thirty women who had responsibility for all household bills were trying to manage on sums of money which ranged from 51 per cent to 80 per cent of their family's supplementary benefit standard; a further four women had income which was 50 per cent of the supplementary benefit level but had, variously, between 61 per cent and 80 per cent of household bills to meet. Problems did not end there, however, for many women had the additional task of finding money for their husband's entertainment and paying off debts not included in the calculations. Inequality was apparent even where women had low scores on the responsibility scale since these were in the basic areas of family food and clothing, as the study below reveals. Conversely, men with few financial responsibilities had these in relation to personal expenditure or a television rental.[10]

Case study

Caroline had only the £4 weekly child benefit payable for her three-year-old son, Sean, although her husband had a weekly wage in the region of £100. He paid the mortgage and heating bills but made no other provision for Caroline and Sean. Caroline described how her friends and family gave them both food:

> 'Irene used to come, and her Dad used to buy me some food or something, you know. He would give me money to make sure I got something to eat. Then Terry moved in. I said she could stay with us a few days. When she was getting her dole money she was buying Sean and I food. If it hadn't been for her we would have had nothing to eat. I had another friend June, she worked in an hotel and she brought me pieces of meat home. Sometimes I used to go to my sister who lived three miles away. I used to walk up there to see if she could give me something to eat, or I used to go to his Mother's. His Dad used to come in about four o'clock if he was on the right shift and I knew that either we'd both get something to eat or at least Sean would.'

Half of the women whose only source of income was child benefit were in the same grim situation as Caroline, who felt, 'We would not have survived another year'. Although such extreme circumstances affected only 5 per cent of the sample, our findings show that the majority of women experienced a depth of poverty far beyond that revealed by reference to their family income level.

The extent of primary poverty

Table 5 relates both family income and the women's income to the supplementary benefit and the Townsend poverty standards for all seventy-eight women in this study.

Table 5: Income level and women's money related to S.B. standard

Income as % of S.B. Standard	Family		Women*	
	No.	%	No.	%
0–100	35	44.9	57	73.1
101–140	14	17.9	13	16.7
141+	24	30.8	8	10.2
Not available	5	6.4	–	–
Total	78	100.0	78	100.0

* Includes women from all allocative systems.

The study of family income has revealed serious deprivation, especially among the long-term unemployed. Yet family circumstances are insufficient to explain all the hardship discovered; as we have shown, much of the primary poverty of women and children existed regardless of family income level, as a result of distribution of income within families.

Living standards

The following examination of family expenditure shows the effect of financial deprivation on living standards. In order to appreciate the actual effect of the financial arrangements described as 'living standards', the material conditions of the families were investigated, their ownership of consumer durables, and what kind of life-style they were able to achieve. Women were also asked whether they felt the lack of particular items or opportunities.

Table 6 shows possession of consumer durables. 'Vacuum cleaner' was added to the list drawn from current official studies, since we were aware that even this basic household aid could not be taken for granted.

The employed, of course, fare better in these stakes. Peter Townsend's concept of the effect of poverty being to exclude people from participation in the usual standards and activities of society is well

Table 6: Possession of consumer durables

Item	Families in study N=78		1981 OCPS[11] low income families	1981[12] F.E.S.
	No.	%	%	%
* Washing machine	64	82	84	81
* Refrigerator	63	81	88	96
* Vacuum cleaner	59	76	N.A.	N.A.
** Television				
Colour	32	41	97	97
Black & white	41	53		
+ Central heating	25	32	43	61
Car	20	26	50	46
Telephone	31	39	37	76

* Many second-hand, often in need of repair.
** Includes portable, second-hand and slot-meter.
+ Owned but not many used because of costs.

illustrated in this study. Without modern household equipment, housework was done by Victorian methods.

'I hated not having a vacuum cleaner or a washer, because washing for the three of us was difficult. I used to stand and scrub with washing soap – I never had any washing powder either. It was bloody hard work. Everything had to be spotless for when he walked in otherwise it was a cause of another row.'

Shortages

Table 7: Items which women could not afford prior to the Refuge

Item	No. of families	% N=78
Clothes for self	43	55.1
for child	27	34.6
Furniture and household goods	14	17.9
Food: fresh meat/fish/fruit	8	10.2
any at times	13	16.7
Other (holiday, 'little luxuries')	5	6.4

The concern with very basic needs shown here goes some way to indicate the desperation of the situation especially with some interpretation of the items. For Angela 'furniture' meant having a chest of drawers to put the children's clothes in instead of having two plastic waste bags; Jean wanted to cover bare boards upstairs and buy a pair of curtains; for others it meant being able to replace the chairs, crockery and furnishings destroyed by violent men. There were families where fresh food was rarely afforded and those who were uncertain at times of getting food at all.

Many Refuge residents have never had a holiday of any kind. More than half of those in the study group said that they have not had a holiday since they were married, and 40 per cent had not had a holiday in their entire lives. This included visits to relations. The large numerical discrepancy between the women who had never had a holiday and those who said they could not afford one (Table 7) supports other evidence of low expectations. As Barbara said: 'No – I've never had a holiday. The only holiday I've had is when I go in the hospital to have the kids – and it's not even that now, they get you up so quick.'

Property and savings

The 18 per cent owner-occupiers in the sample were the only people with property at all, and this is tied up while the family is living there. However, loans for repairs and modernization of the property were felt as millstones round the neck of owners. There was little prospect of benefit through selling up because of the slump in the market, the condition of property, debts, etc.

There were twenty-one saving accounts reported among the seventy-eight families, with understandably meagre amounts of money (usually between £50 and £70). Only four couples had joint savings, of less than £300 in each case. Some women, mainly employed, had been scrimping to achieve a little independence against virtually impossible odds.

Debts and loans

Even greater difficulty than expected was found in this connection with thirty-four families (44 per cent) having debts, many in more than one area of expenditure.

Table 8: Distribution of debt by type for thirty-four families

Category	No.	N=62 %	N=78 %
Clubs/catalogue	5	8.1	6.4
Hire purchase	10	16.1	12.8
Rent/mortgage	19	30.6	24.4
Rates	11	17.7	14.1
Fuel	12	19.4	15.4
Other	5	8.1	6.4
Total	62 (34 families)	100.0	

Housing and fuel debts were found among employed and unemployed alike. Nineteen of the thirty-four families in debt also had bank and credit company loans, occasionally incurred to pay off an older debt, more usually for property alterations and repairs.

Women's work and earnings prior to the Refuge

In the three-month period before coming to the Refuge nineteen women (24 per cent) had been employed, four full-time, fifteen part-time. However, very few women are employed when they arrive at the Refuge, partly because there is a tendency to give up work when the domestic situation deteriorates.

The four women in full-time employment not only had the highest wages, but also more status, being in supervisory or organizational work. The highest weekly take-home pay in 1982 was £75. The highest gross rate of pay was 210p per hour (national average for non-manual workers 252.2p).[13]

The fifteen part-time workers were almost all in low status, badly paid jobs such as cleaning, kitchen and bar work. The lowest rate of pay recorded was 50p per hour, the highest, for clerical work, 157p per hour. Rates were well below the national average for female part-time work. Welsh Women's Aid found similar results in South Wales, an area much like Cleveland economically.[14]

Fourteen of the nineteen working wives (74 per cent) had partners also in work. Three of the four full-time workers were married to men at the top of the income scale used. This echoes other findings which show that where need among two-parent families is greatest it is less likely that women will be employed outside the home. Where twenty-four men were unemployed for over a year, only four wives worked. Supplementary benefit regulations, low pay and domestic cares discourage women from working; men's control over wives is an additional factor. Several women told of giving up work because they had been told to do so by their partners. Others explained that they had not dared to suggest going out to work. 'He'd have killed me', Lee said, a claim not necessarily extravagant given the circumstances.

How women's wages were spent

It was found that none of the women went out to work for 'pin money'. On the contrary their wages were vital to the household economy. Among the twenty-four families whose income was above the Townsend line of 140 per cent there were fifteen wives contributing to that total. Furthermore, whatever the contribution of wives to the overall income, their input to the housekeeping money was proportionately higher. For example: where partners were out of work wives contributed an average of 36 per cent to the family income but 53 per cent to housekeeping money; where husbands were employed, women's wages were an average of 21 per cent of family income and 48 per cent of their housekeeping. This inequity not only means that a woman may be personally no better off for working; it may also result in women, and their children, remaining in poverty despite their efforts to improve matters. The frustration which women experience was bluntly expressed by Marilyn who had two part-time jobs, 'I kept my kids, he didn't. I was lucky if I got £10 to keep him'. Lena, who made ice-lollies at 50p an hour, told us: 'If I hadn't that job I wouldn't have been able to manage. I tell you this – he used to take half of the family allowance as well. He said that was his Tuesday money.'

Furthermore the loss of employment by women seems to be of some significance in the deepening crisis within the marriage. Reasons for this are not hard to find: women's limited financial independence is lost, there is a tightening of control by husbands, especially when men are unemployed, and further general strain on the family purse.

Conclusions

To sum up, where poverty is part of the oppression that women want to escape, it is clearly a hindrance to their efforts to do so. The financial problems of the women in the study were enormous and affected attempts to make decisions as well as to implement them. The extent of their difficulties is immediately apparent when they arrive penniless at the Refuge, sometimes with only the clothes they are wearing. The struggle to establish themselves as single parents is sometimes abandoned because of poverty and the weight of responsibilities.

However, on coming to the Refuge, the more usual reaction to having a regular income and, moreover, full control of it is one of satisfaction and relief. 'I know what I have in my purse' expresses the new found autonomy, limited as it is, of the 55 per cent of the sample who felt better off once they were living on supplementary benefit at the Refuge.[15] Since only 15 per cent actually had more money this control, coupled with reduced responsibilities, plays a large part in the sense of improvement.

Financial hardship, the burden of responsibilities and the prospect of deeper poverty ahead can preserve a violent relationship. Almost half of the women in the study whose family income level was between 100–140 per cent of the poverty line, returned to their violent partners, a higher proportion than among the rest. This group seemed most hampered by their financial circumstances, e.g. debt problems, where women were being held equally responsible for rent and fuel debts incurred by partners. At the same time, most of the women had found that the close control of money and of them by partners, unequal distribution of income and the burden of their responsibilities combined to make their relationship untenable. Where these circumstances coexisted women were less likely to return to husbands who were unemployed than to those in work: 79 per cent of the wives of the unemployed remained single parents as compared with 43 per cent for women whose husbands were employed. In addition, heavy responsibilities for women together with little or no control of income correlated with ending the relationship, especially where women's employment had made little difference to their attempts to 'make ends meet'.

The experience of the women interviewed further demonstrates how necessary it is for the current interest in the patterns of income control, distribution and management to be developed within the context of power in the family. Management of income depends on the ability to control its supply and distribution. However, the majority of women in the research group were either powerless to gain an equitable distribution of family resources in the first place, or felt unable to withstand demands made by husbands to give the money back. Hence the nominal patterns of income distribution turned out to be largely irrelevant; for the concept of the husband's 'right' in what Bell and Newby[16] describe as the 'deferential relationship' appears to have been consistently reinforced by his 'might'.

Other researchers have suggested that violence against wives is related to their material dependency, with Kalmus and Straus,[17] for example, having proposed that economic dependency on husbands is a mediating factor in violence against wives, and that the more serious offences are likely to occur where women are the most dependent. While it is not the purpose of this study to examine any possible connection between the beating of wives and a woman's material dependency on her husband, the evidence shows that the husband's exercise of the power of the purse and the force of the fist coincided in the lives of the vast majority of the women interviewed.

It is sometimes suggested (e.g. Pahl[18]) that state benefit should be paid directly to women to overcome the problem of income retention by husbands. Given the evidence of this study, the ameliorative effects of such a measure are unlikely to be great, although it may do much to change public and personal attitudes. There is need for a more fundamental change of perspective, and policies at both national and local level designed to give women more equal access to economic and social resources in their own right. Economic dependency, combined with acceptance of responsibilities for the care and welfare of their children, can become an intolerable burden for women.

Notes

1 Cleveland Research and Intelligence Unit, *Cleveland Statistics in Brief*, 1982.
2 Cleveland County Planning Department, *Unemployment in Cleveland 1968-1974*, 1975.
3 Cleveland Research and Intelligence Unit, *Cleveland Economic and Demographic Review*(CR 366 1982); Lady Bell, *At the works: A study of a Manufacturing Town - Middlesbrough*, First published 1907 (1969 edn Newton Abbott, David & Charles).
4 Cleveland Research and Intelligence Unit, *Cleveland Statistics in Brief*, 1982.
5 Cleveland Research and Intelligence Unit, op. cit., CR 366 1982.
6 I. Knight, *Family Finances*, London, Office of Population Censuses and Surveys, 1981, Table 6.4 (1).
7 B. Abel-Smith and P. Townsend, *The Poor and the Poorest*, London, Bell, 1965; P. Townsend, *Poverty*, Harmondsworth, Penguin Books, 1979.
8 J. Pahl, 'Patterns of money management within marriage', in *Journal of Social Policy*, 1980, 9:3 pp. 313-35; 'The allocation of money and the structuring of inequality within marriage', unpublished report, Health and Services Research Unit, University of Kent, 1982. See also for review of the literature on money management within marriage.
9 J. Pahl, *A Refuge for Battered Women*, London, DHSS, 1978; 'Bridge over troubled waters' unpublished report presented to the DHSS, 1981.
10 M. Homer, A.E. Leonard and M.P. Taylor, *Private Violence: Public Shame*, Middlesbrough, 1984, gives fuller details of methods. Available from 46 Albert Terrace, Middlesbrough, Cleveland.
11 I. Knight, op. cit., Table J, p. 84.
12 Department of Employment, *Family Expenditure Survey*, HMSO, 1981, Table 4.
13 Department of Employment, *New Earnings Survey* (A), HMSO, April 1982.
14 Welsh Women's Aid, *Mrs. Hobson's Choice*, Cardiff, 1980.
15 V. Binney, G. Harkell and J. Nixon, *Leaving Violent Men*, London, Women's Aid Federation England, 1981, found that 65 per cent of the women they interviewed felt better off; D. Marsden, *Mothers Alone*, Allen Lane, Penguin Press 1969, produced a much lower figure of 33 per cent.
16 C. Bell and H. Newby, 'Husbands and wives: the dynamics of the deferential dialectic' in D.L. Barker and S. Allen (eds), *Dependence and Exploitation in Work and Marriage*, London, Longman, 1976.
17 D.S. Kalmus and M.A. Straus, 'A wife's marital dependency and wife abuse' in *Journal of Marriage and the Family*, May 1982.
18 J. Pahl, op. cit., 1980.

Personal relationships: help and hindrance

Marjorie Homer, Anne Leonard and Pat Taylor

Abstract

This paper shows the extent to which the lives of battered women are controlled by their violent partners. Women are prevented by physical means or threats from seeking help from, or even having any contact with, family, friends and neighbours. Isolation is a prominent feature of their lives. Many men fail to recognize that there is a problem and they behave aggressively towards health visitors, social workers or anyone else who comes round to the home.

Nevertheless, there is evidence to suggest that when battered women begin to seek help they turn first to family, friends and neighbours, and the main purpose of this paper is to examine these informal sources of assistance. An important consideration was that 25 per cent of the women had no accessible parents, but there were other constraints which reduced the degree to which women turned to relatives and friends for help. These included feelings of shame, ideas about privacy and the need for independence, the need to protect family members, friends and neighbours from the man's violent behaviour and the unwillingness of some of those approached to become involved. Women who overcame these constraints spoke warmly of the support they received.

The economic circumstances of the eighty women in the Middlesbrough study were considered to be important as an indication of the point from which the struggle to escape violence was begun.[1] In analysing the women's economic dependency, a picture emerged of the patterns of control that existed within the relationships with their partners. This control extended beyond financial matters into all areas of the women's lives, affecting not only the ability to find and keep employment but women's contact and relationships with everyone outside the partnership: children, wider family, friends, neighbours and formal social agencies. The husband's control within the marriage was often manifested and reinforced by his ability to forbid his wife contact with family and friends. Linda's husband prevented all access between Linda and her parents for a year before she came to the Refuge. Lorna described how her husband tore the dress off her back when she tried to go to a neighbour's party:

> 'I had no friends – there was an atmosphere coming to my house. My friend round the corner – I couldn't even go to her clothes party because of his jealousy – so what chance have I of her coming round here and feeling comfortable?'

By such means some women were almost completely cut off from their old friends or prevented from making new friends of their own after marriage. For these women their only 'friends' were those approved of by their partners, and as we were told over and over again, 'I couldn't ask for help because my friends were his friends'.

Indeed, sheer physical force was used to prevent women reaching any source of help; for example, after being beaten they were locked in to prevent them revealing what their partners had done. This inherent physical ability to enforce constraints was extended when men were unemployed. That situation, for some women, led to every movement being monitored. For example, several women were timed when they went shopping, which meant they had to dash round the shops and so had no opportunities to make contacts that might provide information or support that would allow them to leave. Beryl said that her partner followed her to the telephone box and listened in to her conversations with friends and her social worker. Even when unemployed men went out, women's fears that they might return at any moment restricted their movements, as failure to be at home when a partner returned often led to accusations of infidelity and violent attack. These strategies effectively isolated women in all areas of their lives, thwarting even their efforts to go out to work to relieve financial problems. Amy explained how her husband reacted to her decision to take a part-time job as a barmaid in order to reduce the ever-growing pile of debts.

> 'I took a job as a part-time barmaid to help pay the bills that were piling up. I was only there for a few weeks and he decided I had to pack it in – 'cos he wouldn't go to work – he used to come and sit in the pub and make sure I didn't speak to anyone.'

Some men circumscribed women's access to possible sources of help through their attitude to officialdom. For example, health visitors were often discouraged from coming to the house either by wives because they feared their husband's reaction on discovery, or by the attitudes and behaviour of the men. Again, women whose partners were unemployed were likely to be more restricted in their contacts than those whose husbands were in work. Even when the woman managed to instigate action the uncertainty of her situation could mean that proceedings were delayed and even dropped altogether. For example, Sara told us about her difficulties when trying to initiate legal proceedings while still sharing a house with her husband.

'I had to sneak out to see him [the solicitor] , and most of the time I used to miss the appointment. Then when they got to court, they had to adjourn it because he [her husband] wouldn't let me out of the house. . . . Then one day his mother said, "There's a solicitor round the corner". One day I was going to pick S. . . up from school and I called in at the solicitor, I always made the appointments when I had to go for S. . . so he didn't find out until he got a letter from them.'

Even when the monitoring of women's lives was not so manifest there was still a high degree of control over their actions; both the violence they had suffered in the past and their experience of partners' reactions to past attempts to communicate their problems were often sufficient constraints. For example, Ann explained she did not divulge the source of her injuries to the nurses at the hospital because she was afraid her husband would discover what she had done and give her 'another good hiding'. Some women feared that the agency would take action that would lead to their partner discovering what she had done. Joy, who rang the Samaritans in the middle of the night told us: 'I could hardly talk because I was frightened he would hear me . . . and in the end I put the phone down. I thought what if they send me a letter and he finds out . . . ' whilst others simply felt, fatalistically, that he would always find them. 'My friend, she offered me this place of her Dad's to go to and stay at for a couple of weeks, but I said "No", because if he came looking for me he'd find me in the end and it would have just been worse.' The women were also thwarted in their efforts to improve the situation by their partners' unwillingness to co-operate. Women who felt their partners' drinking to be the source of the problem asked them to go for counselling but men rarely agreed to do this. Women also asked their husbands to go with them to agencies like marriage guidance, but again the answer was usually 'No'. We were told that men's reactions were related either to their assumption that there was nothing wrong with the domestic situation or to their refusal to accept any responsibility for problems. Women found that by even broaching the subject they placed themselves in further danger of physical attack; for those women who had approached an agency before talking to their partners then the risk was likely to be even greater. Sometimes agencies wrote to the man suggesting that he come to see them but the letters were usually torn up or ignored. When men did agree to cooperate we were told any benefit was usually short-lived, maybe lasting for a week or two. There was no firm evidence that men were really concerned to work for improvement. Several women expressed sorrow and resentment at their husbands' reaction to their efforts to improve the situation. Linda told us sadly that although she was really trying to save the marriage her partner didn't care and Julie explained: 'They [Marriage Guidance] told us we both had to work at the marriage – but I know I was doing all the work and he was doing nothing.' It was usually only the woman who went for help about domestic violence. Because she was the one who defined the situation as unsatisfactory, only she was likely to take action to change it. So her responsibility for the problem was emphasized and at the same time, because of her lack of power, the likelihood of her effecting change, however hard she tried, was minimal.

Children made women even more vulnerable in the conflict. For example, Chloe explained how her husband moved to battering their daughter:

> 'He knew he could get to me through her [their daughter] so he started having a go at her . . . till he went too far one day – he cut all her back open and when he went to work I just went to my sister's. I'd got that used to him hitting me – but I don't think she could have stood it.'

Beryl told us of a visit to the doctor about a second pregnancy at a time when the marriage was in a particularly shaky condition. The doctor had offered her an abortion but she refused because her husband would have to know and she was sure he would not allow this because another child was 'another shackle round my wrist'. Threats of counter custody proceedings by husbands could sometimes frighten women into giving up legal proceedings because they felt they had few rights in the situation and were prepared to continue to live with their violent partners rather than risk losing their children. Even when women recognised they were likely to get the children, they sometimes were not prepared to take a chance.

The man's willingness to use physical force to subdue his partner together with his denial of responsibility for the success of the marriage and happiness of the family usually meant that the woman was severely hindered in her attempt to achieve a satisfactory environment for herself and her children within the existing situation. The decision to leave home was similarly hampered in most cases, with only a few women meeting little or no resistance.

This degree of control by partners is only part of the problem. Women's acceptance of responsibility for family well-being, their unwillingness to assert their own needs and rights, their strong feelings of privacy, guilt or shame, and their ignorance about services and legal procedures arising from the enforced narrowness of their lives combine with partners' control almost to incarcerate women in the violent relationship.

Most of the women in the study accepted that the main burden of responsibility for the 'good health' of the family rested on their shoulders. For those women whose partners had apparently abdicated all responsibility then that burden was even more complete. We were told over and over again 'I felt it was *my* problem to solve'. This meant that some women had accepted for many years that they should stay within the marital relationship; they only tried to escape when the circumstances became so dire they found them intolerable.[2] They learned to modify their behaviour in order to keep the situation as stable as possible. For example, Lena, who was kept very short of money to feed and care for the family, said:

'I used to fight with him – about taking the child benefit and everything. But then I just gave in – I thought it isn't worth the hassle, at least it gets him out of the house. So although there's no money at least there's peace for a while.'

There was obviously a great deal of concern for the welfare of the children and it was often only when the battering extended to the children, or women became aware of how the children were suffering through seeing their mother battered, that a decision was made to break up the family: 'I was frightened for the kids – because I didn't want them brought up with it for the rest of their lives. They were the things that made me leave in the end.' Despite the hurt and indignities that women suffered, many told us that they felt a sense of responsibility for their partners. This not only deterred them from leaving their husbands but was an important factor in securing their return when they did leave. Several men either threatened or attempted suicide after their wives had left them, and women often felt compelled to act to prevent their death. For example, Nicola explained how she had tried to leave her violent and domineering partner several times. Even when she had the promise of a council house she was persuaded to return home by telephone calls from her mother-in-law, 'She told me he'd tried two or three times to commit suicide. She said, "come home" and I did because I felt responsible. I wouldn't want anyone to lose their life because of me.' Because of their strong feelings of duty women felt bad about their efforts to escape from the marriage. Feelings of guilt, shame and failure were expressed. Sometimes these feelings were so strong that women returned home repeatedly, finally accepting they would never escape. As Marie fatalistically explained:

'I didn't try again. Because I knew it wouldn't work. I knew that in the end I would pay for it. So I left it – and I'm still not free. I know it wouldn't work for me – he'd always be there, I'd never be free.'

The family as a resource

In order to appreciate fully the strength of these attitudes, they need to be understood in the context of relationships and values that are worked out within the wider family. An analysis of these might provide insight both into the extent to which kinship and friendship networks operated as a resource for the women in the study, and into the cultural dimension of their predicament.

The colloquial use of the term 'family' to refer sometimes to parents, brothers and sisters including occasionally grandparents, aunts, uncles, cousins (the extended family), and at other times to husband and children (the nuclear family) seemed to present no problems of interpretation to the women we questioned. The women's age range meant that all phases of family life were observed in the study.

Several factors influenced both the degree to which women turned to relatives for help and the response to their appeals. Among the more important considerations are: availability, the search for independence, and the values surrounding the family and marriage. Each of these will now be examined.

(a) *Availability:* Casual observation at the Refuge suggested that family support was often unavailable to the women either through loss of parents as a result of death or desertion, or through the pressure of other problems in the family (ill-health, poverty, etc.).

On enquiring which family members existed and were available, it emerged that sixteen of the eighty women had neither father nor mother; for a further three neither was available; and one woman with no mother had no available father; effectively, therefore, twenty women (25 per cent) had no accessible parents. Five of these (6 per cent) had no access to brothers or sisters either. This bore out our original impression that lack of family support is probably a deprivation that makes the Refuge an essential resource for many of the women who turn to it when leaving violent men.

Additionally the relatives available outnumbered the requests made to them in all cases. This seems to indicate the by-no-means automatic support of the family in the crisis of violence. The explanations of why it was difficult or impossible to get help from this source reveal important aspects of the family and of the situation of women within it which may throw light on the complexity and intractability of female inequality. Paradoxically, in their initial answers, women sometimes forgot or overlooked family help which later in the interview it emerged had been given – perhaps a result of the sometimes 'taken-for-grantedness' of family life that makes objective data hard to collect.

In evaluating the data reported in this study it is important to remember that the women had all used the Refuge. There is no way of knowing how representative the sample was of battered women generally. It is possible that some of the women not using refuges have rather more support from relatives than the women we interviewed.

As has already been noted, for twenty women, the relatives most likely to give support, parents, did not exist or were not available. However, the term 'available' runs into the problem of varying definition: while Mary's parents in Wales were considered eminently available, Bertha, who said she had a 'good family', was sure 'I'd get a lot of support from my three sisters if I was near them, but it's the distance and my feet'. The distance was, in fact, not much more than two miles but bus services are infrequent and expensive, and the quotation points to other deprivations in the speaker's life which reinforce isolation from the family. Mary was one of the few women in the study with further education and a professional career. Bertha was one of the group with no father and a mother who had disappeared early in Bertha's childhood. Bertha described her as 'only coming to life a year ago'. She still seems to have made no contribution to solving her daughter's difficulties.

Two women, Angela and Laura, were very young at the time of

interview and had been orphaned. Angela said, 'Since my mother died, we all [brothers and sisters] just split up. Now we have no contact at all. We do speak if we see each other in the street.' She also lost contact with local friends, as a result of being 'in care' in the South. When she was asked how she had felt when faced with her husband's violence in this situation of no support at all, she replied, matter-of-factly, 'desperate most of the time'. She had been nineteen at the time she referred to. The depths of isolation of some of the respondents is matched by the often tragic complexity of the reasons for it, and is reflected in the depression, despair or resignation they expressed. Betty, whose elder sisters had devotedly replaced parents who died while she was still tiny, had been cut off from them after her husband had sexually assaulted two of her nieces. The break was due not to her sisters, but to Betty's inappropriate, but inevitable, sense of guilt and responsibility for the situation. She had then to cope with her husband's violence entirely alone.

(b) *Independence:* By far the largest category of reasons for not turning to the family for help, even when it was known to be available, and relationships were warm and supportive, was that of the highly valued independence of the woman concerned, an independence thus being valued above personal safety or convenience: 'I've an independent nature, I couldn't just present myself on the doorstep'; 'I didn't feel I wanted to put on them really'; 'I don't like burdening other people with my problems, I'd rather try to sort things out myself'; 'It's my problem'; 'It's not their problem'; 'I wanted the trouble to be in my back-yard and no-one else's'. These quotations reflect the spectrum of concerns that preoccupied the women in the study where the various possibilities tended to merge and blend: concern for others, with assertion of independence, with fear for autonomy and personal integrity. There is irony that women's sense of independence should militate against their seeking necessary help to establish freedom from the violence which is surely a severe limitation on their actual independence and autonomy. We here confront the problem of the significance of generally held values of independence and individualism for women who remain socially and economically handicapped. A well-worn phrase was much used to express a woman's own sense of her situation, 'It's my bed, I've got to lie on it'.

This last telling comment, however much of a cliché, has its counterpart in the reported remarks made by family members in rejection of appeals for help, or in response to the suspicion that help might be needed. The fatalism of self-imposed stoicism is replaced by the harshness of a command, quoted more than once, 'You made your bed you lie on it'.

(c) *Values surrounding the family and marriage:* Ironically, the taken-for-granted value and meaning of family life as a focus of warmth, affection and security, and of the paramountcy of the married relationship within that framework, are sometimes the very factors which seem to isolate women within the horror of a violent relationship, even, and perhaps especially, from close kin.

On the one hand, the family can be perceived as sympathetic and caring: 'With being on her own [i.e. speaker's mother] that was why maybe I didn't tell her, because I knew how upset . . . what it would do to her'; 'I can't go to my mother's like this, she'll go mad'. On the other hand, relatives may be critical and judgemental, e.g. the parents of one woman (who had initially disapproved of her marriage) have 'only got talking now I've left him'. They offered no help while she endured the violent marriage. In either case, the net product is often lack of support for the woman in difficulties.

Another paradox is that, while the woman's perception of violence as deviant or aberrant can isolate and trap the woman suffering from it, acceptance of it as normal can have the same effect. 'I just thought it was normal, really, for blokes to hit their wives'. 'My mother-in-law said she'd had worse – made me feel I had to put up with it'.

A further irony is that where family intervention is likely to be whole-hearted and unequivocal, this can also cause problems and 'cover-up' on the part of the woman for fear of escalation and spreading of the violence. For example, 'My brothers hit him and he came home and hit me', with the result that 'I protected myself and them'. Judy said helplessly, 'My brothers would sort him out, but it causes more trouble all round'. Family support can have other counter-productive results. In Pauline's case, her sympathy for her husband was restored when her 'whole family picked on him': she returned home to him next day. The tangle of conflicting loyalties and emotions of women brought up with certain ideas of marriage is well illustrated by that case.

An important constraint on a woman turning to her family is the fear that the violence will encompass them. This is the case, even where the family's response is not itself violent, and especially where family members are themselves seen to be vulnerable and unprotected. One woman was guilt-stricken when her father died shortly after her husband had 'been round', and she felt she was to blame. The function of values of familiar concern and caring in deterring women from seeking help can be seen in the way these values both stigmatize violence and therefore tend to keep it hidden and make a woman reluctant to invoke her family's anxiety on her behalf. There is an extra turn to the screw here, in that the norm of concern does not just operate at the level of the family's response, but at the level of her concern for them and awareness of their problems. Thus we see the operation of internalized values of concern and consideration in cutting off women from the help they need. 'My mam and dad were both getting on see, so I wouldn't put them in a predicament, you know.' 'I didn't want to burden her, she'd already had a hard life. She was getting on, in her sixties.' 'My brother and sister had their own problems, they had their own families.' 'I was worried about the effect on her – she's a diabetic.' To prevent problems for her mother one woman went back home while another was reluctant to burden further her supportive father who had coped throughout his own marriage with his wife's severe mental illness. For one of the older women in our sample the offer of accommodation from married children was refused as 'it wasn't right for me to be with them; they are only young': an example of the shifting focus as family life evolves, but informed by the same values which tend, by recognizing the needs of other relatives first, to handicap women in help-seeking.

Both respondents and their families frequently expressed views which reflected the considerable importance attached to marriage and the essentially private nature of the relationship. Wendy, like several others, refrained from telling her brother and sister of her troubles for fear they would tell her parents since she believed that, 'really, it's a fight between your two selves'. Within the intimacy of the family there is thus the further, more sacrosanct, intimacy of marriage itself, generating the problem of the segregation of public and private life, and making it an issue even within the privacy of the kinship network. Mary's brother refused to help because he 'wouldn't come between man and wife', while independence is linked to the high value of marriage in Sylvia's comment, 'I tried to prove to them that it would be a marriage that worked; they weren't keen on the idea when I got married'. This remark shows the acceptance of the importance of marriage with the obvious problems that result when 'failure' has to be faced up to. Another variation on the same theme is shown when the break-up itself is a source of disapproval, 'My parents didn't really approve of the break-up'. A mother advised 'talking things over', while an uncle attempted reconciliation. One woman's parents threatened to have the children removed (from the Refuge) as 'she had no right to leave and take the bairns'. In their view she should have 'stuck it out'. Jenny's reason for not seeking help from her mother was that she knew her mother believed that 'marriage is for keeps, you have to make it work'.

In asking relatives for help, as in other help-seeking processes, the strong tendency is for the interaction and its implications to undermine the woman's self-esteem and autonomy, subjecting her to further control and stigmatization which amount to perhaps unintentional sanctions against her for her partner's intolerable behaviour. She is somehow guilty by association in her own eyes, if not always in those of her helpers. Lack of support leaves a woman unaided in an unequal contest.

The sense of despair and desolation that was witnessed when support is not available for any of the reasons described is in strong contrast to the sense of gratitude for the strength derived when family solidarity was available and used. Sadly, the mentions of isolation and helplessness outnumber the expressions of gratitude in our survey (twenty-four to thirteen). The latter are the more vivid and telling for the contrast they make with what has been recorded so far in this paper. Thus, Julie's parents, who occupied limited accommodation, pleaded 'stay here and we'll rough it'. Julie also observed: 'Funny enough his mam was good as well, 'cos she'd been battered – his father had been violent to her.' The following is an extract from the same interview:

I: 'What help did you get from your sister?'

J: 'Oh, a lot of help. If I hadn't had the support of the family I'd have cracked up a long time ago. I would definitely have taken a bottle of tablets, me and the kids.'

Debbie's family gave her constant support which was valued the more, since, as she said, 'there were no strings'. Nevertheless, she felt restrained in the degree to which she turned to her family: 'I didn't feel I wanted to put on them really.' This ambivalence, even where a family is supportive, is more common than total straightforward appreciation.

Glenda provides an example of the help occasionally to be found from in-laws when her mother-in-law, who had often helped her, encouraged her to 'stay away – you've got the bairn to think about' and agreed to remain ignorant of Glenda's present whereabouts for reasons of security. June's experience introduces an optimistic note in another unforeseen way by showing that the flow of need, help and support can sometimes be reversed, indicating a different perspective on the family from that adopted so far in this paper. She found her seven-year-old daughter 'the mainstay of her sanity' throughout all her marital troubles and afterwards when living alone. Glenda used almost the same words in describing her grandmother and the part she had played in helping her to escape: 'She is the mainstay of my life'. Thus the very old and the very young, far from occupying a role of total dependency, can be a source of strength and support.

To what degree the problematic nature of family help has only become visible as a result of the pressure now being put upon it by women refusing traditionally submissive roles, or to what extent changing norms concerning family obligations and priorities have undermined the supportive function of family, are questions this paper cannot attempt to answer, although clearly they are raised by this evidence. One handicap suffered by the families we studied is that they cannot usually supply the practical needs of women leaving violent men – the need for accommodation and protection. Women therefore must generally turn to the wider society to obtain the practical help they need, while emotional and personal support, even where it is available from the family, often brings its own problems.

Friends and neighbours

Personal experience shows that friends can be a great source of comfort and support during crisis. Women who came to the Refuge confirmed this, especially where they did not have family help. Some women seemed even to prefer to turn to friends who are 'chosen' rather than to family who are 'given'.

It was necessary to make the distinction between friends and neighbours because, although many married women, especially those with small children, find their friends among neighbours, this might be difficult for women subject to violence, either because of their own shame and embarrassment or because of the neighbours' reluctance to become involved. Despite this, many women did see their neighbours as friends although others made a clear distinction. When this was the case, it was not seen as appropriate to discuss with neighbours private matters concerning the woman's relationship with her partner. 'I was reluctant to involve strangers in my problem.' This was sometimes part of the already noted sense that it is not appropriate to discuss marital problems with anyone.

Where this attitude extended even to friends, approaches were made only in a crisis. The women's sense of failure and shame was another reason for this – a barrier that was removed where friends had similar experiences of violent treatment. 'There was one – I didn't mind telling her because she had problems with her husband as well. But my other friend who had a really good husband - I didn't always like to tell her.' Even when women felt able to talk to friends and neighbours about their problems, the response they met with often reflected the same attitudes that created difficulty in asking, and only added to their loneliness. Linda commented: 'You really feel isolated in that situation, because they just turn away - they just don't want to know about you and your problem.' Another woman said: 'I had plenty of friends and neighbours . . . they knew I was getting beat up but they put it this way - that it was our lives and that we had to sort it out for ourselves.' Such reactions by friends and neighbours can be seen as at least an implicit acceptance of a man's right to beat and control his wife, but women were also sometimes told that such situations were 'normal' and therefore to be endured. 'When I told them, they were getting bashed up as well. One far worse than me - so in the end I thought it was just one of those things.' Thus, prevalent attitudes to friendship and neighbourliness, husband's control, values of privacy and notions of what family life should or has to be combine to make help-seeking in this area a complex process.

Friends were also deterred by fears for their own safety. This was particularly so if they were neighbours as well and so both heard the violence occurring and felt vulnerable to attack themselves. Freda explained how this prevented her from accepting help from the women next door: 'She offered for me to go there - and I used to go for a few hours sometimes when he locked me out and went out fishing. But I couldn't stay there - because she was as frightened of him as I was.' Despite the barriers that discouraged women from turning to friends and neighbours fifty-seven of the women in our study (71 per cent) had approached someone from either or both categories for help. As we have seen, for many women their friends were neighbours, or lived close by, and this meant that they were able, if willing, to provide a wide range of help, sometimes unasked for. For example, neighbours often contacted the police or other agencies in an emergency, either at the instigation of the woman or because they heard the noise and were worried for her safety. They were also available to provide first aid and to look after the children while the woman coped with the aftermath of her husband's violence. However, the proximity and availability that makes friends such a good potential source of help, can also mean that the help they offer must be refused because they are known to the husbands.

As with family, the women felt very upset at the thought of creating problems for their friends, and some gave this reason for refusing proffered accommodation: 'I went to my friend's house – and he followed me there. So I went home to avoid problems.' Because they have no official status, friends and neighbours are particularly susceptible to the pressures and controls men may try to impose on them. Women spoke with great gratitude of the support and help they did receive from friends and felt that this had been a key factor both in their survival whilst within the violent relationship, and in their escaping when the situation became intolerable. For example, Enid who had, together with her daughter, suffered great material deprivation told us simply:

> 'If it hadn't been for her we would have just wasted away to nothing. She was a good friend – very helpful. I would have been on the streets if it wasn't for her. And in the last few months when there was no money – she gave me food.'

Women were particularly grateful to those people who had told them of the Refuge and therefore allowed them to escape. This research confirms data from other studies:[3] where friends and neighbours are involved with a woman's problems related to domestic violence they can be a very important source of help, as the following clearly shows:

> 'It was good. You could always – you could show her what he'd done and get a bit of sympathy at the same time. And I suppose I needed someone who'd tell me often enough how stupid I was to live with him before I left. . . . She was saying to me, 'You're going to be dead before you're so and so age – and what about the kids, you've got them to think about". I think it was talking to her that made my mind up that last time it happened it was really time to go – it was time to give up!'

The information gap

The control that men exerted in the relationship, the subjective feelings and point of view of the women themselves, and the complex nature of relationships and attitudes within personal networks contributed to major practical problems in the predicament in which women found themselves. For instance, information is an important source of power, an essential resource for anyone wanting to take action to change their situation. The women in our sample had very little information about where they could go for help and the kind of help they might expect.

The privatization of women's lives has been well documented, but for these women the isolation was even more complete. The control their husbands kept over their movements meant that they were often denied the informal contacts that provide a great deal of information about the world. Also, perhaps because of the many demands made upon them through their responsibility for family needs, many of the women had not picked up the kind of knowledge that is available, for example, through the media. We were told, 'I never thought such things existed'. One woman told us she had never even heard of social services and many had not approached the voluntary agencies on our list because they had not heard of them. The limited knowledge that some did have about services often meant that they did not turn to them. This was particularly evident in relation to voluntary organizations but women also had perceptions of statutory agencies that prevented them asking for help. In addition, knowledge about legal rights, particularly in relation to such things as custody and housing, was so limited that women were prevented from taking advantage of them. Uncertainty about their legal situation meant that women were afraid that going to agencies would result in their children being taken away from them, particularly if the help they wanted did not include leaving the violent situation. Lynn felt this danger very clearly: 'I think it was because of the children, that if I wasn't prepared to leave for their sake then I might be thought to be unfit to look after them.' It is necessary to describe in detail women's circumstances in order to understand the process that is set in motion when and if women finally turn to outsiders for help.[4] To the internalized and external constraints under which women have to operate are then added the problems of the attitudes and values which underlie the provision of more formal kinds of help.[5] These assumptions often reflect and re-inforce the problems we have already observed, while the practical accessibility and extent of help available does little to offset women's difficulties. The nature of women's private lives makes movement into the public sphere neither likely nor easy; the nature of the response they then meet rarely takes account of the complexity of their problems.[6]

Notes

1   See paper in this Monograph by same authors, 'The burden of dependency'.
2   Ibid.
3   See A. Elsey, 'Battered women – an appraisal of social policy, unpublished M.Sc. study, Department of Social Policy, Cranfield Institute of Technology, 1980.

4   See M. Homer, A. Leonard and P. Taylor, *Private Violence—Public Shame*, 1984. Available from 46 Albert Terrace, Middlesbrough, Cleveland.
5   C. Cavanagh, 'Battered women and social control', unpublished M.Sc. study, Stirling University, 1978; R.E. Dobash and R.P. Dobash, *Violence Against Wives*, Shepton Mallet, Open Books, 1980.
6   See papers in this Monograph by S. Maidment, N. Johnson and M. Brailey.

Police, social work and medical responses to battered women[*]

Norman Johnson

Abstract

Battered women frequently experience difficulties in seeking help from formal sources. They do not always know what services are available and they may be deterred by feelings of embarrassment, shame and even guilt. They may also fear reprisals. A further problem is that services are poorly co-ordinated.

This paper examines the response of the three agencies most frequently approached by battered women seeking help. The police, social workers and medical and paramedical personnel reveal the same or similar attitudes towards marital violence and the problem is either ignored or redefined (usually in terms of child care). There is a marked reluctance on the part of all practitioners to become involved in cases of marital violence which they see as peripheral to their main concerns. The privacy of the family and of marriage is constantly stressed and women are viewed primarily as wives and mothers. When practitioners do become involved, therefore, the emphasis is on reconciliation rather than firm action.

This response has the effect of trivializing the problems, and the legitimacy of male violence as a means of controlling women remains largely unchallenged. It is small wonder that battered women frequently express dissatisfaction with the services concerned.

* The author's interest in this topic stems from involvement in a research project into marital violence conducted at the University of Keele. The research, under the direction of Professor R.J. Frankenberg, was funded by the DHSS. We wish to express our gratitude for this financial support.

109

Introduction

The preceding paper dealt with informal sources of help and with the constraints which often prevent battered women from seeking outside assistance. This paper deals with the response of three key statutory services when they are approached by battered women. The services chosen for consideration are the three most frequently used by battered women: police, social work and medical services.[1]

The evidence suggests that battered women usually turn first to informal sources of help, relatives, friends and neighbours, bringing in statutory agencies only when the violence becomes more frequent or more brutal or when the children appear to be threatened. Dobash and Dobash make the following observation:

> When women first reveal to an outsider that they are being beaten, they usually approach those whom they judge to be closest to them personally and/or those whom they judge most likely to give some help or consolation without making their private problem any more public than necessary.[2]

When women do feel the need to approach formal sources of help their choice of agency will depend upon how they perceive their need and upon their knowledge and perception of the services available. One problem is that many battered women, in common with other sections of the population, have little knowledge of statutory agencies and their functions; and if they are unaware of the full range of options, they will choose an agency which they know something about rather than the one which corresponds most nearly to their needs. A second problem is that battered women may have several different needs, so that even if they do know the sources of help available to them, they will have to either approach several different agencies or decide which of their needs is most pressing and approach the agency they believe to be most appropriate.

Most studies indicate that battered women usually approach several agencies over a period of time. This may have several implications: it may be a reflection of the diversity of needs; it may be an indication of several unsuccessful attempts to secure assistance; it may reflect the referral practices of different agencies. In a study of 636 women, a Women's Aid Federation/ Department of Environment research team found that a total of 3,090 agency consultations had been made and that the average number of agencies or individuals approached for help was five.[3] Dawson and Faragher found a similar pattern of agency use, but noted that the activities of the various sources of help were wholly unco-ordinated so that women were 'placed in the situation of having to start afresh with each new agency'.[4] The fragmentary nature of the services will become more apparent as the responses of individual agencies are examined.

The police

It is sometimes claimed that, apart from hospital accident units, the police is the only service available to battered women for 24 hours a day, every day of the week. This is not entirely accurate: local authority social services departments have emergency teams which are on duty when the offices are closed. However, the service is a minimal one, usually with one small team covering the whole of a county, and it is not widely known. The police is therefore the most accessible service and this accessibility is enhanced by the emergency telephone system. Round-the-clock availability is important because most assaults occur at night after 10 pm and at weekends.[5] Ease of access helps to explain why contact with the police is so frequently reported by battered women. Binney, Harkell and Nixon found that 61 per cent of the women they sampled had sought help from the police,[6] and Pahl found that 63 per cent had done so.[7]

An important feature of all police work is the considerable element of discretion it entails. This is particularly true at the lower levels in the hierarchy where officers come into direct and daily contact with the public. McCabe and Sutcliffe state that:

> The decision to accept or reject a report that a crime has been
> committed is an essential part of the discretion exercised by all
> police officers but particularly by those of the lowest rank who are
> in closer contact with the community.[8]

Individual police officers will decide whether a particular situation warrants their intervention and, if so, what form of action is most appropriate to the circumstances.

The exercise of discretion is directly relevant to cases of marital violence. All studies reveal a reluctance to intervene in what are referred to as domestic disputes – a bland term which disguises the fact that serious assaults may have occurred. Pahl argues that: 'The category of "domestic dispute" includes many other types of incident besides the assault upon wives by their husbands, and it seems likely that this

111

categorisation itself tends to trivialise such incidents.'[9]

Police reluctance to intervene may be explained in several ways. First, there is the notion of privacy:[10] privacy of the place (the home) and privacy of the relationship (marriage). Police evidence to the Select Committee on Violence in Marriage emphasized the need to respect people's privacy.[11] However, the police do have powers of entry when they have reason to suspect that an offence has been committed. Privacy is not apparently such an important issue in cases of child abuse or when evidence of other crimes is sought. Furthermore, the evidence indicates that entry is seldom refused or resisted in cases of domestic violence. A second reason for lack of police readiness to intervene is the belief that dealing with 'domestics' is not 'real police work'. After a detailed study of one police force Faragher concluded: 'It can be said with confidence that sizeable proportions of police officers see the task of dealing with marital violence as lying outside the scope of police work.'[12]

This view and views about privacy will obviously affect the kinds of action police officers are willing to take once intervention occurs. Police roles are frequently divided into two categories: law enforcement, the prevention and detection of crime, and keeping the peace. Intervention in domestic disputes is seen as an aspect of their peace-keeping role and this leads to attempts to achieve reconciliation rather than to arrest and prosecution. This emphasis on reconciliation is expressed very clearly in the following statement made by the Association of Chief Police Officers in its evidence to the Select Committee on Violence in Marriage: 'We are, after all, dealing with persons "bound in marriage", and it is important, for a host of reasons, to maintain the unity of the spouses.'[13] Faragher cites a case in which 'the conditions under which the police could have made an arrest were all clearly present'.[14] The assault had been a serious one leaving visible signs of injury; the man admitted responsibility for the assult and the woman wanted legal action to be taken, but no arrest was made. Police action seemed to be directed to two ends: calming the situation and preventing a recurrence of the violence that night. Other studies show that this example is not untypical. Pahl, for instance, found that 'it is often taken for granted that "re-uniting" the couple and preserving family relationships is desirable'.[15] Arrest in cases of marital violence is therefore rare. There is a reluctance to define violence by husbands against their wives as a crime. Faragher and McCabe and Sutcliffe report that police records of domestic incidents are often sketchy and incomplete and that assignment to the 'crime' or 'no-crime' category takes place after the officers dealing with the case have decided what action to take. If they decide not to take legal action then a 'no-crime' report is recorded. McCabe and Sutcliffe show that when arrest does occur the charge is often for some other offence. Thus, marital violence may result in a charge of 'drunk and disorderly'. In this respect, then, assaults in the streets and upon strangers are treated differently from assaults in the home upon intimates.[16]

Jeffery and Pahl maintain that finer distinctions than those suggested above are made by the police. They hypothesize that

> when a couple are married and are living in the same house, especially when that house is registered in the name of the husband, the police are less likely to interfere effectively if the woman is assaulted, and are less likely to record the incident.[17]

They argue that if a couple are living together but are unmarried or if a couple are married but living apart then the police are more likely to take firm action. Evidence from the United States suggests that another variable may be important. Pagelow claims that the longer a violent relationship has lasted, and the more frequently the police have been called, the less helpful the police response is likely to be:

> In violent relationships of long duration police officers are less inclined to offer assistance or exert effort beyond what is obviously required for the performance of their duties to protect life. As 'problem families' become identified, police responding to repeat calls from the same house become disenchanted with the idea that anything they do will be followed by victim action to effect change, so they tend to handle these 'repeaters' with a detached, peace-keeping attitude.[18]

In their evidence to the Select Committee the Association of Chief Police Officers of England, Wales and Northern Ireland said that in deciding whether to arrest and prosecute the following criteria were applied:
  (i) the seriousness of the assault;
 (ii) the availability of witnesses;
(iii) the character of the alleged assailant;
(iv) age, infirmity, etc. of the complainant;
 (v) previous domestic history;
(vi) the wishes of the complainant;
(vii) if prosecution ensued against the wishes of the complainant would the domestic situation be adversely affected.[19]

113

Although it is difficult to know what significance to attach to the information, Borkowski, Murch and Walker have produced interesting evidence of a tendency among senior police officers to overestimate the proportion of marital violence cases which resulted in prosecutions. Divisional Commanders' estimates varied from 20 per cent to 5 per cent. In fact the highest rate recorded by the researchers was 3.2 per cent. The research also revealed wide variations in the proportion of prosecutions from one division to another.[20]

The police give several reasons for their reluctance to prosecute. In the first place, they claim with some justification, many women have no wish to pursue legal action; they call the police for immediate protection and perhaps to frighten their partner. In other instances women may be afraid to press charges because they fear it may provoke further violence. On the other hand, there is ample evidence that police officers actively discourage women from seeking prosecution, so that even when a woman clearly indicates that she wants her partner to be prosecuted, the police will accede to her request only with the greatest of reluctance. The main reason given by the police for this attitude is that frequently women withdraw their complaints before cases reach court. This point is made in the evidence of the Metropolitan Police to the Select Committee: 'Experience has shown that prosecutions have failed or could not be pursued because of a withdrawal by the wife of her complaint or because of her nervous reaction to the prospect of giving evidence against her husband.'[21] It is undoubtedly true that some women do withdraw their complaints, but the evidence does not support the contention that they do so frequently. Dobash and Dobash, for example, found that only 6 per cent of the assault charges were dropped by the women in their study before the final adjudication. In all instances there had been considerable delay in bringing the cases to court.[22] Successful prosecution will often prove difficult, however, for quite different reasons: lack of witnesses and unwillingness on the part of neighbours and doctors to give evidence.[23]

In the circumstances described it is hardly surprising that battered women frequently express dissatisfaction with the assistance they receive from the police. Binney, Harkell and Nixon reported that 64 per cent of the women who had approached the police had not found the contact useful.[24] Jeffery and Pahl reported that 51 per cent of the women in their survey who had sought assistance from the police found them to be unhelpful.[25] The position in the United States is similar. Pagelow reports that only 32 per cent of women who had approached the police reported favourably on their attitude and behaviour.[26] It would be interesting to know whether the police officers involved in these cases considered their intervention to have been help-ful or not.

Social workers

Local authority social services departments have no statutory responsi-bility for battered women. This is especially important at a time when resources are restricted and the pressure of work is growing. In these circumstances, it is not surprising that local authorities concentrate upon those client groups towards whom they have a statutory duty. This does not mean that local authority social workers have no dealings with battered women, but their involvement is usually as a consequence of contacts established with families for other reasons. Cases will be categorized according to the initial reason for contact, and this presents problems of identification and measurement. A study by Maynard found, surprisingly, that over a third of the caseload in four areas of a northern town included elements of marital violence.[27] This contrasts with figures produced by Borkowski, Murch and Walker (12.5 per cent)[28] and by Leonard and McLeod (13 per cent).[29] The wide dis-crepancy is explainable by the methods used by the three studies. Maynard had access to case files, whereas the other two studies relied upon social workers' own reports. All three studies agree that social workers are likely to underestimate the proportion of their cases involving marital violence.

For a variety of reasons social workers see domestic violence against women as a peripheral part of their work and, in some instances, do not define it as a problem at all. The social work evidence to the Select Committee included the following comment:

> The incidence of violence in marriage is much greater than the prob-lem of violence in marriage. Social workers deal with many families
> where violence occurs but where violence has not been the reason
> for the referral and where violence is not seen by any of the parties
> concerned to be a problem.[30]

Maynard was warned by the social services department before the commencement of her research that she was wasting her time because she would find only two or three cases of marital violence. In fact, twenty-six fully documented cases were found, but only three were identified by social workers as being centrally concerned with marital violence.[31] The overwhelming impression from all the studies is the

115

marked inclination of social workers to redefine the problem of marital violence – almost always in terms of child care. The welfare of the woman is subordinated to that of her children. The following quotation illustrates this point:

> Comments like these seem to us to imply that the practitioner is redefining the problem of marital violence as one of potential child abuse. This may be another way by which marital violence and the woman's plight is relegated to the margins of the practitioner's concern and in some cases is in effect rendered invisible.[32]

Sometimes social workers will urge a woman to remain in the marital home and attempt to make it up to her partner 'for the sake of the children', although it is difficult to understand how the children's welfare is served by remaining in a violent home. As with the police, there is an emphasis in social work on reconciliation and the maintenance of the nuclear family. A report from a working party formed by the British Association of Social Workers made the following comment:

> To support a wife who seeks separation from her husband has often in the past been seen as undermining the institution of the family grouping. Support and maintenance of the family grouping has always been a major part of the social worker's job (as defined both by social workers themselves and by government directives). Social workers are, therefore, likely to define the problem of wife battering in terms of a marital problem for which therapeutic counselling is appropriate.[33]

On the other hand, Binney, Harkell and Nixon, while generally agreeing with the assessment of the working party, found that social workers were far and away the most common source of referral to refuges: 37 per cent of the women had been referred by social workers.[34]

Views about the sanctity of marriage and the importance of the family include assumptions about the role of women. A paper written by a practising social worker and endorsed by the North-West Region of the National Women's Aid Federation stated that 'the ideology and supporting theories of the social work profession . . . are based fundamentally on the notions of the sanctity of the family and marriage' and that they 'accept and reinforce the traditional and oppressive attitudes to women in our society'.[35] The primary roles of women are seen as those of wife and mother, and this has a profound effect on the help offered by social workers. As Maynard says: 'Assumptions concerning the nature of women's role in the family lead social workers to offer very little positive support to those who are being beaten.'[36] Since the woman is responsible for family matters she is always the social workers' primary contact and the men responsible for the violence are seen much less frequently, and sometimes not at all. Leonard and McLeod found that:

> the social workers undertook very little direct work with the men involved in marital violence; overwhelmingly, they visited and interviewed the women, were concerned with a wide complex of material and emotional problems, usually associated with the children and often found the women not prepared to admit and discuss the clear evidence of marital violence that existed.[37]

To be fair to social workers, it has to be said that their training does not really fit them to deal with cases of marital violence. Training courses give scant attention to the problem, and social workers are taught to work with families and to seek solutions within the context of the family. This helps to explain the emphasis on reconciliation. Furthermore, social work training stresses the need for neutrality in dealings with clients, although it is difficult not to take sides when one party is maltreating the other. The social workers interviewed by Leonard and McLeod admitted fears and uncertainty in this area of work and said that they lacked both the skill and the confidence to deal with it.[38] They also felt that there was little they could effectively do, not least because of the lack of resources available to them. As resources are reduced there is increased pressure on social services departments to concentrate upon statutory duties with a high priority going to child care. This tendency to emphasize child care responsibilities is heightened by the media attention which alleged mistakes receive.

According to Binney, Harkell and Nixon, social services departments are the second most frequently contacted statutory agency after the police: 54 per cent of their sample had at some time sought assistance from the personal social services. More than half of the women (52 per cent) said that they had found the contact useful, and this is a much higher level of satisfaction than in the case of the police. The authors concluded that responses by social workers to assaults on women in the home 'varied considerably and depended on the discretion and knowledge of the individual'.[39] Where satisfaction was expressed it was usually because of some practical help which the social worker had been able to offer. One form of practical help which the social worker may be able to give is assistance in finding alternative accommodation.

Medical services

Three kinds of medical services are relevant to battered women: general practice, hospital accident departments and health visiting. Although much more is known about general practicioners than about the other two, it is difficult to assess with any degree of confidence the extent to which battered women consult their GPs about the problems arising from beatings. Any researchers trying to obtain this information from doctors (e.g. Borkowski, Murch and Walker) are faced with several problems, not the least of which is the issue of confidentiality and the difficulty of gaining access to medical records. Even if access were to be granted, a reliable picture may still not emerge. References in the records to the cause of injuries will often be cursory, and instances of marital violence may not always be identified.

The alternative approach is to ask the women themselves about contact with general practitioners. The problem here is that researchers have arrived at very different results. An American study by Pagelow reported that 45 per cent of the sample had received medical treatment at least once.[40] A survey in England by Binney, Harkell and Nixon found that 52 per cent of the women had contacted a doctor.[41] A Scottish study conducted by Dobash and Dobash produced a figure of 80 per cent.[42] A study by Pahl, again in England, reported that 64 per cent of the women interviewed at a refuge had consulted a doctor.[43] The low American figure may possibly be explained by the financial barriers to medical care in the United States, but the discrepancy between the other figures is capable of no such simple explanation. It should be stressed, however, that although 80 per cent of the women in Scotland had *at some time* consulted a doctor about injuries resulting from marital violence, Dobash and Dobash estimate that among the women they interviewed 'only 3 per cent of all the beatings they received throughout their married lives were ever reported to a doctor'.[44]

All three studies, therefore, reveal a reluctance to consult doctors about injuries. This reluctance may stem from feelings of shame, from the fear or the threat of reprisals or the woman may be physically prevented by her partner from going to the doctor. Pagelow found in her study that 44 per cent of the women who did not seek the medical assistance they needed said that their spouses would not let them go to the doctor.[45]

Even when battered women do consult their GP it is unusual for any discussion of the marital violence to occur. Dobash and Dobash report that 'only 25 per cent of the women who went to a doctor ever discussed the beatings with him and on such occasions he usually was noncommital and just listened'.[46] In Pagelow's study, although only 45 per cent of the women consulted their doctors a higher proportion (49 per cent) of those who did see the doctor told him what had happened.[47] Sometimes women give doctors fictitious accounts of how the injuries were sustained. Again, shame and fear may play a part in this. Other factors may be perception of the doctor's role as a healer of bodily ailments and a belief that the doctor is too busy to be bothered with personal problems. Doctors, anyway, may not inquire too closely into the cause of the injuries, suspecting or knowing that the woman's account is untrue but not wishing to become involved in marital conflict. Dobash and Dobash make the following comment: 'The doctor's failure to question the woman about the injuries or his willingness to accept a clear fabrication concerning the cause of the injury results in a mutual denial of the violence leading to it.'[48]

Only half of the doctors interviewed by Borkowski, Murch and Walker saw treating the marital problems of patients as 'real medicine'.[49] What counts as 'real medicine' is the diagnosis and treatment of illness and injury. In the case of battered women this entails the dressing of their wounds and a prescription for tranquillizers or anti-depressants. Drugs may very well make matters worse. Borkowski, Murch and Walker write:

> We are concerned that there are cases where a man's frustration
> might be increased by his wife's lack of emotional responsiveness
> induced by tranquillizing drugs. We think there is need for a more
> technical investigation of this matter, since a high proportion of
> women with marital problems are taking such drugs, particularly
> librium and valium.[50]

The tendency of professionals to define problems in terms of their own specific competence is well-documented. Doctors define marital violence as a purely medical problem rather than as a social problem with some medical implications. Many GPs restrict themselves to medical treatment because they are unsure what to do in cases of marital violence, and they are unaware of other sources of help; very few referrals are made by doctors to other, non-medical agencies. Doctors also share the general views about the importance of marital privacy, and they stress the importance of adopting a non-judgmental approach. In spite of these limitations, however, 56 per cent of the women in the Binney, Harkell and Nixon study had found contact with the doctor useful, and this is a higher level of satisfaction than that recorded for either the police or social workers.[51] In Pahl's study 53 per cent of the women found contact with doctors helpful. It may be supposed that some of those women defined purely medical treatment as helpful, but Pahl reports that many women regarded some aspects of medical treatment, particularly the prescribing of drugs, as an inappropriate, short-term response. The doctors regarded as most helpful were those who listened sympathetically and offered both medical and non-medical advice.[52] According to Dobash and Dobash, when doctors do proffer non-medical advice they almost always urge the women to leave the man.[53] Similar findings were reported by Binney, Harkell and Nixon: a third of the women who had not found contact with a doctor helpful criticized the prescribing of tranquillizers.[54]

As compared with general practitioners, there is very little information about hospital accident departments in so far as battered women are concerned. The great advantage accident departments have over general practitioners is that no appointments are necessary and they are open 24 hours every day. Some women may prefer the relative anonymity of accident departments, neither expecting nor receiving anything more than emergency medical treatment. There are no entirely reliable statistics about the use of hospital accident departments by battered women. It is clear, however, that battered women will form only a very small proportion of total accident admissions.

According to Borkowski, Murch and Walker, battered women also constitute a small proportion of the clients of health visitors – 1.8 per cent on average of total caseload.[55] Binney, Harkell and Nixon found that 23 per cent of their sample had been in contact with health visitors, and that 55 per cent of these said that the contact had been useful.[56] In their dealings with battered women, health visitors share many of the characteristics of social workers. There is the same overriding concern with the welfare of children; indeed, this concern may be even more pronounced among health visitors than it is among social workers. There is the same reluctance to intervene, the same emphasis on respecting a couple's privacy and the same importance attached to neutrality. One interesting difference is the greater readiness of health visitors to refer battered women clients to other services or agencies, especially to social workers, solicitors and general practitioners.[57]

Conclusions

This paper has considered the responses to marital violence of the three statutory services which have most contact with battered women. It is the similarity in the attitudes and responses displayed by the three agencies which strike one most forcibly. Much of the similarity stems from the view, shared by all practitioners, of women primarily as wives and mothers. Much stress is laid on the importance of keeping the family together and, more often than not, this leads to a redefining of the problem as one of child care.

Dealing with battered women is peripheral to the main concerns of all practitioners. In the case of social workers this arises partly because local authority social services departments have no statutory responsibility for battered women. For GPs, health visitors, accident departments and the police, cases of marital violence represent only a small proportion of their total work, although not so small a proportion as the practitioners themselves appear to believe. Many battered women complain that practitioners do not treat their cases seriously, but this is almost inevitable if dealing with marital violence is regarded as being not 'real medicine', not 'real social work' or not 'real police work'.

Views about the privacy of what occurs in the home and within a marital relationship lead to a reluctance on the part of all practitioners to intervene. The view of the family as an institution built on love, security and the growth of the individual leads to efforts to sustain the family unit even when women are being treated violently by their partners. As Jones says: 'For our own security and peace of mind, we tend to cling to an idealised picture of family life: to see the family as a centre of solidarity, love and acceptance rather than of conflict and potential violence.'[58] With the exception of GPs, the emphasis of practitioners is on reconciliation. Doctors rarely give non-medical advice, but when they do they invariably tell the woman that she should leave the man. They apparently see this as a relatively simple matter, not recognizing the immense difficulties facing women who try to break away from a violent relationship.

One of the most obvious weaknesses in the services is their fragmentary, unco-ordinated nature. The Select Committee recommended 24-hour family crisis centres which would:

be specially responsible for the co-ordination of the local arrangements already available to women and children in distress. We have been impressed by the fact that one of the prime problems for the family in stress is the need to consult with several different agencies, very often not relating together very effectively.[59]

Unfortunately, few such centres have been established.

The overall impression of the services covered by this paper is of a general lack of effectiveness in their dealings with battered women. This is certainly the case if levels of dissatisfaction among the women using the services is taken as the measure: the proportions of women not finding contact with the services useful, according to Binney, Harkell and Nixon, range from 64 per cent in the case of the police to 44 per cent in the case of doctors. The failure to respond adequately has the effect of diminishing the importance of the problem. In this way the statutory services both reflect and reinforce the view of women as 'appropriate victims' of violence.[60] The services do not present a serious challenge to the legitimacy of male violence as a means of socially controlling women.

Notes

1 Papers by Maidment and Brailey in this volume deal with the responses of local authority housing departments.
2 R.E. and R.P. Dobash, *Violence Against Wives*, Shepton Mallet, Open Books, 1980, p. 167. The same point is made by M. Borkowski, M. Murch and V. Walker, *Marital Violence, The Community Response*, London, Tavistock, 1983 and by J. Pahl, 'A bridge over troubled waters: a longitudinal study of women who went to a refuge', unpublished report for DHSS, 1981.
3 V. Binney, G. Harkell and J. Nixon, *Leaving Violent Men*, London, Women's Aid Federation England, 1981, p. 13.
4 B. Dawson and T. Faragher, *Battered Wives Project: Interim Report*, Department of Sociology, University of Keele, 1977, p. 98.
5 Dobash and Dobash, op. cit., pp. 120–1.
6 Binney, Harkell and Nixon, op. cit., p. 14.
7 J. Pahl, *A Refuge for Battered Women*, London, HMSO, 1978, p. 37.
8 S. McCabe and F. Sutcliffe, *Defining Crime*, Oxford, Blackwell, 1978, p. 85. See also S. Holdaway, *Inside the British Police: A Force at Work*, Oxford, Blackwell, 1983.
9 J. Pahl, 'The police response to marital violence', *Journal of Social Welfare Law*, November, 1982, p. 337.
10 A good treatment of this topic is to be found in Borkowski, Murch and Walker, op. cit.
11 House of Commons, *Report from the Select Committee on Violence in Marriage*, HC 553, London, HMSO, 1975.
12 T. Faragher, 'The police and domestic violence', unpublished paper, 1981, p. 25.
13 House of Commons, op. cit., p. 365.
14 Faragher, op. cit., pp. 13–15.
15 Pahl, op. cit., 1982, p. 341.
16 McCabe and Sutcliffe, op. cit., pp. 78–9.
17 L. Jeffery and J. Pahl, 'Battered women, the police and the criminal law', unpublished paper, 1979, p. 11.
18 M.D. Pagelow, *Women-battering: Victims and Their Experiences*, Beverly Hills, California, Sage, 1981, p. 125.
19 House of Commons, op. cit., pp. 367–8.
20 Borkowski, Murch and Walker, op. cit., p. 21.

21 House of Commons, op. cit., p. 376.
22 Dobash and Dobash, op. cit., p. 222.
23 Borkowski, Murch and Walker, op. cit., pp. 93–4.
24 Binney, Harkell and Nixon, op. cit., p. 14.
25 Jeffery and Pahl, op. cit., p. 10.
26 Pagelow, op. cit., p. 141.
27 M. Maynard, 'The response of social workers to domestic violence', unpublished paper, 1979.
28 Borkowski, Murch and Walker, op. cit., p. 18.
29 P. Leonard and E. McLeod, 'Marital violence: social construction and social service response', unpublished paper, Department of Applied Social Studies, University of Warwick, 1980, p. 44.
30 House of Commons, op. cit., p. 532.
31 Maynard, op. cit., p. 18.
32 Borkowski, Murch and Walker, op. cit., p. 89.
33 British Association of Social Workers, 'Home violence – is there an answer?', *Social Work Today*, vol. 6, no. 13, pp. 409–13.
34 Binney, Harkell and Nixon, op. cit., p. 20.
35 North-West Region of the National Women's Aid Federation, 'Battered women and social work' in J.P. Martin (ed.), *Violence and the Family*, Chichester, Wiley, 1978, p. 322.
36 Maynard, op. cit., p. 5.
37 See Leonard and McLeod, op. cit., p. 54.
38 Ibid., p. 53.
39 Binney, Harkell and Nixon, op. cit., p. 20.
40 Pagelow, op. cit., p. 140.
41 Binney, Harkell and Nixon, op. cit., p. 20.
42 Dobash and Dobash, op. cit., p. 181.
43 J. Pahl, 'The general practitioner and the problems of battered women', *Journal of Medical Ethics*, 5(3) 1979, p. 117.
44 Dobash and Dobash, op. cit., p. 180.
45 Pagelow, op. cit., p. 140.
46 Dobash and Dobash, op. cit., p. 183.
47 Pagelow, op. cit., p. 140.
48 Dobash and Dobash, op. cit., p. 181.
49 Borkowski, Murch and Walker, op. cit., pp. 157–65.
50 Ibid., p. 64.
51 Binney, Harkell and Nixon, op. cit., p. 14.
52 Pahl, op. cit., 1979, p. 117.
53 Dobash and Dobash, op. cit., p. 187.
54 Binney, Harkell and Nixon, op. cit., p. 20.
55 Borkowski, Murch and Walker, op. cit., p. 17.
56 Binney, Harkell and Nixon, op. cit., p. 14.
57 Borkowski, Murch and Walker, op. cit., p. 37.
58 C.O. Jones, 'The family as a conflict prone institution' in Social Work Services Group, Scottish Education Department, *Violence in the Family*, Edinburgh, HMSO, 1982, p. 3.
59 House of Commons, op. cit., para. 20.
60 The term 'appropriate victim' is used by Dobash and Dobash, op. cit., chs 2 and 3.

Doing his best to sustain the sanctity of marriage

Michael D.A. Freeman

Abstract

Freeman's paper deals with marital rape, a specific form of marital violence which has been virtually ignored in the literature on violence against women. Battering and rape, the author argues, are closely related and frequently occur together. Both forms of violence stem from a patriarchal society designed to protect the interests of men and maintain male dominance.

At present men who rape their wives are immune from prosecution in England. This is also the case in most other countries, but the paper also considers what has happened in places where the immunity has been removed or modified. Freeman traces the history of the immunity in England and casts doubt on its legal foundation and on the contemporary arguments used in its defence. The immunity rests on two shaky foundations: that married women are part of their husbands' property and that man and wife are one flesh. The first of these ideas may still have some currency, but it is as outmoded as the immunity itself. The author considers various modifications that could be made to the exclusion rule but concludes that abolition is the only satisfactory solution.

Women made a fuss about it in books, but in the cool judgement of right thinking men, of other men of the world, such as he recollected often received praise in the Divorce Court, he had but done his best to sustain the sanctity of marriage, to prevent her from abandoning her duty . . . . No, he did not regret it.

Thus spoke Soames in Galsworthy's *Forsyte Saga*. He had just raped his wife, Irene. In the last decade considerable attention has been devoted to rape,[1] and where once the literature was 'largely concerned with the difficulties of protecting a man accused of rape from a spurious or vindictive charge', now it commonly emphasizes 'the problems involved in protecting raped females from what is seen as particularly odious behaviour on the part of components of the criminal justice system',[2] the police,[3] defence counsel and the judiciary.[4] Twice in recent years, in 1975 and 1982, there has been something of a rape crisis in Britain.[5] At the same time, violence against women in the home has emerged as a social problem of considerable dimension and has demanded and received responses from a wide spectrum of organizations.[6] Twice the UK legislature has responded to the plight of the battered woman by creating new,[7] or refashioning existing,[8] remedies: twice the House of Lords has considered the meaning and scope of these remedies.[9] The 'sexual harassment of working women' has also caused concern:[10] greater attention has also been given to the implications of pornography[11] and the economic violence of prostitution.[12] There have been searching examinations of the institution of marriage[13] and of sexist justice.[14]

Despite all this, comparatively little concern has been shown for victims of marital rape.[15] Neither De Crow's *Sexist Justice* nor *Sexism and the Law* by Sachs and Wilson devote any space to what is the archetype of partriarchalism and is entrenched in the law of most 'civilized' countries. Yet as John Stuart Mill commented over a century ago:

A female slave has (in Christian countries) an admitted right . . . to refuse to her master the last familiarity. Not so the wife . . . her husband can claim from her and enforce the lowest degradation of a human being, that of being made the instrument of an animal function contrary to her inclination.[16]

This paper is an exploration of the marital rape immunity. In the course of it I doubt the legal foundation of the existing English rule, while showing its origins in liberal democratic theory. The history of the immunity is traced and contemporary justifications are questioned. The approaches of a number of other legal systems are also sketched. The paper begins with a discussion of the relationship between the acknowledged problem of wife battering and marital rape, still, it seems, seen as a 'personal trouble'.[17]

Michael D.A. Freeman

Violence against women and marital rape

There is no objective behaviour that we can automatically recognize as wife abuse. It may be easy enough to distinguish 'normal domestic disputes' from 'real domestic brutality'. As an example of the latter, Jack Ashley MP gave 'the crushing of spirits'.[18] Whether emotional assault comes within the category of 'domestic brutality' depends on who does the defining and for what purpose. For centuries husbands had the right to chastise their wives.[19] Thus, a sheriff in Scotland in 1975 expressed his support for the ancient principle that 'reasonable chastisement should be the duty of every husband if his wife misbehaves' (quoted in *Ms* (1975)). This may be an isolated judicial pronouncement:[20] on the other hand, it may reflect an underlying *Volksgeist*.[21] Gelles certainly found women who would agree with the Scottish sheriff.[22] There are clear parallels, of course, in the case of child abuse. Is the infliction of moderate and reasonable corporal punishment to be regarded as abuse? With children there is another label, 'non-accidental injury', but what is an 'accident'? All of these concepts are problematic and depend on numerous situational contingencies.[23] So it is with marital rape. It is surprising that violence against women and marital rape should have been kept conceptually so distinct,[24] but it is true to say that sexual intercourse without a wife's consent would not be regarded as abuse by most people. But the relationship between violence and rape, if not self-evident, is such that it is only in a situation where marital rape is not considered legitimate that violence against women in the home can ultimately be eliminated. The aetiology of both phenomena is to be explained in terms of current definitions of male-female relationships, and it is only with a redefinition of these that we can hope to limit the incidence of violence against women, whatever form this takes.[25]

But violence against women and marital rape are not just connected conceptually. There is empirical evidence of causal links as well. Thus, women may accede to sexual intercourse with their husbands to avoid being battered. One woman, interviewed by Gelles, 'viewed being beaten up as a more acceptable alternative to marital rape'.[26] But they are not always alternatives. Both Rape Crisis Centres and Women's Refuges report instances of women who are both violently assaulted and raped. Some husbands seem to regard a wife's refusal of intercourse as grounds for beating or intimidating her. One wife is quoted by Gelles as saying:

He was one of those – he liked to strike out a lot and hit you and a lot of that was based on sex . . . he thought I was a cold fish – I wasn't affectionate enough . . . Sometimes he took a shotgun to me.[27]

According to the first annual report of the London Rape Crisis Centre in 1977, 'the majority of battered women and many women in so-called "normal" marriages describe their sexual relations with their husbands at times as rape'.[28] Sometimes sexual demands lead to a conflict which precipitates domestic violence. One woman, quoted in the Australian Royal Commission report on Human Relationships, described a sequence of events thus:

> If I had my period and didn't want sex he used to bash me up. Another time when I was pregnant (and didn't want sex) he rolled me on my stomach and lashed my buttocks so I couldn't lie on my back for a week.[29]

Sometimes women are raped and then beaten. Sometimes it is the other way about. Faulk describes cases where sex was forced on a wife after she had been beaten.[30] Sexual assaults other than rape are also perpetrated on married women by their husbands. These may range from indecent assault to fellatio and buggery. In one reported case a husband struck his wife and then dragged her upstairs by her hair. He committed buggery on her saying during the act, 'I'm doing it this way because I know it will hurt you'. (She suffered from haemorrhoids and this was known to him.) (*R v Hornby* 1978).)

Despite all this evidence, few of the many books published on the subject of violence in the family discuss marital rape, just as, until recently, few treatises on child abuse incorporated the problem of sexual exploitation of children. Marital rape clearly exists. It can be no coincidence that the most publicized recent cases about rape have involved husbands (though the husbands themselves could not be charged with rape).[31]

How much marital rape exists cannot be determined with any precision. If rape is the most under-reported of crimes, marital rape, which is not even a crime, must be the least complained about category of rape. Marital rape is probably only reported where it is accompanied by other violence. In the absence of violence (or even in its presence), the majority of wives probably do not perceive forced sexual intercourse as rape. Some will consider it their fault.[32] Others will be ashamed to talk about it. Many will have adopted cultural definitions of the act and will see themselves as property at their husband's disposal. Gelles argues that 'the pervasive ideology of "women as men's chattels" has served to deny women the opportunity to perceive their own sexual victim-isation'.[33]

Accordingly, little is known of its incidence. There are no official statistics: that much is obvious since the law does not regard marital rape as a crime. We do, however, know that a high percentage of rape victims know the offender. In Amir's research[34] (1971), 48 per cent came into this category. In Bart's study[35] (1975), 8.4 per cent of women were raped by men with whom they had intimate relations (0.4 per cent by husbands): a further 12 per cent were raped by 'dates' and 23 per cent by acquaintances. In Walmsley's study[36] (1980), 50 per cent knew the offender, of whom 3 per cent were relatives. The London Rape Crisis Centre reports that 3.6 per cent of the cases referred to it between April 1978 and April 1979 involved rape of a woman by her husband or lover (the statistics do not dis-tinguish between them).[37] Such statistics reveal only the tip of the iceberg. It may be that women only regard marital rape as rape where it is accompanied by other violence. If this is so, the removal of the husband's immunity would only open the floodgates (a common fear of those who defend the status quo) from marriages where there was other domestic violence. There is some support for this hypothesis in findings by Willis and Chappell in South Australia (a state which has removed the husband's immunity from prosecution, though in a rather con-voluted way). They found that when women were asked whether they had been raped in marriage, they stated that they had not. But when the question was rephrased as 'have you ever had sexual intercourse against your will with your husband', the respondents poured out stories of numerous violent assaults endured prior to submitting to sexual intercourse.[38]

The English law of rape: Hale but not hearty

According to Susan Brownmiller, 'the exemption from rape prosecu-tions granted to husbands who force their wives into acts of sexual union by physical means is as ancient as the original quaint phrase of biblical origin, "unlawful carnal knowledge"'. 'To our Biblical fore-fathers', she continues, 'any carnal knowledge outside the marriage contract was "unlawful". And any carnal knowledge within the mar-riage contract was by definition "lawful".'[39] Too little is known about the historical origins of the exemption to make a statement as categori-cal as Brownmiller, though it has a ring of truth about it. What, how-ever, cannot be doubted is that the law regarding rape developed to protect not women but the interests of men.

To maintain the same about the law today will be contentious in the eyes of many, but rape is a crime about which many myths have been constructed.[40] It may be that the male interests protected by the contemporary law of rape do not coincide with the interests of men which the medieval law protected, but they are male interests nonetheless. The earliest pronouncements of our institutional writers make it clear that the law of rape was designed to prevent the abduction of propertied virgins. The severity of the penalties prescribed reflects the fact that rape was perceived as akin to the defilement of another man's property. The prosecution of a husband for raping his wife would in this context make no more sense than prosecuting a man for stealing his own property.[41]

Women today may not be commodities in the marriage market or pawns in the property accumulation process in quite the same way as they were in earlier ages, but hangovers from such notions remain potent forces for the exploitation of women. Ours remains a society in which men are or are expected to be on top[42] with women, it may cynically be added, on tap.[43] In a patriarchal society 'male dominance must be maintained at all costs because the person who dominates cannot conceive of any alternative but to be dominated in turn'.[44] This ideology is to a considerable extent sustained by women, and, as Bell and Newby note,

> might remains very close to the surface. Deference stabilises the
> hierarchical nature of the husband–wife relationship, but . . . the
> relationship is embedded in a system of power – and the naked use
> of this power can be, and is, resorted to if the relationship threatens
> to break down.[45]

The recognition that a husband commits no crime when he forces his wife to have sexual intercourse reflects this ideology. Rape is the denial of self-determination,[46] the rejection of the victim's physical autonomy:[47] it symbolises 'ultimate disrespect . . . the exercise of the power of consent over another person'.[48]

It is usual today to trace the origin of the marital rape exemption rule to Sir Matthew Hale (1609–76).[49] It is generally maintained that Hale can in no way be said to have created the rule: that he was merely declaring what for centuries the law had generally been believed to be. There is some evidence for this in William Lambarde's *Eirenarcha, or Of The Office of the Justices of the Peace*, published in 1611. He held that a man could not rape his own mistress, but could be prosecuted for raping the mistress of another.[50] Hale's actions – he presided over an infamous witchcraft trial in Bury St Edmunds in 1662 – have been said to be saturated with systematic biases against women.[51] Francis North has him saying that with women 'there is no wisdom below the girdle'.

Hale's statement on immunity is a bare assertion. There is no citation to support it which is contrary to his usual practice. Given his views on women it cannot, therefore, be ruled out that he did, indeed, create or at least institutionalize the marital rape exemption rule. His abstention from citation of authority may be the result not only of absence of authority to support his assertion but of authority the other way. There is some evidence for this hypothesis. In 1631, Lord Audley was convicted of rape of his own wife 'for holding her by force, while one of his minions forcibly, against her will, had carnal knowledge of her'. The report in *State Trials* states that 'she was the party wronged; otherwise she might be abused'.[52] Another report of the case states 'she may have the peace against her husband'.[53] What is remarkable about this case is that there is no argument to the effect that, if a husband himself raped his wife he was not to be convicted, it must follow *a fortiori* that it could not be rape by a husband where he personally did not penetrate her. Hale was aware of this case. Of it he wrote: 'Tho in marriage she hath given up her body to her husband, she is not to be by him prostituted to another.'[54] But this statement does not explain why such a husband should be convicted of rape. He could be convicted of other offences while the actual perpetrator could be convicted of rape. I am not convinced as to the adequacy of Hale's explanation. The so-called legal foundation of the marital rape exemption may, therefore, not be as substantial as has been usually assumed.

Legal ideas, however, are not conjured out of thin air. We should, therefore, not be surprised to find support for Hale's implied irrevocable contract in the writings of the political theorist, John Locke, who was a near contemporary of Hale. His *Two Treatises of Government*, published in 1690, was written explicitly as an attack on the patriarchalism of Filmer. But he excludes from his criticism 'women': only men count as individuals and only they may assume natural individual freedom and equality. Women are held to be born to subjection. Locke takes it for granted that a woman will, through the marriage contract, always agree to place herself in subordination to her husband. Wifely subjection has 'a Foundation in Nature'. In the family, Locke argues, the husband's will as the 'abler and the stronger' must always prevail over 'that of his wife in all things of their common Concernment'. Of course, if women are naturally subordinate, the question of their consenting to this arrangement does not arise.

Carole Pateman makes this point:

> If the assumption of natural subjection did not still hold, liberal democratic theorists would long ago have begun to ask why it is that an ostensibly free and equal individual should *always* agree to enter a contract which subordinates her to another such individual. They would long ago have begun to question the character of an institution in which the agreement of a wife deprives her of the right to retract her consent to provide sexual services to her husband, and which gives him the legal right to force her to submit.[55]

That they, Mill apart, have not done so says something about their schizophrenia. There is no one writing today who would gainsay a woman's right to take part in democratic political processes. But, if women can exercise consent and freedom in the public area, how can we justify denying them this freedom in the most private of spheres?

To return to legal sources, it was not until *R v Clarence* in 1888 that the doctrine was properly considered by an English court.[56] But all the statements in this case regarding the culpability of a man for the rape of his wife are *obiter*. Clarence was charged with 'unlawfully and maliciously inflicting grievous bodily harm upon his wife' and with an assault upon her occasioning actual bodily harm. He had had sexual intercourse with her with her consent, when he was suffering from venereal disease. He knew this: she did not. He was convicted, but on appeal his conviction was reversed. Those judges who pronounced on the rape issue, and it was clearly not incumbent on them to do so, were divided.

Only one judgement (that of Baron Pollock) unequivocally states that a wife's consent given to intercourse upon marriage can never be revoked: 'she has no right or power to refuse her consent'.[57] Stephen J. also did not think that a husband might be indicted for the rape of his wife, though his reasoning is more ambivalent.[58] Hawkins J. is probably also on Hale's side though his judgement is thoroughly confused and contains gross inconsistencies so that it is best ignored.[59] A.L. Smith J.'s judgement is also equivocal: a wife's consent, though implied, might apparently be revoked.[60] Two of the judges, Wills J. and Field J.,[61] were clearly opposed to Hale's proposition. Wills J. said:

> If intercourse under the circumstances now in question constitute an assault on the part of the man, it must constitute rape, unless,

indeed, as between married persons rape is impossible, a proposition to which I certainly am not prepared to assent, and for which there seems to me to be no sufficient authority . . . I cannot understand why, as a general rule, if intercourse be an assault, it should not be rape.[62]

The issue came before the courts again in 1949 in *R v Clarke.*[63] This does not help us much. The wife had secured a separation order.[64] By this 'process of law', opined Byrne J., 'her consent to marital intercourse was revoked'.[65] Once more Hale was relied on and *Clarence* was cited uncritically. *R v Miller*[66] in 1954 is the next authority. A husband forced his wife to have sexual intercourse after she had filed a petition for divorce but before the action was heard. He was, it was held, guilty of assault but not rape. Lynskey J., applying 'the law as it stands', stated that 'the law implies consent to what took place in so far as intercourse is concerned'.[67] Lynskey J. relied on the judgements in *Clarence*'s case. These, he argued, showed that Hale's assertion was accepted by the judges. He quoted, however, *inter alia* from Wills J., who did not agree with Hale, and Hawkins J., whom Lynskey J. argued 'took a strong view that a husband could not be convicted of a rape on his wife'[68] (*sed dubitante*). He concluded with the strange comment that 'the view which I take of the *dicta* of the judges in *Clarence* is that the statement of the law in Hale was still accepted by them because their observations are only *obiter dicta*'.[69] Of course, the statements of the judges in *Clarence* are only *dicta*. But it is a *non sequitur* to argue that because of this the judges were accepting Hale's statement.

As Scutt has also argued, *Miller* is the case which lent itself most opportunely to a reappraisal of the so-called rule.[70] But the opportunity was not taken. It is arguable, indeed, that *R v Miller*, a case from 1954, is the only direct decision on the subject. Is our authority then only thirty years old? That a rule like the marital rape exemption rule could date from a time when the status of women was supposed to have improved says a lot about that supposition. That we should wish to attribute the anomaly to a seventeenth-century luminary says much about contemporary society and the role of ideology.

More recent cases are particularly helpful, concerned as they are with limiting what is assumed to be Hale's doctrine. *R v O'Brien*[71] concerned rape of a wife after a decree nisi of divorce. Park J. stated:

There can be no question that by a decree nisi a wife's implied consent to marital intercourse is revoked. Accordingly the husband commits the offence of rape if he has sexual intercourse with her thereafter without her consent.[72]

Park J.'s reasoning was that a 'decree nisi effectively brings the marriage to an end'.[73] But it is submitted that this is not the relevant question which is: did the wife withdraw her consent to sexual intercourse? In *R v Steele*[74] the Court of Appeal decided that when a husband gave an undertaking to the court not to 'assault, molest or interfere with his wife' he also gave up his sexual rights, so that he could be charged with raping her. It was, the Court of Appeal said, equivalent to the granting of an injunction.

The judges have carved out exceptions to what Lord Hailsham recently called (almost certainly wrongly, as this paper has demonstrated), the 'ancient common law doctrine'.[75] For this at least we may be grateful. In Canada, by contrast, there were no exceptions.[76] Smith and Hogan have, however, argued that the statutory formulation of rape in the Sexual Offences (Amendment) Act 1976 as 'unlawful sexual intercourse' not only affirms the Hale doctrine but may also have reversed *R v Clarke* and *R v O'Brien*, thus leaving the wife in a worse position than she was until these recent developments. They conclude that this 'was certainly not Parliament's intention' and argue that 'the section should not be so interpreted'.[77] With this I agree. Smith and Hogan go on to argue that 'intercourse constituting a matrimonial offence is "unlawful" and capable of being rape if the other conditions are satisfied'.[78] But, since there can be no doubt that the behaviour of a husband who forces his wife to have sexual intercourse with him against her will is such that she cannot reasonably be expected to live with him (to be in other words a breach of matrimonial obligation sufficient to ground a petition for divorce),[79] it would follow that the rape of a wife constitutes 'unlawful sexual intercourse'. The marital rape exemption would thus be swept away by a side-wind. This was clearly not Parliament's intention since it expressly refused to uproot the exemption. 'Unlawful' usually means 'outside matrimony'. But there is no reason why this should be its exclusive meaning. I would, therefore, suggest that Parliament, which gave no attention to the meaning of the word 'unlawful', intended to affirm the Hale doctrine and to accept those exceptions engrafted upon it by judges in the last thirty-five years. It must also be assumed that the judges in *R v Steele* thought this.

In the most recent case (*R v Caswell*) the immunity was extended 'logically' to indecent assault. The commentator to the report stated:

'It would make nonsense of the immunity if the husband could be
convicted of attempted rape. The acts constituting the attempt
would inevitably amount to indecent assaults and it would be
wrong to allow the immunity from conviction of rape . . . to be
evaded by describing those acts as indecent assaults.'

In *Caswell* the act was fellatio: surely wives in marriage do not impliedly consent to this as well?

Hale and implied consent

Hale's rationale is that a wife consents to sexual intercourse by marry-
ing. That this is clearly a legal fiction may be seen by examining the
matrimonial law context. Marriage may, as Lenore Weitzman[80] has so
ably shown, be a contract different from any other, but it is clear that
in terms of matrimonial law a wife is not bound to submit to her
husband's demands for sexual intercourse. She can refuse his sexual
demands where they are inordinate or unreasonable.[81] She may refuse
sexual intercourse if he is suffering from a venereal disease.[82] American
courts, which also followed Hale uncritically, even held that a husband
has the 'duty of forbearance . . . at the reasonable request of the
wife'.[83] A wife's refusal to have sexual intercourse with her husband
has never in itself constituted a ground for divorce.[84] Matrimonial law
principles, in other words, have developed separately from Hale's doctrine. There have even been situations where a wife has been expected
not to have sexual intercourse with her husband: for example, where
this would condone his adultery.
  Hale's reasoning is thus inconsistent with matrimonial law generally.
It is, furthermore, quite untenable. Even if it were acceptable that on
marriage a wife consented to all sexual relations with her husband,[85] it
is unreasonable to conclude from this that she has consented to the
force and even to the injury which her husband may inflict upon her in
enforcing his 'right'. Yet a husband may not be convicted of rape no
matter how brutally he forces himself upon his wife or how seriously
he injures her. It is true that he may be convicted of assault in such
circumstances. But the existence of alternative remedies hardly justifies
the exemption from prosecution for rape. All rapists assault their
victims: should rapists generally only be charged with assault? (This is
rather different from the question of whether a separate crime of rape
should exist at all.)[86] Any suggestion that assault laws provide an
adequate alternative remedy for wives raped by their husbands fails to

appreciate the real violation inherent in a rape. Rape laws should protect not just bodily safety but the sexual integrity and autonomy of women. Rape causes more than just physical injury; the emotional and psychological repercussions are incalculable.

The courts both in the United States[87] and in England[88] have affirmed that a husband has no right to prevent his wife aborting their child. This is a recognition that women have some autonomy, at least *vis-à-vis* their husbands, when it comes to the decision as to whether they should give birth to a child. More than a hundred years ago women linked demands for freedom from their husbands' demands for sex and demands for voluntary motherhood. Thus, in 1871, at the American National Woman Suffrage Association, Paulina Wright Davis attacked the law 'which makes obligatory the rendering of marital rights and compulsory maternity'.[89] Despite the very much more vocal demands today for an end to compulsory maternity, the link between this and the compulsory rendering of marital rights is seldom forged.

The notion that women impliedly consented to their husbands' sexual demands may have been meaningful when all decisions were taken by husbands. But society has changed enormously since those times, and both legislation and case law reflect this. What Denning L.J. said over thirty years ago about the location of the matrimonial home is surely apposite with reference to sexual relationships in marriage. 'The decision where the home should be,' he said, 'is a decision which affects both the parties and their children. It is their duty to decide it by agreement by give and take, and not by the imposition of the will of one over the other. Each is entitled to an equal voice in the ordering of the affairs which are their common concern. Neither has a casting vote. . . .'[90] Why, then, should one party have the 'casting vote' in relation to sexual activities?

At root, Hale's idea rests on two closely related notions. One emphasizes that a married woman is really part of her husband's property, a mere chattel, so that forced sexual intercourse is really a husband making use of his own property. The second (see, for example, Blackstone, 1765) stresses man and wife as one flesh adding to that the Pauline conclusion 'and I am he'.[91] Neither of these ideas can stand scrutiny today. The first, as has already been indicated, may live on. But anachronisms cannot be rationally justified by finding in their support ideological sentiments which too must be rejected. Hale's statement is thus the shakiest of foundations upon which to rest the marital rape exemption.

In defence of the immunity

There are five other justifications found in the literature which must be considered. The first emphasizes the inappropriateness of using the criminal law in disputes between husbands and wives. This view is not new: it is common to find commentators on the problem of marital violence generally putting it forward. Parnas used to do so;[92] Susan Maidment still does. It is worth pondering her reasoning. She writes:

> Serious consideration must be given to whether prosecuting a
> husband for a criminal offence . . . will achieve anything in terms of
> improving the marital relationship, the mutual respect which the
> husband and wife should have for each other, or the husband's
> ability to understand and control his aggression.[93]

She favours the Family Court mediation-oriented approach to be found in a number of American cities. But why should 'improving' marital relationships be the goal? Why, to quote evidence to the House of Commons Select Committee on Violence in Marriage, should 'every effort . . . *be made to re-unite the family*'?[94] It is all very well wanting the family to function as it should but, when it has not done so, it may very well not be in the victim's best interests to use social work intervention to restore the *status quo ante.* I have argued elsewhere that the state should treat violence against a wife as it treats violence against strangers.[95]

Similar ideas have found their way to the marital rape debate. Thus, the South Australian report, which produced legislation which has partially removed the marital rape exemption stated:

> it is only in exceptional circumstances that the criminal law should
> invade the bedroom. . . . The wife who is subjected to force in the
> husband's pursuit of sexual intercourse needs, in the first instance,
> the protection of the family law . . . and not the protection of the
> criminal law.[96]

Similarly, Joanna McFadyen 'by no means suggest[s] the application of the full force of the criminal law in every case'. She advocates its use 'as a last resort on a continuum, of resources focused on the increased well-being of the family unit and each of its members'.[97] The significance of marital rape must not be underestimated. Rape is the most extreme example of legal sexism.[98] It is, to quote Medea and Thompson, 'at one end of a continuum, of male-aggressive, female-passive patterns'.[99] The McFadyen approach concentrates not on the well-being of the family unit but on the welfare of the husband and men everywhere. There is no reason why rape in marriage should be regarded differently from rape of a stranger. There may be a case for a grading of penalties but that would have to be based not on the fact of marriage but on that of previous sexual contact, as in Sweden or Delaware. If the criminal law has no place in the bedroom *à propos* rape, then why has it a place as regards assault, kidnapping[100] and theft?[101] And why does the exemption not extend to those who cohabit?[102]

Secondly, the immunity is sometimes justified on the basis of the difficulties of proving marital rape.[103] There are cases where it would be difficult to prove marital rape. There are unlikely to be witnesses. But many crimes are difficult to prove, and no one has suggested removing them for that reason. This is particularly so in the case of rape. With rape the most difficult thing to prove is lack of consent. But this applies to all prosecutions for rape, particularly where the accused and victim have had a sexual relationship prior to the incident in question. Is it seriously being suggested that the only rapes that should be prosecuted are those where rapist and victim are complete strangers? An alternative, outside the scope of this paper, might involve changing certain rules of evidence such as those relating to corroboration in order to facilitate the prosecution of men alleged to have committed rape.[104]

A third alleged rationale for the marital rape exemption is linked to the second, though arguably inconsistent with it. It asserts that the possibilities exist of a vindictive wife bringing a malicious prosecution based on fabricated evidence, possibly for an ulterior purpose such as blackmailing her husband into making a favourable property settlement or custody arrangement. The 'vengeful wife' rationale is not convincing. If, as the second rationale argues, rape in marriage is difficult to prove, a threatened rape prosecution would hardly be a potent weapon in a vindictive wife's hands. It is assumed that the repeal of the immunity would open the floodgates, but this has not materialized in those jurisdictions which have done away with it. Wives can now prosecute their husbands for assault and sodomy and there is no evidence that they are doing this commonly and, in cases where they are, vengefully. Of course, the initiation of criminal proceedings is a potentially dangerous weapon that can be used by anyone against anyone else. Do we believe that women are more spiteful or more vengeful? If we do, we are failing to appreciate the current context of rape trials, the stigma, trauma and tribulation involved for the victim.[105] Women in rape trials often feel *they* are on trial. In these circumstances, only a mentally unstable wife is likely to initiate a prosecution except in the most serious of circumstances.

A fourth line of defence stresses the possibility that a wife, having accused her husband of rape, will change her mind and become reconciled to him (e.g. *The Times*, 22 May 1976). This argument was used when an attempt was made in 1976 to get rid of the marital rape exemption. The argument is a weak one. It is said (for example, by the police in their evidence to the House of Commons Select Committee on Violence in Marriage) that women who bring assault charges against their husbands change their minds the next day, so that police time has been wasted and little more achieved. Whether that is so is debatable, but there are few calls for husbands to be immune from prosecution for assaulting wives. It may well be that prosecutions for marital rape should not take place where the spouses are subsequently reconciled, though it should not be forgotten that the state, as the protector of married women generally, has an interest in the prosecution over and above that of the victim; it is difficult to argue from this that the act should not be a crime. The pros and cons of making the wife a compellable witness cannot be considered here: suffice it to say that the decision of the House of Lords[106] that she is not a compellable witness has not assisted the cause of those who wish to see the exemption removed.[107]

A fifth defence of the exemption states that a wife does not need the protection of the criminal law because she has alternative remedies in family law (as well as limited remedies in criminal law itself: she can prosecute for assault). It is true that she can seek injunctions against molestation and exclude her husband from the matrimonial home. She may bring divorce proceedings against him.[108] She may seek financial provision in the magistrates' courts. This defence overlooks a number of things. Firstly, it is not easy for working class women particularly to leave their husbands, set up elsewhere and bring divorce proceedings. That is one of the reasons why there is such an urgent need for extensive refuge provision.[109] Secondly, there is no evidence that family law remedies offer sufficient protection. The cases of *Clarke, Miller, O'Brien* and *Steele* are testimony to the inadequacy of those when faced with a determined husband. Thirdly, the defence once again ignores the rationale of rape laws: rape is not just matrimonial misconduct. It may leave emotional and psychological scars. It may lead to the birth of a child. It is an offence of sufficient moment for women to be able to claim the protection of the criminal law. Finally, it may be noted in parenthesis, husbands whose wives deny them sexual intercourse have remedies in family law, in nullity and divorce. Oddly, though perhaps it is not all that odd, the courts (or at least Lord Dunedin)[110] have advocated that a husband should use 'gentle violence' on a wife unwilling to consummate their marriage. The husband in question was chided for exercising insufficient virility. The judge, it seems, was oblivious to the fact that he was advocating assault and thus was an accessory to any crime which subsequently took place! No judge has suggested that, since rape is a 'remedy' for non-consummation of marriage, the existing remedies in nullity should be removed. But that is the logic of those who argue that the existence of alternative remedies is a reason for marital rape not being a crime.

Other systems

Most countries follow the rule that exempts the husband. An increasing number, however, do not. In the USSR, Czechoslovakia and Poland the law provides that any person can be guilty of rape by the use of physical violence against the victim. Marriage is not considered to remove the sexual freedom of women.[111] In Sweden, it has been possible to prosecute a husband for marital rape since 1965,[112] though the crime is considered less grave in view of the spouses' relationship,[113] Denmark has a similar law of a similar vintage. More recently, in 1980 the Supreme Court of Israel rejected the English common law and applied Talmudic law to Jewish residents of Israel. Justice David Bechor said of Hale's statement that it 'outraged human conscience and reason in an enlightened country in our times'. A man was sentenced to three years for forcing his wife to have intercourse against her will, beating her and then threatening to kill her if she refused to withdraw her complaint to the police.[114] In 1981 French law was changed to permit prosecution of a husband for spousal rape. In 1983 the Scottish courts appeared to reject the Scots common law basis for the marital exemption rule,[115] though there remains some doubt as to what the Scottish position actually is: it may be that a prosecution can only take place where the spouses are factually separated.[116] Even with this limitation Scottish law would still go further than English law in permitting prosecutions. Canada repealed the immunity in 1983.

The major, and most publicized, developments have taken place in the United States. The *New York Times* reported in 1981 that at least forty-seven husbands had been charged with raping their wives; twenty-three had come to trial and nineteen had resulted in convictions.[117] The first case, *State v Rideout*, in 1978 attracted worldwide publicity.[118] The prosecution took place in Oregon, one of the first states to remove the husband's immunity. The first one was South Dakota in 1975 but it reinstated the exemption two years later. A number of states have now removed the immunity. Others have limited it rather as the English judges have done.[119]

In England there was an attempt to remove the exemption in 1976 when the Sexual Offences (Amendment) Bill was at its committee stage in the House of Commons. An amendment carried at this stage was subsequently reversed. A private member's bill in 1983 was lost when Parliament was dissolved. The Criminal Law Revision Committee (1980) first recommended that marital rape should be an offence but insisted that as a safeguard prosecution should only be brought with the consent of the Director of Public Prosecutions.[120] In its final report (1984)[121] it has recommended that a woman living apart from her husband should be able to charge rape but has advocated the retention of the immunity during cohabitation. If implemented, there would be marginal improvement: the legal position in England would be assimilated to that in Scotland. But such limited reform is unacceptable. So is the Committee's reasoning. Women are denied responsibility for their own decisions. The Committee even suggests that 'a category of rape which was dealt with leniently might lead to all rape cases being regarded less seriously'. This begs the very question that is being asked.

Three choices are now open to Parliament: (i) the retention of the existing law. The arguments against this have been fully stated. The law is an indefensible hangover from an earlier age when different sentiments about marriage prevailed. The law is, furthermore, certain. (ii) They could adopt the approach found in Sweden and Delaware, for example, and distinguish between rape of a stranger and rape of someone with whom there has been previous sexual contact. The offence in both situations would be the same: only the available statutory maxima sentences would differ. Though preferable to choice (i), this solution is not recommended. The principal objection is that it supports the idea that sexual intercourse is not a woman's choice: she would be assumed to have consented by reason of having consented before. (iii) The marital rape exemption could be removed.

I believe the onus rests with those who do not wish to adopt choice (iii). Thus far, they have not provided any convincing argument at all.

Conclusion

In 1898 an American feminist, Alice Stockham, wrote that we had to get away from the tradition of 'men's necessities and woman's obedience to them'.[122] Lucy Stone, another, wrote to Elizabeth Cady Stanton: 'I very much wish that a wife's right to her own body should be pushed at our next convention'.[123] These women were writing primarily about birth control. But what they wrote can be generalized and can certainly embrace the question of rape in marriage. As long ago as 1891 it was held that a husband cannot detain his wife against her will.[124] In 1971, in *R v Reid* Cairns L. J. expressed the opinion that 'the notion that a husband can, without incurring punishment, treat his wife . . . with any kind of hostile force is obsolete'.[125] It is statements like this one and that of Denning L. J. in *Dunn v Dunn*, already quoted, which should be in the minds of the legislature. If they were, there would be no way in which the existing doctrine could be supported. Parliament has just permitted a couple to divorce after one year of marriage.[126] When Hale wrote, marriage was indissoluble. A woman who can change her mind about whether she wishes to be married can also change her mind on sexual relations with her husband. So much for Hale's logic and Soames's. Neither can prevail any longer: the marital rape exemption must be consigned to the dustbin of historical relics.

Notes

1 See, for example, S. Brownmiller, *Against Our Will*, London, Secker and Warburg, 1975; D. Chappell *et al. Forcible Rape*, New York, Columbia University Press, 1977; B. Toner, *The Facts of Rape*, London, Hutchinson, 1982; H. and J. Schwedinger, *Rape and Inequality*, Beverly Hills, Sage, 1983.

2 D. Chappell *et al.*, 'Forcible rape: a bibliography', *Journal of Criminal Law and Criminology*, vol. 65, 1974, p. 248.

3 This was brought to public attention by a BBC documentary in January 1982 on the Thames Valley Police: discussed in *The Times*, 19 and 20 January 1982.

4 Legislation in 1976 was thought to have effected some improvement but see Z. Adler, 'How the rape law really works', *The Times*, 10th February 1982.

5 In 1982 a MORI poll showed that more than half the British public wanted long prison sentences for convicted rapists, 22 per cent of them favouring life imprisonment and 7 per cent the death penalty. See *The Sunday Times*, 24 January 1982. See also the excellent leading article in *The New Statesman*, 23 July 1982, 'The mythology of rape'.

6 M.D.A. Freeman, *Violence in the Home*, Farnborough, Gower, 1979; R.E. Dobash and R.P. Dobash, *Violence Against Wives*, Shepton Mallet, Open Books, 1980; M.D. Pagelow, *Woman-Battering*, Beverly Hills, Sage, 1981;

S. Schechter, *Women and Male Violence*, London, Pluto Press, 1982; M. Borkowski *et al.*, *Marital Violence: The Community Response*, London, Tavistock, 1983; E. Wilson, *What is to be Done About Violence Against Women*? London, Penguin, 1983.

7 Domestic Proceedings and Magistrates' Courts Act 1978, sections 16–18.

8 Domestic Violence and Matrimonial Proceedings Act 1976, sections 1–3.

9 In *Davis v. Johnson* [1979] A.C. 264 and *Richards v Richards* [1984] A.C. 174.

10 See C. Mackinnon, *Sexual harassment of Working Women*, New Haven, Yale University Press, 1979; A. Sedley and M. Benn, *Sexual Harassment*, NCCL, 1982.

11 L. Lederer, *Take Back the Night: Women in Pornography*, New York, Morrow, 1980; A. Dworkin, *Pornography: Men Possessing Women*, London, The Women's Press, 1981; Wilson, op. cit.

12 J. Walkowitz, *Prostitution and Victorian Society: Women, Class and the State*, London, Cambridge University Press, 1980; E. McLeod, *Women Working: Prostitution Now*, London, Croom Helm, 1982.

13 L. Weitzman, 'Legal regulation of marriage', *California Law Review*, vol. 62, 1974, pp. 1169–288; L. Weitzman, *The Marriage Contract*, New York, Free Press, 1981; D.L. Barker, 'The regulation of marriage: repressive benevolence' in G. Littlejohn *et al.*, *Power and the State*, London, Croom Helm, 1978, pp. 239–66; K. O'Donovan, 'The male appendage – legal definitions of women' in S. Burman (ed.), *Fit Work for Women*, London, Croom Helm, 1979, pp. 134–52; C. Smart, 'Regulating families or legitimating patriarchy? Family law in Britain', *international Journal of the Sociology of Law*, vol. 10, 1982, pp. 129–48; C. Smart, *The Ties That Bind*, London, Routledge & Kegan Paul, 1984.

14 K. de Crow, *Sexist Justice*, New York, Random House, 1974; A. Sachs and J.H. Wilson, *Sexism and the Law*, Oxford, Martin Robertson, 1978; S.S.M. Edwards, *Female Sexuality and the Law*, Oxford, Martin Robertson, 1981.

15 The subject is barely discussed in rape literature. The discussion by Brownmiller, op. cit., p. 380, is very brief. J. Reynolds, 'Rape as social control', *Catalyst*, no. 8, pp. 62–7, one of the best known feminist accounts of rape, does not appear to be aware of the omission. S.S.M. Edwards, op. cit., discusses it briefly (pp. 33–5).

16 J.S. Mill, *The Subjection of Women*, London, Longmans Green, 1869.

17 The term is taken from C.W. Mills, *The Sociological Imagination*, Harmondsworth, Penguin, 1970. Battered women are, by contrast, in his terminology, a 'public issue'.

18 J. Ashley, *Hansard*, H.C. vol. 884, col. 214, 14 January 1975.

19 J. Hecker, *A Short History of Women's Rights*, London, Putnam, 1910.

20 See Freeman, op. cit., 1979, pp. 177–8.

21 C.F. von Savigny, *System of Modern Roman Law*, 1840. The term is explained in D. Lloyd, *Introduction to Jurisprudence*, London, Stevens, 1972.

22 R. Gelles, *The Violent Home*, Beverly Hills, Sage, 1974, p. 59.

23 For a discussion of these see M.D.A. Freeman, 'Child welfare: law and control' in M. Partington and J. Jowell (eds), *Welfare Law and Policy,* London, Pinter, 1979, pp. 223–31. Also, M.D.A. Freeman, *The Rights and Wrongs of Children*, London, Pinter, 1983.

24 Marital rape is considered briefly in the 'battered wives' literature, but see

R. Gelles, *Family Violence*, Beverly Hills, Sage, 1979, ch. 7.

25 Freeman, *Violence in the Home*, op. cit., 1979, pp. 141–8. See also C. McGrath, 'The crisis of domestic order', *Socialist Review*, vol. 43, 1979, pp. 11–30; D. Klein, 'Can this marriage be saved? Battery and sheltering', *Crime and Social Justice*, no. 12, 1979, pp. 19–33; D. Klein, 'Violence against women: some considerations regarding its cause and its elimination', *Crime and Delinquency*, vol. 27, 1981, pp. 64–80.

26 Gelles, op. cit., 1979, p. 131.

27 Ibid., p. 130.

28 London Rape Crisis Centre, *First Annual Report*, 1977, p. 18.

29 Report of Australian Royal Commission on Human Relationships, 1977, vol. 4, p. 135.

30 M. Faulk, 'Sexual factors in marital violence', *Medical Aspects of Human Sexuality*, vol. 11, 1977.

31 *Morgan v DPP* [1975] 2 All E.R. 347; *R v Cogan and Leak* [1976] Q.B. 217.

32 The woman may see her husband's response as legitimate punishment for her giving the appearance of violating traditional female expectations. Cf. Reynolds, op. cit.

33 Gelles, op. cit., 1979, p. 124.

34 M. Amir, *Patterns in Forcible Rape*, Chicago, University of Chicago Press, 1971.

35 P. Bart, 'Rape doesn't end with a kiss', *Viva*, June 1975.

36 R. Walmsley, 'Rape: rates, trends and sentencing practice', *Home Office Research Bulletin*, no. 10, 1980, pp. 32–5.

37 According to the London Rape Crisis Centre, of a sample of 281 rapes, thirteen were committed by husbands/lovers (the categories are not differentiated), that is, 4 per cent. London Rape Crisis Centre, *Sexual Violence: The Reality for Women*, London, The Women's Press, 1984.

38 See also R. Hall *et al., The Rapist Who Pays The Rent*, Bristol, Falling Wall Press, 1984 (2nd edn). Research in 1982–3 suggested that one in seven women are raped by husbands.

39 Brownmiller, op. cit., p. 380.

40 See S. Griffin, 'Rape – the all-American crime', *Ramparts*, September 1971, pp. 26–35.

41 Toner, op. cit. provides a useful outline of the historical background.

42 Reflected in the so-called missionary position – see E. Figes, *Patriarchal Attitudes*, London, Faber and Faber, 1970, p. 52.

43 What Judge Felix Frankfurter said of sociologists – see Lloyd, op. cit., p. 354.

44 Figes, op. cit., p. 52.

45 C. Bell and H. Newby, 'Husbands and wives: the dynamics of deferential dialectics' in D.L. Barker and S. Allen (eds), *Dependence and Exploitation in Work and Marriage*, Harlow, Longman, 1976, p. 164.

46 Griffin, op. cit., p. 34.

47 L. Clark and D. Lewis, *Rape: The Price of Coercive Sexuality*, Toronto, Women's Press, 1977, p. 167.

48 C. Schafer and M. Frye, 'Rape and respect' in M. Vetterling-Braggin *et al.* (eds), *Feminism and Philosophy*, Totown, New Jersey, Littlefield, 1977, p. 340.

49 See R. Heilbron, *Report of Advisory Group on Law of Rape*, Cmnd. 6352, London, HMSO, 1975, p. 3. Also Toner, op. cit.

50 N. Bashair, 'Rape in England between 1550 and 1700' in London Feminist History Group (eds), *The Sexual Dynamics of History*, 1983, p. 38.

51 See G. Geis, 'Lord Hale, witches and rape', *British Journal of Law and Society*, vol. 5, 1978, p. 43.

52 3 *State Trials* 401, 402.

53 123 *English Law Reports* 1140.

54 *Historia Placitorum Coronae*, p. 629; quoted with approval in *R v Cogan and Leak* [1976] Q.B. 217, at p. 223.

55 C. Pateman, 'Feminism and democracy' in G. Duncan (ed.), *Democratic Theory and Practice*, London, Cambridge University Press, 1983, p. 212.

56 [1888] 22 Q.B.D. 23: on which see J. Scutt, 'Consent in rape: the problem of the marriage contract', *Monash Law Review*, vol. 3, 1977, pp. 257–61.

57 [1888] 22 Q.B.D. 23, 64.

58 In the first edition of his *Digest of the Criminal Law*, he expressed the opinion that in certain circumstances a husband might be indicted for the rape of his wife. He subsequently withdrew this.

59 He states: (i) 'a husband cannot be convicted of rape committed by him upon the person of his wife': (ii) 'even if to hold a husband liable for an assault under such circumstances would be to subject him also to a charge of rape, the opinion I have expressed would not be changed': and (iii) 'I can, however, readily imagine a state of circumstances under which a husband might deservedly be punished with the penalty attached to rape' (see pp. 46–55).

60 [1888] 22 Q.B.D. 23, 37.

61 Ibid., pp. 57–8.

62 Ibid., p. 33.

63 [1949] 2 All E.R. 448.

64 Now abolished by the Domestic Proceedings and Magistrates' Courts Act 1978, s. 3 and 'replaced' by personal protection orders (s. 16). We may assume that a rape committed after such an order could be prosecuted.

65 [1949] 2 All E.R. 449.

66 [1954] 2 Q.B. 282.

67 Ibid., p. 290.

68 Ibid., p. 287.

69 Ibid.

70 Scutt, op. cit., p. 263.

71 [1974] 3 All E.R. 663.

72 Ibid., p. 665.

73 Ibid.

74 (1977) 65 Cr. App. Rep. 22.

75 In *Morgan v D.P.P.* [1975] 2 All E.R. 347.

76 J. McFadyen, 'Inter-spousal rape: the need for law reform' in J.M. Eekelaar and S.M. Katz (eds), *Family Violence*, Toronto, Butterworths, 1978, p. 193. Immunity repealed 1983.

77 J.C. Smith and B. Hogan, *Criminal Law*, London, Butterworths, 1983.

78 Ibid., p. 406.

79 See Matrimonial Causes Act 1973, s. 1(2) (b). 79a [1984] Crim. L.R. 111.

80 Weitzman, op. cit., 1974; Weitzman, op. cit., 1981.

81 *Holborn v Holborn* [1947] 1 All E.R. 32.

82 *Foster v Foster* [1921] P. 438.

83 *Hines v Hines* 185 N.W. 91, 92 (1921). See also *Griest v Griest* 140 A. 590, 593

(1928).

84 See *Sheldon v Sheldon* [1966] P. 62.

85 There is one sexual act (buggery) which is a criminal offence for both, even where the wife consents.

86 There is a strong case for replacing it by a form of aggravated assault to reflect the fact that rape is now recognized as a crime of violence rather than one of sex.

87 *Planned Parenthood of Central Missouri v Danforth* (1976) 428 U.S. 52.

88 *Paton v Trustees of BPAS* [1978] 2 All E.R. 987.

89 N.M. Blake, *The Road to Reno: A History of Divorce in the United States*, New York, Macmillan, 1962, p. 108.

90 In *Dunn v Dunn* [1948] 2 All E.R. 822, 823. See also Law Reform (Husband and Wife) Scotland Act 1984, s. 4.

91 O. McGregor, *Divorce in England*, London, Heinemann, 1957, p. 67.

92 Compare R. Parnas, 'Judicial response to intra family violence', *Minnesota Law Review*, vol. 54, 1970, p. 584 with the same writer's view in 1978: R. Parnas, 'The relevance of criminal law to inter-spousal violence' in Eekelaar and Katz (eds), op. cit., p. 188.

93 S. Maidment, 'The law's response to marital violence: a comparison between England and the USA' in Eekelaar and Katz (eds), op. cit., p. 124.

94 House of Commons, *Select Committee on Violence in Marriage*, H.C. 533, 1974–5, London, HMSO.

95 Freeman, *Violence in the Home*, op. cit., 1979, pp. 192–4.

96 South Australian Criminal Law and Penal Methods Reform Committee,

97 J. McFadyen, op. cit., pp. 197–8.

98 L. Davidson and L.K. Gordon, *The Sociology of Gender*, Chicago, Rand McNally, 1979, p. 182.

99 A. Medea and K. Thompson, *Against Rape*, New York, Farrar, Straus and Giroux, 1974, pp. 11–12.

100 *R v Jackson* [1981] 1 Q.B. 671 and *R v Reid* [1972] 2 All E.R. 1350.

101 Theft Act 1968 s. 30.

102 The American Law Institute, Model Penal Code (1980), pt II, vol. 213.6 recommends that the exemption extend to cohabiting couples.

103 See University of Chicago Law Review, Note, vol. 43, 1976, pp. 613–41.

104 The Sexual Offences (Amendment) Act 1976 has made steps in this direction but see Adler, op. cit.

105 See Brownmiller, op. cit. and L.R. Walum, *The Dynamics of Sex and Gender*, Chicago, Rand McNally, 1979, p. 117.

106 See *Hoskyn v Metropolitan Police Commissioner* [1978] 2 All E.R. 136.

107 The Police and Criminal Evidence Bill 1983–4 will do this.

108 See *Bradley v Bradley* [1973] 3 All E.R. 750.

109 V. Binney, G. Harkell and J. Nixon, *Leaving Violent Men*, London, Women's Aid Federation England, 1981.

110 In *G v G* [1924] AC 349, 357.

111 E. Livneh, 'On rape and the sanctity of matrimony', *Israel Law Review*, vol. 2, 1967, pp. 425–22.

112 Swedish Penal Code 1962 Ch. 6 s. 1 (1) and (2).

113 See G. Geis, 'Rape-in-marriage: law and law reform in England, the US and Sweden', *Adelaide Law Review*, vol. 6, 1978, pp. 284–301.

114 *Jerusalem Post*, 'Husband who rapes wife guilty of criminal offence',

26 September 1980.

115 See *HM Advocate v Duffy* [1983] SLT 7.

116 A. Forte, 'Marital rape – a cautionary note', *Law Quarterly Review*, vol. 99, 1983, pp. 513–14.

117 *New York Times*, 3 June 1981, p. 16, col. 1.

118 B. Hoggett and D. Pearl, *The Family, Law and Society*, London, Butterworths, 1983, p. 34.

119 M.D.A. Freeman, 'But if you can't rape your wife who(m) can you rape? The marital rape exemption re-examined', *Family Law Quarterly*, vol. 15, 1981, pp. 1–30.

120 Criminal Law Revision Committee, *Working Paper on Sexual Offences*, London, HMSO, 1980. See J. Temkin, 'Towards a modern law of rape', *Modern Law Review*, vol. 45, 1982, pp. 399–417.

121 Criminal Law Revision Committee, *Sexual Offences*, (15th Report), Cmnd 9213 (1984).

122 L. Gordon, *Woman's Body, Woman's Right*, Harmondsworth, Penguin, 1977, p. 102.

123 V. Bullough, *The Subordinate Sex*, Harmondsworth, Penguin, 1974, p. 328.

124. In *R v Jackson*. See [1891] 1 Q.B. 671.

125 [1972] 2 All E.R. 1350.

126 Matrimonial and Family Proceedings Act 1984, s.1.

Woman-battering, child abuse and social heredity: what is the relationship?*

Evan Stark and Anne Flitcraft

Abstract

This paper explores the relationship between child abuse and woman-battering. In so doing the authors test and reject the hypothesis, common in the violence literature, that 'violence begets violence'. The vast majority of woman-batterers do not come from homes where they were beaten, and the vast majority of men who were beaten as children do not later batter their wives.

Child abuse experts deny the importance of woman-battering. Interventions to stop child abuse focus on changing the 'mother's' behaviour. Wife abuse is, however, the major precipitating context of child abuse. Children whose mothers are battered are more than twice as likely to be physically abused than children whose mothers are not battered. When women are battered and children are abused it is usually the male batterer who is responsible for the maltreatment of the child. In other cases women may turn to child abuse when their own battering is already well-established. Battered women who abuse their children are more likely to be treated punitively than non-battered mothers who treat their children in a similar manner. They are, for instance, more likely to have their children removed.

These findings have important implications for policy. The authors point out that those who are concerned about child abuse 'would do well to look toward advocacy and protection of battered mothers as the best available means to prevent current child abuse as well as child abuse in the future'.

---

* Support for this research was provided by a grant from the National Institute of Mental Health, 'Medical Contexts and Sequelae of Domestic Violence' (MH–30868–01A1) as well as by the Department of Sociology, University of Essex.

Introduction

In previous work we demonstrate that fully 19 per cent of the women presenting with injury to a major metropolitan hospital have a documented history of battering, making battering the single most important context for serious injury to women in the U.S.[1] In addition, a comparison of the complete medical charts of 600 battered and 600 non-battered women revealed a 'battering syndrome' that unfolds over time and includes, in addition to multiple and escalating injury, a disproportionate risk of alcohol and drug abuse, attempted suicide, rape, abortion and miscarriage, mental illness and 'fear of child abuse'. Since this disproportionate risk appears only after battered women present an initial violent episode to the hospital, the psychosocial components of battering are its sequelae, not its precipitants. Extrapolating from the sample data to the medical population as a whole, we hypothesize that physical abuse of women may be the most important stimulus for a number of psychosocial problems, child abuse prominent among them.

The most provocative conclusion in the earlier work is that clinical intervention directly contributes to the progression from an initial incident of abuse to the full-blown syndrome observed on hundreds of adult records. Regardless of whether abuse is recognized as such and irrespective of age, presenting problem, marital status, employment status or race, abused women are significantly more likely to receive pain medication (even when contraindicated by the nature of the injury), to be prescribed major or minor tranquilizers, to be 'sent home' without follow-up, to be labelled and to receive punitive referrals (e.g., mental hospitalization with no indication of psychiatric disease). Content analysis of a hundred complete medical records verified the initial impression.[2] The clinical response helps lock abused women, who seek help from medical and social services, into brutal relationships and a pattern of psychosocial behavior that is destructive to self and others.

To verify that battering is a major source of child abuse, it is necessary to gather information on a population of abused children and their mothers. The purpose of this paper is to review critically the major theories of how the battering of women and child abuse are linked, if at all, and then to present evidence bearing on this link. Part I considers the political context in which child experts have received and adapted the growing evidence that male battering is both a direct and indirect precipitant of child abuse. Part II presents data on the prevalence of child abuse among battered women and on the significance of wife-battering in child abuse. In both sections critical attention is paid to the dominant view in the field, that child abuse and battering are 'inherited' through 'intergenerational transmission'. The original findings presented here are drawn from two target groups, the sample of battered and non-battered women referred to above (the 'trauma sample') and a population of abused children and their mothers.[3] On the basis of earlier analyses of the trauma sample, we hypothesize that purposive violence by male intimates against women is the single most important context for child abuse. If supported, this would challenge the prevailing view of family violence as a by-product of social inheritance and individual pathology. A second hypothesis, also based on the analysis of the trauma sample, is that the way in which child abuse is 'known' and 'treated' contributes to the violent context in which it is evoked.

Part I
The social knowledge of child abuse and woman-battering

'The battered child syndrome'

Medically speaking, a 'syndrome' is a group of concurrent problems which appear to comprise a single clinical entity but for which no single patho-physiological or psychiatric pathway has been identified. To clinicians, the term signifies that diverse medical events are evoked by a single cause, are not independent signals of disease and require no lengthy probe. The approach is pragmatic. Clinicians want to get on with business.

Prior to Kempe's (1962) classic description of child abuse as a 'syndrome', pediatricians often confronted a history of apparently unrelated bruises by resorting to complex blood and metabolic workups in search of a unifying explanation.[4] By stipulating that these bruises and accompanying behavioral and psychological problems such as 'sleep disorders', 'failure to thrive' and 'secretiveness' comprise a 'syndrome' set off by parental assault, Kempe relieved frustration among professionals and facilitated diagnosis and disposition. Ambroise Tardieu, a French professor of legal medicine, described a similar set of symptoms in 1860.[5] And nineteenth-century feminists and welfare reformers like Francis Cobbe and Jane Addams had depicted child abuse, incest and battering in some detail.[6] Even some pediatricians had already pointed to the importance of 'non-accidental injury' among children.[7] What was new, therefore, was not the discovery of child abuse as such but its peculiar dramatization as 'the battered child syndrome' and the apparent readiness of Kempe's clinical audience to admit his image into its reconceptualization of the family as a context for pathology.

The recognition of a child abuse 'syndrome' has significantly contributed to its widespread identification. But it has also had several negative consequences. For one thing, public attention has been increasingly distracted from the non-medical components of child abuse, including the possible malfeasance of the welfare and health establishments. This 'medicalization' process has accompanied a growing public willingness to subject abused children and their mothers to clinical management, although there is little proof that the prospects of either child or mother are improved as a result. For another thing, the consensus that child abuse is a 'syndrome' has led to its widespread treatment as a problem with a single cause and a certain inevitable course but no ongoing logic of determinacy. Child abuse is viewed as a 'moment' (an injury) or as a series of moments, but not as an unfolding process located in identifiable cultural, political and subjective milieus. While the parent's intentionality is acknowledged, it is alternately trivialized by reduction to psychological 'risk factors' or depoliticized by links to environmental conditions such as poverty or class which are too far removed from living history to be meaningful. Thus, the so-called social definitions of child abuse which stress environmental factors give us little more sense of the situational dynamics that produce and perpetuate violence against the young than Kempe's purely clinical description.[8]

The tendency to conceptualize child abuse as a clinical problem primarily transcends important cultural differences in the relative power of organized medicine. In Great Britain and the United States and regardless of whether doctors, psychiatrists, social workers, home visitors or the police are assigned major responsibility for managing the problem, it is the behaviour of 'mothers' that is the universal object of scrutiny. What began as a pragmatic decision to 'treat' a number of coincident childhood problems as interrelated, despite a clear understanding of their links, ends by asking whether the women who bring these children for help are adequate persons or, instead, are 'immature', 'overly aggressive' and 'without impulse control'.

One question is what impact this clinical view of mothers as the key to child abuse has had on the development and prevalence of the problem. A related question involves the political basis from which certain problems such as child abuse, rape or battering come to be defined as clinical 'syndromes'. It is tempting to suggest that the projection of child abuse as a 'syndrome' provides a convenient means for the health and welfare establishment to 'enter' the family and 'police' women's behavior in the home.

The ideology of child abuse and the emergence of woman-battering as an issue

The entire corpus of child abuse literature revolves around two outstanding assumptions, that the mother is ultimately responsible for the child's welfare and that an injury to a child is a primal offense which becomes imprinted on family history and evokes subsequent family misfortunes. These presumptions set the framework for interpreting and conducting research and are themselves largely immune to evidence. In effect, the research and treatment prompted and shaped by these assumptions carry a certain political bias towards women into the world and lend it an aura of scientific legitimacy.

Representative sample surveys have established the fact that fathers are as likely or more likely to abuse children as mothers. An American Humane Society survey (1978) concluded that males were the assailants in 55 per cent of reported cases of child abuse.[9] And Gil estimates that whereas 40 per cent of the children in a national survey were abused by fathers, fathers were responsible for two-thirds of the incidents where men were present.[10] Smaller studies have produced somewhat different results, estimates of child abuse by fathers running as low as 25 per cent.[11] But male violence against children is clearly a serious problem.

Despite this evidence, there is as yet no major study focusing on paternal neglect and/or abuse as an independently motivated social process. In a recent literature survey, Martin identifies only two articles out of seventy-six focusing on men.[12] Almost half of the articles Martin surveys look at women only and the rest consider both parents. In the latter cases, however, women are typically the only source of direct information, little or no attempt is made to control for gender or differentiate parental behavior and/or motivation by sex, and 'abusing parent' is often revealed to be a euphemism for 'mother'. Perhaps more importantly, studies considering both parents tend to have an environmental focus with little interest in the immediate precipitants of violent behavior. By contrast, the closer research comes to clinic populations, the greater the attention paid exclusively to women.[13] In sum, child abuse studies either fail to differentiate by sex or focus on the mother only.

There is no hint in the literature that violence in the family might emanate from a purposive defense of male privilege and authority in the family. Instead, mother is responsible when things go 'wrong'. Of course, this is true of the helping literature more generally. Howell in the U.S. and Oakley in Britain have pointed to the tendency for pediatricians to blame mothers for a range of children's problems.[14] 'Mother' is used in these accounts to describe a role through which women are presumed to express a natural propensity for nurturing. Child abuse is read as a failure of this function. If the father harms the child, this is because the mother is not present when the child returns from school, because adults other than the mother care for the child when ill or because unsatisfactory care arrangements have been made by working mothers.[15] In a London survey, More and Day are more explicit still.

> In the 20 cases where the father or step-father had hit the child, the following pattern emerged. . . . In 7 of these cases, the mother's behavior acted as a trigger for the assault. Either she had provoked her husband in some way and then made sure – perhaps by going out – that the child got the full weight of the anger produced, or she had complained to her husband about the child's behavior (sometimes, perhaps, to take the spotlight off herself in an explosive situation).[16]

Thus, the presentation of problems about which professionals feel they can do little provides an occasion for defining feminine identity and reinforcing women's exclusive responsibilities for social reproduction.

The singular attention to mothering appears even more problematic when euphemisms like 'explosive situation' are replaced with data showing that males not only abuse children but their mothers as well. Throughout the 1970s, the child welfare establishment has felt increasing pressure from researchers and service providers to acknowledge that child abuse is linked to the battering of women.

Elsewhere, we show how the very different political contexts in which battering was discovered in Britain and the U.S. led to different images of its causes and dynamics.[17] But in both the U.S. image of battering as a component of 'the violent family' and the British picture of abuse as one moment in a 'cycle of deprivation', violence against women and against children are linked. This link entered the public imagination through its dramatization in the mass media, e.g. via Erin Pizzey's authentic accounts of her multiproblem clients or the council estate exploits of the BBC's late police captain-turned-social worker Juliet Bravo. Survey data strengthened these images. Thus, psychiatrist J.J. Gayford was able to generate rates of child abuse among battered women simply by posing the question and omitting controls or any other basis for comparison.[18] Gil's more compelling work in the U.S. demonstrated that where a woman was being abused, men were also the child's assailant in 70 per cent of the cases.[19]

Still, what appears to have impressed the child welfare establishment most were the reports of woman-battering from child health providers and case workers, particularly as program funds began to shift from the protection of children exclusively to 'at risk families' and 'abused wives'. For 1977–8, for instance, 20 per cent of the child abuse reports to the American Humane Society were accompanied by descriptions of wife abuse.[20] And in Britain, a 1975 'Memorandum on Battered Wives' by the Royal College of Psychiatrists asserted that child abuse by both parents 'is found in some frequency . . . where the wife is also assaulted'. In both cases, strictly child-oriented efforts were replaced by an integrated 'team' approach.[21]

Although the new attention to the battering of women identified male violence less as a cause of subsequent problems than as part of a complex fabric of pathological behaviors, those whose access to women and families was primarily through children felt their credibility threatened. Beyond this, the new emphasis on the criminality of violence suggested a closer alliance between caseworkers and the police. To defend itself against the growing sentiment that it take a broader approach to maternal and child health, the child welfare establishment appealed to the economic, professional and political self-interest of its constituents. Compared to the significant child-welfare edifice, the institutional response to woman-battering was still embryonic. One policy maker asked:

> Can we assume that new funding on a relatively large scale will be forthcoming? If not, we should [ask] . . . who will [be] winners and who losers, since it will be necessary to redistribute a limited pie. That redistribution will obviously be at the perceived expense of child abuse and neglect agencies.[22]

There were also sound humanitarian and professional reasons to keep the issues of child abuse and wife-battering separate.

> We should ask whether the conceptual joining of these problems is likely to affect . . . the approach to families in which violence occurs. . . . At a time when a concerted effort is underway to move away from a punitive approach to parents who maltreat their children [there is a prevalent view] that violence against spouses is essentially a police problem. . . . Will joining the two issues result in an attitudinal and institutional retrogression to a reliance on punishment?[23]

But these appeals merely rationalized a fundamental political concern which links the child establishment and the liberal welfare state. 'Perhaps,' conceded the Region II Director of the National Center for Child Abuse and Neglect (NCCAN), 'the dynamics of child abuse, wife and husband beating and rape are interrelated in ways that lend themselves to a common form of intervention.' But 'are we prepared to follow the implications of this linkage?' Having taken up the search for links, he warned, 'we are unlikely to end with the intrafamilial dynamics of violence'. The Director continued: 'The discussion will almost certainly be extended to a systematic examination of the social causation of all forms of family violence. For example what role do joblessness and underemployment play in the physical abuse of family members?'[24]

For thousands of state employed mental health workers this suggested that looking beyond childhood injury could open a political Pandora's Box. Besides, added the Director, a comprehensive theory of family violence implied a level of social change that was clearly beyond the scope of the present establishment. In sum, it was unwise, impractical, economically disastrous and even inhumane to add battered women to the spotlight in which the abused child now stood alone. Rarely have policy makers appealed so explicitly for ideology over science.

Despite this resistance, the battered woman's movement, publicists and family researchers evoked images of violence against women that were as inviting to policy-makers, case-workers and the public as the imagery developed around child-saving. As the child-protectionists feared, when the center of concern shifted from innocent children to women who had been victims of male violence, so did funds, media coverage and political interest. Though only slightly less conventional in their view of appropriate family roles, in the U.S. at least, specialists on woman-battering seemed more catholic in their willingness to acknowledge family violence (and even joblessness) in their perspective. Indeed, the link between battering and child abuse was grist for their mill because it proved what American family sociologists Murray Straus, Suzanne Steinmetz and Richard Gelles claimed, that the home was a 'cradle of violence'.[25]

It was amidst the scramble for resources, prestige and public attention that the child abuse experts were forced to come to terms with their competitors in family research and treatment. What is notable is that the accommodation to mounting evidence that violence was aimed at women as well as children was made without compromising a quasi-psychoanalytic and genetic perspective in which the earliest experience of the young is determinant. Whatever other issues still divide the fields of child abuse and battering, there is agreement that violence in the present family is the result of violence (or abuse) in the family of origin, that an injury to a child (whether imprinted through witness or direct assault) is carried from one generation to the next. 'Violence begets violence' claim Straus and his colleagues because of 'social heredity'.[26] Straus writes that 'the idea that child abusing parents were themselves victims of abuse and that wife-beating husbands come from violent families is now widely accepted'.[27] But does this idea have a basis in fact?

Part II
Woman-battering, child abuse and social heredity:
the evidence

Intergenerational violence

The assumption that family pathology derives from a primary wound inflicted on the young is most consistently expressed in the theory of intergenerational violence in which harsh treatment of children is seen as extending across one or more generations.[28] Supportive evidence is offered at two levels: on the childhood experience of woman-batterers and child abusers and on the current penchant for persons who witnessed or suffered childhood abuse to 'transmit' violence to their spouses and/or children.

U.S. hospitals have recorded child abuse since the mid-1960s. But estimates of its general prevalence in the U.S. still vary by a factor of twenty or more, ranging from 2.5 to 4 million cases down to 41,000.[29] There are few longitudinal studies of abused youngsters and none of which we are aware that trace children from violent homes into adult life. Until recently, the belief that woman-batterers and/or child abusers come from violent homes was based exclusively on self-reports from small criminal subgroups, anecdotal information from battered women about their assailants, individual case histories and reports from service providers.

In their book-length summary of a national family violence survey, Straus, Gelles and Steinmetz contend that 'researchers who have studied child abuse find that children who are abused grow up to be abusing parents'.[30] But not one of the studies they cite offers any concrete evidence for intergenerational transmission. Gayford reports that Chiswick residents are beaten by men with 'disturbed or violent childhoods'.[31] But even if such second-hand reports are believed, without baseline data there is no way to tell whether a disturbed childhood is any more likely to lead to battering than any other childhood experience. Other psychiatrists support the thesis by examining prominent murderers such as Charles Manson, presidential assassins, delinquents, and small groups of convicted murderers.[32] Since none of these studies employs controls, establishes representativeness or otherwise establishes the quality of information secured, they become transparent the moment we suspend complete faith in the underlying presumption of inheritance.[33]

Another limit of the available 'proofs' is that the definitions of 'abuse' and 'violence' differ too widely to make studies comparable. One of the most frequently cited authorities on the transmission of violence, Steele, writes that 'the single most common element in the lives of violent or abusive adults is the experience of being neglected or abused to some degree by caretakers during the earliest years'.[34] But by 'abuse' and 'neglect', he means 'lack of empathetic mothering' or, as he puts it elsewhere, 'a variety of less than ideal responses of the caretaker (usually the mother) to the infant which leads to a "lack of confidence" or "trust" in the child as an adult'. However insightful such a reading in a particular case, it is far too ambiguous to provide a useful tool in aggregate analysis.

To their credit, Straus, Gelles and Steinmetz actually compare the reported childhood experience of 'non-violent' adults with the experience reported by current abusers. Since these are the only randomized survey data which support the intergenerational thesis, they bear some critical attention.

On the basis of their national sample of intact couples, Straus, Gelles and Steinmetz conclude that 'the *majority* of today's violent couples are those who were brought up by parents who were violent to each other'.[35] Substantiating information is provided on the prospects of children hit by their parents and on the childhood of current abusers. For example, report the authors, compared to men from non-violent families of origin, men who saw their parents attack each other are three times as likely to 'hit' their wives and ten times more likely to 'abuse' them (e.g. to use weapons as well as fists). Only 2 per cent of the men from non-violent homes hit their wives while fully 20 per cent of the men from the 'most violent' families do so.[36] Even if only children who witnessed 'wife-beating' (hits without punches or weapons) are considered, 10 per cent are violent adults. Conversely, among the 13 per cent who report being hit as teenagers, fully 35 per cent (or 4 per cent of all persons interviewed) now hit their wives. By contrast, only 10.7 per cent of those *not* hit as teenagers are currently abusive.

There is a 'clear trend for violence in childhood to produce violence in adult life'. The data 'provides striking evidence for the idea of social heredity in violence - that violence by parents begets violence in the next generation'.[37]

The limits of the survey instrument - the Conflicts Tactics Scale (CTS) - have been pointed out elsewhere.[38] It equates actual hitting with threats, considers 'acts' irrespective of consequence, makes a number of dubious assumptions about the validity of self-reporting and disregards the possibility that remembering how one was treated as a child may rationalize current beliefs and behaviors. Each bias exaggerates the 'violence' (e.g. threats taken as acts) and any association of violence past and present. But it is impossible to support the authors' conclusions even if the evidence is accepted at face value.

The continuum of violence along which Straus and his colleagues locate their sample is so broad that the vast majority of couples interviewed (63 per cent) fall into the 'violent' group. Since it would be hard to identify a peculiar component of violence among so broad a stratum, the evidence on intergenerational violence is compiled by comparing two extremes, men from 'non-violent' homes (approximately 37 per cent) with the small subgroups of persons who witnessed wife-abuse as children (about 5 per cent) or came from 'the most violent' homes, the 1 per cent of families where weapons as well as kicks and fists were used in spouse abuse. Note, while a boy who witnessed wife-abuse is three times as likely to abuse his wife now, given the relative proportion of children from 'violent' and 'non-violent' homes in the general population (5 per cent to 37 per cent), a current batterer is more than twice as likely to have had a 'non-violent' rather than a 'violent' childhood (7:3) and seven times more likely to have come from a 'non-violent' home than from a home classified as 'most violent'. More to the point, 90 per cent of the children from 'violent' and 80 per cent of the children from the 'most violent', homes are not now currently abusive. At best, social heredity appears a weak medium. The data on the transmission of parent-child violence are less convincing still. For while three times as many men who recall having been hit as teenagers currently abuse their wives than men with 'non-violent' parents, from a consideration of the relative proportions of these groups we learn that for every abuser who has been hit as a youngster, two have not been hit.

Something more than bad sociology is involved here. By inverting the findings, a small group from 'violent' homes appear as a 'majority', and this fabricated 'majority', in turn, appears to automatically produce current battering and child abuse. By equating the relatively small probability that extreme violence in childhood will be followed by adult violence with the absolute likelihood that this 'transmission' will occur, the authors effectively 'normalize' pathology. Meanwhile, we 'forget' that the 'real' majority of 'violent' families is constructed by placing spanking and sibling rivalry on a continuum of violence with homicide. Of course, the implication is that the same controls that might be appropriate to the tiny minority who 'pass on' their violence also suit those who are 'at risk' because of a 'violent' childhood. Compared to the determining power of childhood experience, the real actors and their immediate purposes have little significance. And the key finding of this work – that the vast majority of batterers have neither learned nor inherited their behavior – is lost.

Wife-battering and child abuse

Wife-beating is not typically precipitated by witnessing or suffering childhood abuse. It is possible, however, that batterers with violent childhoods are more likely also to abuse their children and that mothers who abuse their children are also more likely than other mothers to have been abused in their own childhoods, a claim that remains widespread.[39] Comparing abusing and non-abusing parents, Herrenkohl, *et al.* conclude that, while a majority of those who report having been abused as children are *not* now abusive, a majority of the abusive parents (56 per cent) were abused as children.[40] This conclusion rests on a probabalistic association between the degree of current discipline reported ('abusive techniques') and reports of childhood punishment or neglect. Even should this association hold in longitudinal studies or studies employing more rigorous definitions and determinants of childhood experience, there may yet be a common process which constrains certain individuals to learn and/or transmit violence.

While childhood experts insist the child-abusing mother is passing on her own childhood experience, less psychoanalytically-minded students of family violence argue that the abusing mother is more often transmitting the violence suffered from a male intimate. The children, in turn, hit one another and, less often, their parents.[41] Here, although violence against women is acknowledged as widespread, again it is merely a medium through which inherited pathology moves to its current diffusion in 'the violent family', an image which makes an emphasis on the purposive violence of a single party seem sectarian.

The 'second level' of intergenerational transmission is constructed from two dubious claims, that child abuse is typical (or common) in families where women are battered and that in these families the abusing parent is typically 'mother'. If child abuse is relatively rare even where mothers are abused or if fathers typically abuse both children and the children's mothers, then the linkage theory of violence has limited applicability. Even if violence is transmitted across generations only rarely, it is still possible that 'mother' links male violence and child abuse.

It is common knowledge in hospital settings that social workers frequently label and remove children from their homes as protection against brutal males. But battering is rarely mentioned in the child abuse literature. Instead, 'family conflict' is used as a contextual metaphor for everything from frequent arguments to random brutality. Meanwhile, treatment protocols are designed to help the intractable or 'immature' mother who cannot adequately manage 'conflict'.[42]

Comparing only the earliest estimates of child abuse and battering, it appears that their prevalence is similar. But, whereas the initial figures on child abuse greatly exaggerate its incidence (e.g. Gil, 1973), the initial reports from institutions on the incidence of woman-battering underestimate its extent by factors of twenty or more. Prior to the demonstration that fully one women in five presenting with injury had a history of abuse, hospitals in the U.S. estimated that, at most, 1.5 per cent of the emergency patients were abused. In Britain, meanwhile, Dewsbury reported finding only fifteen battered wives among 13,000 'at risk' patients, a rate of only 1.5 per thousand.[43] But more accurate comparisons based on recent survey data suggest that between 3 and 5 million women are battered each year in the U.S. compared to somewhere between 50,000 and 200,000 children.[44] This enormous difference makes the linkage theory suspect.

The trauma sample

To estimate the significance of child abuse as a sequela or coincident of battering, reports of child abuse were compared on the records of 600 battered and 600 non-battered women patients. Whereas child abuse or fear of child abuse is noted among approximately 6 per cent of the battered women, fewer than 1 per cent of the non-battered women appear to be mothers of abused children, a highly significant difference.

Clearly, a report of current child abuse on a woman's record is closely associated with her risk of being battered. But the data also suggest that only one battered woman in sixteen has an abused child, a finding which supports the view that even among battered women,

Evan Stark and Anne Flitcraft

child abuse is relatively uncommon.[45]

The reporting of child abuse or fear of child abuse on an adult record is largely haphazard and provides no definitive picture of how frequently battering and child abuse are associated. Conceivably, for instance, the tendency for physicians to use labels disproportionately to describe battered women also makes them prone to 'see' child abuse where wife abuse exists. Even so, while battered women are 'at risk' for child abuse, there is no evidence that child abuse is a common sequela of battering.

Although few battered women appear to be mothers of abused children, 25 of the 28 mothers of abused children in the trauma sample are battered. Extrapolating to the emergency medical population as a whole suggests that as many as two-thirds of those patients who are mothers of abused children may themselves be battered, making battering the single most common factor to date identified among mothers of abused children. To verify this hypothesis and determine the exact relation between battering and child abuse, we turned to a population of abused children and their mothers.

The child abuse population

At a large metropolitan medical complex in the Eastern U.S., children suspected of being abused or neglected are 'darted' and referred for investigation and disposition to a special hospital 'Dart' Committee. By matching Dart Committee reports on children to the medical records of their mothers and subsequently classifying mothers as battered or non-battered on the basis of a comprehensive trauma screen developed and tested in the 'trauma sample' referred to above, it is possible to determine the significance of battering in families experiencing child abuse, the identity of the abuser, whether mothers who are battered come disproportionately from problem families and whether current dispositions acknowledge and/or respond to the battered mother's predicament.

The *study population* includes the mothers of all children referred to the hospital Dart Committee for suspicion of abuse and/or neglect between July 1977 and June 1978, 116 mothers in all. After classifying the children as either 'abused' or 'neglected', the full medical records of the mothers were examined and each injury in their adult history classified into one of four risk categories as follows.

Positive: record states that the patient's injury was inflicted by a male

160

family member or male intimate.

Probable: record states that the patient was the object of blows – she was hit, kicked, beaten, stabbed, etc. but no personal etiology was indicated and it was *not* a mugging, anonymous assault on the street, a robbery, etc.

Suggestive: alleged etiology did not appear to account for the type, location or severity of the injury.

Negative: the pattern of injury was adequately explained by the recorded etiology. Injuries suffered in assaults described as muggings or anonymous assaults were included in this category.

In turn, the injury visits within each record were aggregated into a single 'trauma history' and each woman was assigned a 'battering risk group' according to the injury indicating the greatest likelihood of battering. For instance, women with at least one 'positive' episode were 'positives'. The analysis of medical records was supplemented by data from family background notes in Dart Committee reports.

Among the 116 women 45 per cent (n=52) had a history indicative of abuse, 25 per cent (n=29) were 'positives', 16 per cent (n=18) were 'probables' and 4 per cent (n=5) were 'suggestives'. An additional 5 per cent (n=6) had a history of 'marital conflict' though neither the trauma history nor other medical information indicated abuse. Fifty per cent (n=58) had no documented trauma history indicating abuse and no record of 'marital conflict'.

Frequency of battering

The first point of note is that the frequency of battering among mothers of abused children is 2.4 times greater than the frequency of battering among women presenting injuries to the surgical service (45 per cent compared to 19 per cent) making this the highest at risk site thus far identified.

The fifty-two women at risk presented a total of 217 injury episodes during their adult histories, for a mean of 4.2 trauma presentations per woman. Positives averaged 4.9 episodes each, probables 3.4 episodes each and suggestives 3.4 episodes each. By contrast, the negatives averaged only 1.1 injury episodes, what one would expect from a 'normal' population (i.e. one visit to an emergency service for injury).

161

Interestingly, the six mothers with a history of 'marital conflict' averaged 1.8 trauma episodes each, falling somewhere between suggestives
and negatives. Conceivably this group constitutes a battering risk
category falling outside the purview of an identification method based
solely on the trauma history. The mean frequency of trauma visits for
abused mothers was lower than the corresponding frequency for battered women identified in the trauma sample (5.7 compared to 4.2),
reflecting the younger average age of abused mothers and the fact
that the trauma sample was drawn only from women who presented at
least one injury episode during the study year. Clearly, however, for
battered mothers as for the battered women identified in the trauma
sample, battering is an ongoing process, not an isolated incident. These
data are illustrated in Table 1.

Table 1: Number of trauma episodes among battered and non-battered
mothers of abused children

Mother's Battering Risk Group	n	Number of Episodes in Risk Group	Mean Number of Trauma Episodes/Woman
Positives	29	143	4.9
Probables	18	61	3.4
Suggestives	5	13	2.6
Total at risk	52	217	4.2
Marital Conflict	6	11	1.8
Negatives	58	64	1.1

Family history

To ascertain whether battered mothers were likely to have a family
history of pathology, as at least some versions of the intergenerational
transmission thesis contend, we compared common indicators of a high
risk family history, alcoholism, violence, 'chaos' or 'disorganization',
suicide attempts and incest. Women with a history of 'marital conflict'
were included with the 'negatives'.

As Table 2 on page 163 shows, a significant subpopulation of
mothers come from high risk families of origin. Notably, however,
abused mothers do not typically come from multi-problem backgrounds, are far less likely to come from a background that includes
incest and/or alcoholism and, perhaps most important, are no more
likely to have a family background that includes violence. In sum, if
anything, battered mothers of abused or neglected children are less

likely than non-battered mothers to have a multi-problem family history.

Table 2: Problems in the family histories of mothers of abused children

Problem	number among mothers in the positive, probable and suggestive risk groups n = 52 (%)	number among mothers in the negative and marital conflict risk groups n = 64 (%)
Alcoholism	6 (12%)	12 (19%)
Violence	9 (17%)	10 (16%)
Suicide attempts	5 (10%)	7 (11%)
Incest	1 (2%)	4 (6%)
Chaotic family	12 (23%)	12 (19%)

Reason for 'dart'

Most children are 'darted' because a clinician feels they are 'at risk' of abuse, are neglected, injured under 'suspicious circumstances' or because the mother needs 'support' to help her cope. As Table 3 on page 164 indicates, only a minority are darted because of documented physical abuse. However, children whose mothers have a positive history of being battered are twice as likely as the children of non-battered mothers to be darted for actual abuse. Interestingly, they are also more likely to be darted because the mother needs help coping ('mother needs support'). At best, this is a tacit recognition of the battered mother's predicament since in almost no instance is 'abuse' or 'battering' actually noted.

The mothers in this study were selected because their children were 'darted' in 1977-8. So it is not surprising that the vast majority of their trauma visits precede the child's referral. For this group, then, battering is clearly the context within which child abuse develops. But it is conceivable that women currently classified as non-battered may be abused in the future.

Identity of the abuser

Dart Committee reports give the identity of the parent allegedly responsible for abusing the child. In families where the mother is battered, the

Table 3: Reasons for 'dart'

Mother's Battering Risk Group	n	Mother Needs Support (%)	Neglect and/or Suspicious Injury (%)	Abuse (%)
Positives	29	15 (50%)	5 (18%)	9 (32%)
Probables	18	6 (33%)	8 (44%)	4 (22%)
Suggestives	5	2 (40%)	2 (40%)	1 (20%)
Total at risk	52	23 (44%)	15 (29%)	14 (27%)
Marital conflict and negatives	64	29 (46%)	23 (35%)	12 (19%)

father or father substitute is more than three times as likely to be the child's abuser than in families of non-battered mothers. Approximately 50 per cent of the children darted among at risk women are abused by the male batterer, 35 per cent are abused by the mother who is also being battered and the rest are abused by others or by 'both'. The numbers here are too small, however, to make generalizations with confidence.

Removal of the child

Among children darted for all reasons, almost one third are removed from homes where mothers are being battered; this is significantly higher than the percentage of children removed for all reasons from families with non-battered mothers. But this may simply reflect the greater likelihood that children of battered mothers will be physically abused. To control for this possibility, we compared the disposition only in cases where the child had been allegedly neglected or where mothers needed support. Here too, if the mother was battered, the child was far more likely to be removed from her home than if she was not.

Summary and conclusions

Evidence is now available to suggest that the physical abuse of women by male intimates is second only to male–male assault as a source of serious injury to adult Americans, affecting somewhere between 3 and 5 million women. There are no comparable data from Britain. By contrast, even the most exaggerated estimates of child abuse indicate it is far less common. In a review of a year's sample of medical records, fully 19 per cent of the women using the emergency service for injury had a history of physical abuse. Further, when 600 battered and 600 non-battered women were compared, the battered women appeared to be at significantly greater risk for child abuse (or fear of child abuse). Although the two groups were similar in age and average number of children, 6 per cent of the battered, but only 1 per cent of the non-battered, women had a report of child abuse on their records. Although there are serious methodological problems in generalizing from this data source, it appears as if battering may be a major precipitant of child abuse.

To test this hypothesis, a population of abused children and their mothers was identified and studied. Of 116 abused or neglected children whose mothers' records were reviewed, 45 per cent were battered and another 5 per cent experienced 'marital conflict' though there was no direct evidence of deliberate injury. The prevalence of battering in this population is greater than in any other group yet identified, including female alcoholics, drug abusers, females who attempt suicide, rape victims, mental patients, women filing for divorce, using the obstetrical service or women presenting with injuries to the emergency service.[46] In all probability, battering is the single most important context for child abuse. It also appears that child abuse is an intermediary point in an unfolding history of battering.

The prevalent wisdom is that battering and child abuse are typically a consequence of intergenerational transmission. Neither these findings nor any other set of findings reviewed to date supports this conclusion. To the contrary, the stimulus to this history of deliberate injury and child abuse appears to be repeated assault by a male intimate, not a personal or familial inheritance of pathology. On the one hand, between 80 per cent and 90 per cent of the woman-batterers identified in a national sample come from 'non-violent' families of origin. On the other hand, the battered mothers of abused children have fewer problems in their families of origin than non-battered mothers. The mothers of abused and neglected children are of two types primarily; those whose 'history' or current socioeconomic milieu is associated with 'child neglect' and those whose battering is either directly linked to the child's physical abuse because the male batterer is the child's assailant, or is indirectly linked because the mother abuses the child after her own battering is well established. Children whose mothers are battered are more than twice as likely to be physically abused than children whose mothers are not battered and the father is the typical

165

abuser of the child if the mother is battered. It is tempting to suggest that the battering of women is the typical context for actual child abuse, not merely its most important context.

To those familiar with the child abuse literature cited above, the clinical response to families where mothers are battered will come as no surprise. Like the literature, the medical records of battered mothers are silent about physical abuse and instead emphasize the mother's failure to fulfill her feminine role (mother needs support in coping). And, again like the child abuse literature, battered mothers are punished because things have gone 'wrong'. Thus, even when we control for the level of danger to the child, battered mothers are more likely to lose their children than non-battered mothers. It is also possible that social workers see mothers from multi-problem family backgrounds as 'neglectful' and are more likely to label their children as a result. Jason, *et al*. find that a number of presumed 'risk factors' for child abuse such as teenage mothers, a focus on infants and an emphasis on mothers as abusing parents are functions of the reporting systems but do not reflect actually documented abuse or neglect.[47] Ironically, despite the demonstrated association here between a multi-problem history and neglect and of current battering of the mother and physical abuse of the child, researchers and practitioners continue to insist that child-abusers, and mothers of abused children in particular, are predisposed by their 'history'. This systematic misreading justifies a pattern of psychiatric and social service intervention while concealing the situational crisis battered mothers confront.

Whatever the rationale for the removal of a child in a particular case, the general reasoning is that the problems thought to cause the child abuse are relatively intractable. For the battered mother, this reasoning can have tragic consequences. It projects an inevitability onto her situation which she may internalize and 'read back' to her helpers through a passive or somatic adaptation to her abuse. While factors such as 'immaturity' or a 'family history of disorganization' *are* relatively unresponsive to current therapeutic modalities, what appears to be the most important factor in these cases, and is arguably the single factor about which something decisive can be done, the mother's battering, is 'overwhelmed' by being set in a field of inherited traits and factors.[48] As a result of this way of interpreting the situation which evokes child abuse, both child and mother may be placed at increased risk. When abused or neglected children are removed from their homes the isolation of the battered woman, hence her vulnerability to attack, is substantially increased. And the batterer, as well as his victim, may read the punitive intervention as acknowledgment that she is 'wrong'.

A lengthy and detailed study of hundreds of battered women using the health services indicated that the ways in which abuse is 'known' and treated contribute to the tragic evolution from abusive injury (hitting or fighting) to a full-fledged 'syndrome' of battering. By selecting such consequences of violence against women as female alcoholism or child abuse as the focus of intervention, defining these problems as the inevitable inheritance of a tragic victim of circumstance and adapting family maintenance strategies to manage the secondary problem, psychiatrists, physicians and social workers made it more difficult for women to extricate themselves from violent relationships than before they sought help. At least one national survey indicates that women hit men as often as they are hit.[49] But there is no evidence whatsoever that men, siblings, grandparents or other family members against whom violence may be directed suffer the pattern of injury and psychosocial problems identified as battering. Nor does battering automatically follow abusive injury for all women. Middle class women may escape this pattern. And Marsden and Owens describe nineteen abused wives in a small English town who exhibit none of the problems evident among the poor and immigrant residents of Chiswick.[50] Indeed, the 'syndrome' of battering observed on hundreds of medical records may be characteristic primarily of urban, minority or working class women who depend on institutionalized therapy or welfare rather than on established networks of family, wealth and kin. In this case, battering would appear to be one consequence of the institutional support given to deliberate male violence when it is used to enforce sexual, class and racial subordination.

Is this same argument applicable to child abuse? Perhaps, but we know too little to say for sure. Still, there is some basis for such an argument. Despite firm evidence that men abuse children as frequently as women and that violence against the mother is the most important context for child abuse, child abuse is widely interpreted as the consequence of 'bad mothering', whether in this generation or the previous one. Regardless of who is abusing the child, experts point to the culture (environment), family background and personality that produce mothers who are 'deficient in social learning', are 'immature' or who have other problems in fulfilling their feminine roles.[51] The ideological thrust of this view is suggested by direct pleas from child policy-makers to set aside evidence that battering and child abuse are linked and to abandon the innovative treatment (and political) strategies that might follow from making such links. The discussion of child abuse is the occasion to legitimate the therapeutic management of female behaviour in the home. The few attempts to assess the situational dynamics surrounding family violence conclude it is 'purposeful behavior that occurs in specific situations' and involves struggles around real material problems such as money, sex, housework, child care and the like.[52] But, apart from the feminist polemics against violence aimed at women, students of child abuse and battering have shunned the possibility that men who batter women and assault children are often consciously defending privileges that they feel are threatened by the growing autonomy of women and the young. It is to this defense of male privilege that the knowledge of child abuse and the treatment strategies that follow appear to lend their weight.

At first, the focus on wife-beating threatened the purely child-centered examination of family problems. But differences between the two emphases were reconciled and the genetic thrust of the child abuse literature was extended through the theory that current family violence is the inheritance of injuries suffered directly or vicariously by the older adult as a child. Not only does this view find little empirical support, but the major data set offered to prove 'social heredity' shows the opposite; that the vast majority of persons from violent childhoods do not become abusive and that the vast majority of woman-batterers (and child abusers) do not come from violent families of origin. To the contrary, as the findings here show, current abuse by a male intimate is the single most important cause and context of child abuse.

The knowledge of child abuse is less a description of events than an intervention designed to shape events along certain lines. And the practical incorporation of this knowledge in social service settings may have tragic consequences for mother and child. The actual consequences of current intervention strategies remain to be carefully studied, however. Nor can we claim that the interventions employed by what is widely thought of as an enlightened child abuse program are common elsewhere. In lieu of further research along these lines, case-workers and clinicians would do well to look toward advocacy and protection of battered mothers as the best available means to prevent current child abuse as well as child abuse in the future.

Notes

1 E. Stark, A. Flitcraft and W. Frazier, 'Medicine and patriarchal violence: the social construction of a private event', *International Journal of Health Services*, 9(3), 1979, pp. 461–93; E. Stark *et al.*, *Wife Abuse in the Medical Setting: An Introduction for Health Personnel*, Washington DC, Monograph No. 7, Office of Domestic Violence, 1981.
2 E. Stark, *The Battering Syndrome: Social Knowledge, Social Therapy and the*

Abuse of Women, PhD Dissertation Department of Sociology, State University of New York, Binghamton, New York, 1984.

3 For a detailed description of the 'trauma sample', see E. Stark, *et al.*, op. cit., 1981.

4 C.H. Kempe, F.H. Silverman, B.F. Steele, *et al.*, 'The battered child syndrome', *Journal of the American Medical Association*, 181, 1962, pp. 17–24.

5 R. Bybee, 'Violence toward youth: a new perspective', *Journal of Social Issues*, 35(2), 1979, pp. 1–15.

6 Francis Power Cobbe, 'Wife torture in England', *Contemporary Review*, London, 1878; Jane Addams, *The Spirit of Youth and the City Streets*, New York, 1923.

7 J. Caffey, 'Multiple fractures in longbones of infants suffering from subdural hematomas', *American Journal of Roentgenology* 56, 1946, pp. 163–73; F. Silverman, 'The roentgen manifestations of unrecognized skeletal trauma in infants', *American Journal of Roentgenology*, 69, 1953, pp. 413–26; E. Elmer, 'Abused young children seen in hospitals', *Social Work*, 5, 1960, pp. 48–102.

8 D. Gil, *Violence Against Children, Physical Child Abuse in the United States*, Cambridge, Mass., Harvard University Press, 1973.

9 American Humane Society, *National Analysis of Official Child Neglect and Abuse Reporting*, Denver, Colorado, AHA, 1978.

10 D. Gil, op. cit., p. 116.

11 E. Baher, *et al.*, *At Risk: An Account of the Work of the Battered Child Research Department*, NSPCC, Boston, Routledge & Kegan Paul, 1976.

12 Judith Martin, 'Maternal and paternal abuse of children: theoretical and research perspectives', in D. Finkelhor *et al.*, (eds), *The Dark Side of Families: Current Family Violence Research*, Beverly Hills, California, Sage Publications, 1983.

13 Martin, op. cit., p. 296.

14 M.C. Howell, 'Pediatricians and mothers', in J. Ehrenreich (ed.), *The Cultural Crisis of Modern Medicine*, New York, Monthly Review Press, 1979; Ann Oakley, 'Wisewoman and medicine man: changes in the management of childbirth' in J. Mitchell and A. Oakley (eds), *The Rights and Wrongs of Women*, London, Penguin, 1976.

15 J. Garbarino and D. Sherman, 'High risk neighborhoods and high risk families: the human ecology of child maltreatment', *Child Development* 51(1), 1980; B.A. Robertson and J.M. Juritz, 'Characteristics of the families of abused children', *Child Abuse and Neglect*, 3, 1979, p. 861.

16 J. More and B. Day, Family interaction associated with abuse of children over 5 years of age', *Child Abuse and Neglect* 3, pp. 391–9. Cited by Martin, op. cit., p. 300.

17 E. Stark and A. Flitcraft, 'Social knowledge, social policy and the abuse of women' in D. Finkelhor *et al.*, (eds) *The Dark Side of Families*, Beverly Hills, California, Sage Publications, 1983.

18 J.J. Gayford, 'Battered Wives', *Medicine, Science and Law*, 15(4), 1975, pp. 237–45.

19 D. Gil, op. cit.

20 American Humane Society, op. cit.

21 American Humane Society, op. cit.; L. Daly, 'Family violence: a psychiatric perspective', *Journal of the Irish Medical Association*, 68(18), 1975, pp. 450–3.

22 National Center on Child Abuse and Neglect, *Child Abuse and Family Violence*, Washington DC, U.S. Children's Bureau, February, 1978, p. 8.

23 Ibid.

24 Ibid.

25 M. Straus and S. Steinmetz, 'The family as a cradle of violence', in S. Steinmetz and M. Straus (eds), *Violence in the Family*, New York, Dodd, Mead and Co., 1974.

26 M. Straus, R. Gelles and S. Steinmetz, *Behind Closed Doors*, New York, Doubleday, 1980.

27 M. Straus, 'Ordinary violence, child abuse and wife beating: what do they have in common?' in D. Finkelhor *et al.*, (eds), op. cit., 1983.

28 For example, see L. Silvers, C. Dublin and R.S. Lourie, 'Does violence breed violence? Contributions from a study of the child abuse syndrome', *American Journal of Psychiatry*, 126(3), 1969, pp. 404–7; J.E. Oliver and J. Cox, 'A family kindred with ill-used children: the burden on the community', *British Journal of Psychiatry*, 123(572), 1973, pp. 81–90; D.A. Freedman, 'The battering parent and his child: a study in early object relations', *International Review of Psychoanalysis* 2(2), 1975, pp. 189–98.

29 Gil, op. cit.; M. Straus and R. Gelles, 'Violence in the family', *Journal of Social Issues*, 35(2), 1979, pp. 15–40; S. Cohen and A. Sussman, 'The incidence of child abuse in the United States', *Child Welfare*, 54, 1975, pp. 432–43.

30 Straus, *et al.*, op. cit., 1980, p. 74.

31 Gayford, op. cit.

32 See, for example, A. Solnit, J. Goldstein and A. Freud, *Beyond the Best Interest of the Child*, New Haven, Conn., Yale University Press, 1977; A. Button, 'Some antecedents of felonious and delinquent behaviour', *Journal of Clinical Child Psychology*, 2, Fall 1973, pp. 35–8; R.S. Welsh, 'Severe parental punishment and delinquency: a developmental theory', *Journal of Child Clinical Psychology*, 35(1), 1976, pp. 17–21.

33 Palmer, like Gillen, finds that killers experienced more frequent and severe violence as children than their brothers who did not go on to commit homicide. Even assuming a large enough sample to establish the significance of observed differences, the incredible disproportion between the number of children who become murderers and the number who experience some violence in their childhood suggests how strained causal arguments based on this sort of evidence become. J.L. Gillen, *The Wisconsin Prisoner: Studies in Criminogenesis*, Madison, Wis., University of Wisconsin Press, 1946 and S. Palmer, *The Psychology of Murder*, New York, Thomas Cromwell, 1962.

34 B.F. Steele, 'Violence within the family' in R.E. Helfer and C.H. Kempe (eds), *Child Abuse and Neglect: The Family and the Community*, Cambridge, Mass., Ballinger Co., 1976.

35 Straus, Gelles and Steinmetz, op. cit., 1980, p. 100.

36 Ibid.

37 Ibid., p. 113.

38 R.E. Dobash and R. Dobash, *Violence Against Wives*, Glencoe, Illinois, Free Press, 1979.

39 Silvers, op. cit.; Oliver and Cox, op. cit.

40 Ellen C. Herrenkohl, R.C. Herrenkohl and L.J. Toedter, 'Perspectives on the intergenerational transmission of abuse', in D. Finkelhor *et al.* (eds),

The Dark Side of Families, op. cit., 1983.

41 Straus, Gelles and Steinmetz, op. cit., 1980.

42 Martin, op. cit., Carolyn Kott Washburne, 'A feminist analysis of child abuse and neglect', in D. Finkelhor *et al.* (eds), *The Dark Side of Families*, op. cit., 1983.

43 A.R. Dewsbury, 'Battered wives: family violence seen in general practice', *Royal Society of Health Journal*, 95(6), 1975, pp. 290–4.

44 Stark and Flitcraft, op. cit., 1979; C.H. Kempe and R. Helfer (eds), *Helping the Battered Child and his Family*, Philadelphia, J.B. Lippincott, 1972; R. Light, 'Abused and neglected children in America: a study of alternative policies', *Harvard Educational Review*, 43, 1973, pp. 556–98.

45 The impact of battering on children extends beyond direct physical abuse, of course, and includes numerous psychological and somatic problems (from nightmares, respiratory distress and bed-wetting through poor school performance). Beyond this, numerous writers report an increased risk of battering during pregnancy. In a study of women using a major medical obstetrical service, we discovered that fully 25 per cent of the patients had a documented history of ongoing abuse. Whether or not this constitutes 'child abuse' as such, violence against pregnant women is often aimed at the unborn child.

46 Stark and Flitcraft, op. cit., 1979; Stark, *et al.*, op. cit., 1981; Stark, op. cit., 1984; B.P. Post, S. Back and G. Darcy, 'Victims of domestic violence: a preliminary study of battered and non-battered women psychiatric patients', University of Colorado School of Medicine, unpublished paper, 1979.

47 Janine Jason *et al.*, 'Child abuse in Georgia: a method to evaluate risk factors and reporter bias', *American Journal of Public Health* 72 (12), 1972, pp. 1353–8.

48 J.G. Moore, 'The yo-yo syndrome: a matter for interdisciplinary concern', *Science, Medicine and the Law*, 15(4), 1975, pp. 234–6.

49 Lenore Walker, *The Battered Woman*, New York, Harper and Row, 1979. See also paper by Pagelow in this Monograph.

50 D. Marsden and David Owens, 'The Jekyll and Hyde marriages', *New Society*, 8 May 1975.

51 Moore, op. cit.; Gayford, op. cit.; B. Star, C. Clark and K. Goetz, 'Psychosocial aspects of wife-battering', *Social Casework*, October 1979, pp. 479–85.

52 E. Marx, *Social Context of Violence Behaviour – A Social Anthropological Study in an Israeli Immigrant Town*, London, Routledge & Kegan Paul, 1976; Dobash and Dobash, op. cit.

The 'battered husband syndrome': social problem or much ado about little?*

Mildred Daley Pagelow

Abstract

The newly recognized social problem of wife-beating quickly became clouded by confusion over the introduction of the idea of a 'battered husband syndrome'. The media immediately sensationalized the idea, because the concept of men suffering physical abuse at the hands of the 'little woman' is contrary to role expectations. This article examines the data, statements and generalizations upon which the claims were based. There is not enough scientifically sound empirical evidence to support the notion of a battered husband syndrome, although most of the general public is not aware of that. Much of the evidence put forward for the argument was taken out of context, data were added, altered, or eliminated, and generalizations were introduced as fact. Other evidence that the overwhelming proportion of victims of violence are women was ignored. However, the divisive question of male versus female victims hampered efforts to increase the funding and provision of other resources to female victims of family violence, and the debate tended to trivialize their demands for civil rights.

When the problem of violence between spouses first caught the attention of social scientists and began to be researched, the primary focus of concern was centered on battered women because of their over-

* Sincere thanks to Marilynne Brandon Hampton, Maurice Jackson, Jacqueline Wiseman, and especially Malcolm Spector who read earlier drafts of this paper and gave helpful advice, criticisms and suggestions. They all assisted in the shape and focus of this paper, but the responsibility for the final product lies with the author. The nucleus of this article was a paper presented at the 9th World Congress of Sociology, Uppsala, Sweden, and at the annual meeting of the Society for the Study of Social Problems in San Francisco, U.S.A.

representation in the victim category and the special factors that tended to keep them there.[1] While some writers were describing wife-beating as the most under-reported crime in the nation, a few other voices began to be heard making counter claims. Shortly after the American public became aware of the fact that many women are repeatedly beaten by their husbands, some voices raised the issue of 'husband battering', which was next proclaimed to be the 'most under-reported' type of family violence. Two sources quote sociologist Suzanne Steinmetz[2] as saying: 'The most unreported crime is not wife beating – it's husband beating.' Thus, the newly emerging social problem of woman battering became clouded by confusion over the introduction of the notion of 'husband battering' by a few individuals. Steinmetz, a member of the Straus *et al.*[3] research team, wrote a number of articles about a 'battered husband syndrome' that received worldwide media publicity.[4]

It began in 1977, during a scholarly meeting, when Steinmetz presented a paper entitled 'The battered husband syndrome', a title she later used for an article.[5] She proposed looking at 'the other side of the coin'[6] and apparently claimed that her research findings indicate that 250,000 American husbands are battered by their wives each year. The very idea of husband battering seemed to titillate the collective imagination of the mass media. *Time Magazine*, which never devoted more than a few inches of column space to battered wives, published a full page on 'The battered husbands'.[7] It refers to Steinmetz's book and states: 'Extrapolating from her studies of domestic quarreling in Delaware's New Castle County, she estimates that each year at least 250,000 American husbands are severely thrashed by their wives.'[8]

Large and small newspapers across the United States ran articles on battered husbands,[9] using headlines such as, 'Who struck Jane . . . or John?'[10] The *Chicago Daily News* reported that the 'Husband is more battered spouse',[11] and later a *Chicago Sun Times* article stated: 'Husbands are victims of physical assaults as often as wives, according to a study funded by the National Institute for Mental Health.'[12] Fascinated reporters and national television talk-show hosts latched onto the topic and telecast interviews from coast to coast, and eventually the claim of 250,000 battered husbands exploded into 12 million battered husbands,[13] and spread internationally. Headlines in a Norwegian newspaper article referred to Steinmetz's research and told readers about '12 million battered American husbands'.[14] Officials in Finland were concerned about what provisions should be made to accommodate male victims of spouse abuse in proposed shelters for battered wives.[15] The media continued to show great interest in the 'other side of the

173

coin' and husband battering was paraded before the public just as Steinmetz averred 'the horrors of wife-beating are paraded before the public'.[16]

News of the 'battered husband syndrome' penetrated policy-making circles, and at the U.S. Commission on Civil Rights consultation on 'Battered Women: Issues of Public Policy', the idea was both publicly and privately denounced by many participants as a divisive and destructive tactic.[17] At Congressional hearings on proposed legislation, witnesses carefully chose words describing battered women as 'battered spouses',[18] and substituted the term 'domestic violence' for 'wife-beating, because political acumen indicated that identifying a social problem as a 'woman's issue' meant sure defeat for their goals. One sociologist notes, 'Until the mid-1970s, "domestic violence" meant riots and terrorism. . .'[19] A national organization for professionals, the Sociologists for Women in Society, unanimously adopted a resolution calling it a 'pseudo issue of battered husbands'.[20] Yet the image of thousands, perhaps millions, of husbands suffering as much as wives appeared to trivialize the issue and minimize the needs of battered wives, sometimes resulting in withdrawal of funding. At a White House meeting on family violence in 1978, one woman reported that her group was refused funding for a shelter for battered women and their children on the basis of 'discrimination against men' because the group were unprepared and unequipped to offer identical shelter and services to battered husbands. According to Fields and Kirchner, specialists in family and divorce law:

> Steinmetz's essay on violence against husbands is filled with baseless conjecture which gives substance to what had been a latent backlash against the movement to aid battered wives. The press has made much of her inaccurate conclusion that wives are 'slightly higher in almost all categories' of violence than husbands. In Chicago this incorrect statement was used to defeat efforts to obtain funding for a shelter for battered women and their children.[21]

Examining the claims

It is unclear how Steinmetz arrived at the estimation of 250,000 battered husbands that has been quoted so frequently, but it seems to have occurred in the following manner. From her Delaware sample of fifty-seven intact couples with two children, Steinmetz identified four wives as victims of serious assault.[22] Based on an estimated county population of 94,000 couples, and converting to rates per 100,000, she calculated that this represented 7,016 female victims per 100,000 population. Then comparing her own data against police reports of twenty-six cases of spouse assault (twenty-four women victims and two men victims), and calculating that 'only about one out of 270 incidents of wife-beating are ever reported to the authorities', she concludes:

> Although there were no husbands as victims of serious assault among the study population, in two of the cases reported to the police, the victim was the husband. If the same degree of underreporting was present for husbands, then one could suspect that 540 incidents (574/100,000) occurred in New Castle County during 1975.[23]

This may be how Steinmetz generalized *unreported* cases of husband battering in one county to 47 million couples nationwide, arriving at an estimated figure of 250,000 battered husbands in the United States.[24] This is despite the fact that she failed to find even *one* battered husband in her own 'stratified quota sample of normal American families'.[25]

The table provided by Steinmetz[26] to support her argument is both incomplete and inaccurate. Three categories of the most potentially dangerous types of violence, all of which were engaged in more by men than by women, were omitted.[27] These were: 'beat up spouse', 'push down', and 'choke', Fields and Kirchner object to the discrepancies, saying:

> Steinmetz indulges in a little flim-flam when she presents her version of 'Table1'. . . . The Straus *et al.* data even as set forth on Steinmetz's 'Table 1' do not, as she asserts, show wives to be higher in 'almost all' of the seven categories of violence she presents. . . . When the omitted category, 'beat up spouse' is included, the figures show that husbands exceed wives in the most serious types of violence, 'beat up spouse' and 'used knife or gun'.[28]

In addition, one category was added to Steinmetz's own study which only husbands engaged in – the potentially very dangerous act of 'used knife or gun' – but this item was not in her original reference source.[29] Figures from the reference sources also differ from the table Steinmetz later constructed: the table in her original report of her own study[30] shows a sample size of forty-nine, which changed to fifty-four in the article,[31] a 10 per cent increase in number of respondents. Also, there was an almost 50 per cent increase in the rate of wives 'pushing, shoving and grabbing', because Steinmetz's original report[32] shows that 22 per cent of the wives reported these acts, but the table presented later indicates that 32 per cent of the wives reported such behavior.[33] It should be noted that this category, by virtue of the increase to 32 per cent, is the *only category* in which her own sample wives exceeded husbands in violence - by one per cent. Finally, the data from two other studies included in the table came from Steinmetz's secondary analysis of a small sample of Canadian college students and a 'broad-based non-representative group'.[34]

In sum, the data Steinmetz provided simply do not agree with her claim that 'not only the percentage of wives having used physical violence often exceeds that of the husbands, but that wives also exceed husbands in the frequency with which these acts occur'.[35] Conversely, they argue against these claims, despite the fact that some figures were removed, some were added and others were changed.[36] But there were other kinds of 'evidence' used by Steinmetz to support the notion of a battered husband 'syndrome', such as her references to comic strip characters like 'Maggie and Jiggs' and the 'Katzenjammer Kids', as reflecting 'common family situations'.[37]

Another repeatedly used piece of evidence was a single case taken from a newspaper article about a man severely beaten by his wife.[38] The victim in this instance was a 'wealthy, elderly New York banker' who won a separation from his younger wife by producing evidence of extreme cruelty. Historian Pleck and her colleagues note that economic incentives of divorcing men may lead some to report falsely victimization or to 'overcome their reasons not to report. . .'.[39] Other writers[40] also point out that there may be economic motives for publicly disclosing private shame and embarrassment (which Steinmetz claims keeps battered husbands from reporting). Fields and Kirchner explain that New York state law requires that 'a person must have certain specified complaints about his or her spouse' - which includes cruelty - and so:

> It is in the husband's pecuniary interest to show his wife is guilty of marital fault so that he will not have to pay alimony or give her a share of the property. Even if husbands are shy about voicing complaints as Steinmetz suggests, their lawyers' prodding and their financial self-interest overcome any tendency toward reticence when the husband has a complaint to use in the economic struggle.[41]

Paradoxically, when Steinmetz was presenting the idea of a 'syndrome', besides talking about comic strip characters and newspaper items about a rich old man, she also drew on accounts of the punishment historically meted out to 'a husband who allowed his wife to beat him'.[42] The fact is, a husband beaten by his wife was (and still is) an anomaly, and it was precisely because such events were departures from the general rule that they were mentioned in the book she cited. Pleck *et al*. note that Steinmetz neglected to state that the examples she used were presented by the author as 'conspicuous exceptions to the far more prevalent pattern of wife-beating'.[43]

Finally, Steinmetz points to the classic study on criminal homicide by criminologist Wolfgang.[44] Various statements made by Steinmetz[45] claim that wives are as violent as husbands because there was 'virtually no difference between the percentage of husbands or wives who were offenders' in the Wolfgang study. More recent statistics show that out of 1,814 spouse murders[46] in 1980, 1,027 victims, or 57 per cent, were wives killed by husbands.[47]

Pleck *et al*.[48] respond that Steinmetz overlooks the fact that wives are 'seven times more likely to have murdered in self-defense', and that she avoids the association between excessive violence and spouse slayings found by Wolfgang[49] who points out that: 'Husbands killed their wives violently in *significantly* greater proportion than did wives who killed their husbands.' Violent homicide is defined as 'severe degrees of violence in which more than five acts are involved. . .'.[50]

Probably the most important, and most publicized, contribution Wolfgang's study made to our understanding of homicide was his introducing the concept of *victim precipitation*.[51] Fields and Kirchner's critique of Steinmetz's claims states that: 'Analysis of spouse murders show . . . that wives kill husbands who have a history of beating them, although husbands kill wives without provocation.'[52] Wolfgang not only found that husbands were significantly more likely to have precipitated their own murders than their wives,[53] but he also says:

> The number of wives killed by their husbands constitutes 41 per cent of all women killed, whereas husbands slain by their wives make up only 11 per cent of all men killed. . . . Husbands are often killed by their wives in the kitchen with a butcher knife, but nearly half of the wives are slain in the bedroom.[54]

Steinmetz's claims rest in large part on the study in which she was a co-researcher under principal investigator Murray Straus, who says this about the national study: 'These data do not tell us what proportion of the violent acts by wives were in response to blows initiated by husbands. Wolfgang's data on husband-wife homicide suggests that this is an important factor.'[55] Yet the Straus *et al.* study[56] is the main source of estimations of husband-battering. In this study, a nationally representative sample of 2,143 persons living in intact marital relationships were administered the Conflict Tactics (CT) scales.[57] The survey instrument asked about conflicts between family members in the previous year. Conflict resolution was measured on a continuum from non-violent tactics (calm discussion) to most violent ('used a knife or gun'). The Straus *et al.* research team categorized eight acts ranging on the continuum as 'violent', and five of these acts were categorized as 'severe violence'. Thus it was the researchers' judgment, not their respondents, that defined what was violent and what was not.[58]

Using the CT scales, various types of intrafamily violence reported by one adult member of each family were recorded including husband to wife and wife to husband.[59] This obtained a numerical count of the frequency of violent acts in one year as noted by Safilios-Rothschild,[60] but there was no substantive measure of events preceding or following each act, the intensity of the blows or the severity of injuries (if any) sustained, and the meanings attached to these acts by both the aggressors and the victims. The categories are not mutually exclusive;[61] for example: 'Threw or smashed or hit or kicked something', 'Kicked, bit, or hit with a fist', or 'Hit or tried to hit with something'.[62] There is an important different between hitting and trying to hit, yet reports on these responses subsume both in the category 'hit'.

A limitation to the Straus *et al.*[63] survey is its primary focus on acts committed only in the previous year, 1975. Straus[64] admits that violence occurring at any time prior to that one year received very slight attention in his study, yet these acts may have great significance for the duration of a couple's relationship. Straus explains:

> Unfortunately, our data for events before the year of the survey do not distinguish between who was the assailant and who was the victim. . . . In some cases it was a single slap or a single beating. However, there are several reasons why even a single beating is important. . . . It often takes only one such event to fix the balance of power in a family for many years – perhaps for a lifetime.[65]

There are a number of drawbacks to the questionnaire used in this large survey, some of which were pointed out by the principal investigator and the research team.[66] Critics note some serious methodological problems of survey research in general and limitations imposed by any forced-choice scale, but their major complaints center on theoretical assumptions and conclusions drawn by the research team based on their questionnaire data.[67]

Yet Straus *et al.*[68] claim that violence rates were almost equal for all couples: 12.1 per cent of the husbands attacked their wives and 11.6 per cent of the wives attacked their husbands during the year covered by the survey. Their report states that 4.6 per cent of the acts by wives were included in the husband-beating index, therefore 'That is over 2 million very violent wives'.[69] They cite three other studies done by each investigator separately[70] that 'also found high rates of husband-beating'.[71] A recent article in *Time Magazine*[72] credits Murray Straus with saying that he estimates that 282,000 men are beaten by their wives each year, offering his support to Steinmetz's earlier claims. This latest statement raises questions, in view of Straus's earlier statements. He had written several articles[73] warning about the likelihood of bias in the data of his national study resulting from over and under reporting by respondents, and pointing out the differences (not measured by the CT scale) in severity of injury and lack of alternatives for wives. For example, referring to the national study,[74] Straus explicitly states:

> Although these findings show high rates of violence *by wives*, this should not divert attention from the need to give primary attention to wives as victims as the immediate focus of social policy. There are a number of reasons for this. . . . In short wives are victimized by violence in the family to a much greater extent than are husbands and should therefore be the focus of the most immediate remedial steps.[75]

Examination of the evidence

There was a prompt and forceful response to the notion of a 'battered husband syndrome' by a number of other researchers who largely denounced it as 'much ado about little'.[76] Many others addressed the question of whether or not there is such a thing as a 'battered husband syndrome'.[77] Almost all writers who discuss the question of wife abuse versus husband abuse come to the conclusion that the proportion of male victims is minuscule compared to female victims; even when men stay in violent relationships they have a wider range of alternatives available than women; and there is no way to determine how many wives' attacks are self-defense or victim precipitated. It is known that when battered women do strike back, they tend to use objects or potentially lethal weapons as 'equalizers'.[78]

Of *all* crimes of violence, violence against women by men is approximately six times greater than that of women against men.[79] As assistant district attorney of Milwaukee County, Charles Schudson[80] handled hundreds of spouse abuse cases and only one of these included a battered man. In 1977, Minnesota was one of the first states to require data collection on woman-battering from every medical and law enforcement agency in the state. The following year the law was amended, requiring data analysis and a report on the feasibility of creating shelters and social service programs for men, similar to the ones provided for women.[81] Over 4,000 reports were received in an 8.5-month period, but a data collection form to obtain background information on abused men and on the services needed by them was utilized throughout the state only for the reporting period of 1 July to 15 November 1978. During those weeks, there were 966 reports, 95 per cent of which were incidents of assault on women by men with whom they were or had been residing.[82] The other five per cent consisted of male assault victims who ranged in age from eleven to eighty-seven years old; 50 per cent were twenty-nine years old or younger. They continued to collect data and estimated 86,945 assaults by males on their female partners over a two-year period; out of 3,900 reports in 1981, 3,737 were reports of males battering females, and 163 (four per cent) were reports of females battering males.[83]

As noted earlier, Steinmetz[84] found that out of twenty-six cases of spouse abuse reported in one year in New Castle County, Delaware, two (7.6 per cent) of the victims were male, which is almost double the Milwaukee percentage. Her own data still show that 92.4 per cent of the victims were female, which does not substantiate her idea that wives are as violent as husbands or that there is a 'battered husband syndrome'. Nevertheless, in an effort to determine how frequently women and men turn to social service agencies for victim assistance, an informal survey was taken of a variety of community agencies for this information.[85] Table 1 on pages 182–3 shows that regardless of the source, in no instance does the male victimization rate match or exceed the police rates reported by Steinmetz.[86]

The seven sources at the top of Table 1 supplied the data directly, while the last four were published sources. The percentages of males seeking assistance ranged from 1 per cent or less at nine agencies, 4 per cent at the Fremont Police Department Victim Services, and 7.6 per cent in the New Castle County Police Department reported by Steinmetz. It should be noted that the total number of victims reported by each agency is considerably higher than the few from the Delaware county, which may have biased the data. There are three other sources for statistics on divorce clients who claim abuse by their spouses, and all report that three per cent of the men accused their wives of physical abuse.[87] On the basis of this evidence, it seems safe to assume that about 3 to 4 per cent of husbands are abused by their wives.

Dobash and Dobash[88] provide solid evidence on the relative violence of women and men in society and in the family. Gathering data from police and court records in one year, they found 2,872 cases involving violence in which the sex of victim and offender were known, and males were the offenders in 91.4 per cent of the cases.[89] A study in the United States [90] shows that males were offenders in 91 per cent of the cases. The data from Scotland and the United States are strikingly similar: women in both countries were offenders less than 10 per cent of the time, and they were victims in 39 to 45 per cent of the cases respectively in the two studies. The only large difference is in the percentage of American women arrested for violence against a male victim, which is almost twice the Scotland charges (6.4 per cent compared to 3.5), and female to female violence is less in the United States sample than the Scotland sample.[91] Moreover, when the Dobashes narrowed their inquiry into all cases of violence between family members, they found an even larger differential between males as offenders and females as victims. There were 898 cases involving violence between family members (all assaults on spouses, children, siblings, and parents), and Dobash and Dobash say: 'These data reveal that violence occurring between family members almost always involved male offenders and female victims, a pattern which prevailed in almost 94 per cent of the cases.'[92] Among offenders, males comprised 97.4 per cent compared to 2.6 per cent female offenders.

Other researchers who have concentrated on wife-abuse insist that wives are victims in the vast majority of cases. For example, Walker[93] estimates that one out of every two women is beaten at some point in her life by a man within the context of an intimate relationship, but that is based on her experience as a counselor and observations from her studies on woman-battering, not from a representative sample of wives. On the other hand, Russell[94] obtained a representative random sample of women in the San Francisco, California area, and out of the 644 ever-married women in her sample, 21 per cent reported that they had been beaten by husbands at least once. It was the women themselves who defined 'violence' in response to the question, *'Was your husband (or ex-husband) ever physically violent with you?'*[95] Their definitions of violence were restricted to the more severe levels (slapping, hitting, beating); the minimal levels of force (being pushed, pinned, held down, or struggled with) were not defined by these respondents as 'violence'. Russell[96] notes several reasons why the

Table 1: Social service agencies available for victim services, victimization category and clients served

Time Period	Place and Source of Data	Victimization Category	Number Victims Total	Number Victims Males	Per cent Male Victims
9 months	Assault Crisis Center Ann Arbor, Michigan Kathleen J. Fojtik	Spouse Abuse	404	2	.005
3.5 years	Victims Advocate Program Dade County, Florida Catherine G. Lynch, Director	Documented Spouse Abuse	346	0	.000
1 year	District Attorney's Office San Luis Obispo, California Alan Bond, District Attorney	Spouse Abuse	72	1	.010
3 months	Victim Services, Fremont Police Department, Calif. Donna Hamilton, Victim Services Representative	Battery: Men–Women, Intimate Relationships	70	3	.043
9 months	WomenShelter Long Beach, California Geraldine Stahley, Director	Spouse Abuse	700+	0	.000
13 months	Harbor Area YWCA, San Pedro, California Martha Prumers, Director	Assistance: All Types	1,900+	1	.000

Table 1 (continued)

Time Period	Place and Source of Data	Victimization Category	Number Victims		Per cent Male Victims
			Total	Males	
1 year	A Southern Calif. County Marilynne Brandon Hampton	Specifically Spouse Abuse	278	2*	.007*
6 months	Crisis Centers, New York City Public Hospitals (Fields and Kirchner, 1978:3)	Medical Treatment for Spouse Abuse	490	2	.004
10 years	Miami Florida Mental Health Services Dr Tom Cahill (Storch, 1978:G16)	Battered Spouses Spouses	2,000	0	.000
unknown	Citizens Dispute Settlement Program, Dade County, Florida F. Morgenroth (Storch, 1978:G16)	Battered Spouses	1,750	3	.002
1 year	New Castle County Police (Steinmetz, 1977a:65)	Serious Family Assaults	26	2	.076

*not thoroughly documented

Source: Pagelow, 'Social learning theory and sex roles: violence begins in the home', paper presented at the annual meeting of the Society for the Study of Social Problems, 1978.

violence rates would have been higher for her sample if techniques similar to the Straus *et al.* study had been employed.

Frieze[97] attempted to obtain a control group for her sample of battered women by sampling women living in their same neighborhoods in Pittsburgh, Pennsylvania, matching them on socioeconomic status, ethnicity and age. After the interviews were completed, she found that 34 per cent of the control sample had been physically assaulted by their husbands.[98]

Researchers have found that violence within marriages tends to escalate over time in intensity and frequency;[99] and sometimes this escalation continues[100] after the relationship has been severed. Some spouses become violent only *after* wives declare their intentions of severing the relationships, which can be a very crucial and dangerous period of time. Some men are literally obsessed with the idea that 'if I can't have you, nobody can!' and become extremely violent, even to the point of murder.[101] The Straus *et al.* study did not tap violence during or after the severance of relationships because it was limited to couples cohabiting during the interview,[102] and the refusal rate was 35 per cent,[103] which could have eliminated the most violent families from their sample.

Almost all studies of marital violence involved interviews with one or other spouse, but not couples. Szinovacz conducted one of the very few studies that included *both* husband and wife; she used a modified CT scale and found that spouses tended to disagree considerably on the occurrence and frequency of violent behaviors.[104] This study adds further evidence to the methodological inadequacy of the Straus *et al.*[105] study and support to the Dobash and Dobash[106] contention that there are ambiguities in the forced-choice responses of the CT scale and that scale items should be mutually exclusive. Szinovacz found that no husbands admitted to 'kicking, biting, or hitting' their wives, but that some wives reported that their husbands engaged in these acts. The researcher assumes that husbands may be unwilling to admit to 'feminine' behavior such as kicking and biting, even if they had done so. In the test for scale item reliability and concurrent validity, aggregate data were compared with couple data, and both response inconsistency and biases were discovered; Szinovacz concludes:

> *Aggregate data* (i.e., data based on husbands and wives from *different* marriages) may eliminate distortions in the data that are due to the reliance on one selected group of respondents, but they cannot replace or serve as a substitute for *couple data* (i.e., data based on husbands and wives from the *same* marriage).[107]

Response inconsistency in couple data is very common,[108] but Szinovacz found clear evidence that 'aggregate husband–wife comparisons [as used in the Straus *et al.* study,[109]] are inadequate for concurrent validity estimates and that only couple comparisons . . . ought to be used for this purpose'.[110] Comparing couple data to aggregate data, Szinovacz[111] found 50 per cent more violence by husbands and 20 per cent more violence by wives; it appears that men and women view violent behavior differently:

> [T]hey may very well differ in their definition of violence and accordingly report or fail to report especially minor forms of violence. Thus, husbands may not report or even recall some violent acts by their wives because they did not take these behaviors seriously[112]

Adler[113] also interviewed couples and found approximately equal acts of violence reported by husbands and wives, but while the wives tended to take their husbands' (or their own) violence seriously, many of the husbands saw their wives' violence as ineffective and/or non-threatening. These men perceived their wives' serious attempts to hurt them as amusing or, at most, annoying. One husband is quoted as saying, 'she can beat me all over my head and it won't hurt me',[114] but his wife said: 'I hit him a couple of times in the arm. And as he stood there laughing at me I belted him a couple of times; I belted him again. I felt better after. He laughed. He thought it was hilarious.'[115] Adler notes that the husband added that the episode did not bother him, but his wife hurt her hand and she was so upset she cried.

Analysis of the 'battered husband syndrome'

It is doubtful if there is a 'battered husband syndrome', although evidence indicates that perhaps 3 to 4 per cent of husbands suffer abuse from their wives, but whether the abuse is primary or secondary we have no way of knowing at this time. On the other hand, if we hold our definition of wife-beating to mostly one-directional, repeated beatings (secondary battering), a conservative estimate probably ranges between Russell's[116] under-reported 21 per cent and Frieze's[117] 35 per cent. It is likely that between 25 and 35 per cent of all women in the United States are beaten at least once during the course of intimate relationships, and it would be higher if ex-husbands and ex-lovers were included.[118]

Undoubtedly, many women are violent, and some of them are extremely violent, and can create an environment of real fear and danger for their husbands. There is not sufficient scientific evidence of a large-scale 'syndrome' that compares to the evidence of a widespread and serious battered wife problem, yet there must be many husbands who have been beaten severely by their wives more than once, but who remain for various reasons. Proportionately, a few men are the vulnerable elderly, frail, physically handicapped,[119] or muscularly weaker than their wives. If these men are unfortunate enough to have violent wives, they may be unable to defend themselves or prevent the violence. Although the idea was bandied about that old men are frequently beaten by their much younger and stronger wives, statistics show that it is relatively rare for husbands and wives to have great age differentials. A population report states: 'among married men age 45 and over, only about 1 in 900 had a wife under age 25'.[120] As mentioned earlier, data on battered husbands collected in one state found that half of the men who complained of abuse by wives were under 30 years old, and only three of the men were sixty-five or older.[121]

The vast majority of men are not *physically* or *economically* restrained from walking out of the front door and never returning if and when their wives become violent. Men are, on average, larger and muscularly stronger than women, so if they choose to strike back they can do greater physical harm than is done to them; they can non-violently protect themselves from physical harm; or they can leave the premises without being forcibly restrained.

There are other factors besides the average man's superior size, weight, and muscular strength that mitigate against their being helpless victims of violent wives. Due to the design of men's clothing, they are more likely to carry their wallets containing cash, identification and credit cards on their person, for a hasty exit, than women, who may have to search around for their purses (or have them snatched away when they attempt to flee). If there is any operable motor vehicle available, a man is more likely to have the keys in his possession, or to be physically capable of taking them despite resistance. Even in the case of a vengeful wife who disables the family car to prevent her husband's quick departure, a man is more likely to know how to replace battery cables or distributor wires than a woman in a similar position.

Why then would an able-bodied man remain with a violent wife after being subjected to physical abuse? There are many reasons why a man may stay after one violent episode, but few reasons that can adequately explain why a man would stay until he was subjected to the repeated episodes of increasing violence that many battered wives are unable to prevent or leave. Some men remain for the same reasons most women do not leave after the first assault: the spouse is truly contrite and loving afterward; love for the abuser, the behavior is excused by circumstances, e.g., stress, alcohol and so forth; the abuser has many other positive features; unwillingness to expose private embarrassment to family and friends; the investment made in the relationship; and the children. But among men who remain after an initial attack (primary battering), and stay after the violence has been repeated (secondary battering),[122] their reasons often center on issues such as material and economic concerns, psychological dependency, and fear for safety of the children. These factors indicate a need battered husbands have for legal and psychological counseling, rather than the varied needs of battered wives, the most important of which is usually safety for themselves and often their children. Data obtained from abused husbands confirm that the primary service needs of assaulted men were support groups and counseling, and legal services.[123] One battered husband expressed his situation in these terms:

'She was the first woman I ever loved, and I did love her! There were many nice things about her: she was smart, she was fun to be with, and she was a wonderful mother to our two little girls. But she could be mean as hell, and she'd hit me with anything she got her hands on. I just tried to protect myself – I never could really let her have it – no matter what. But finally, I had enough, and I just took a walk and never went back, except to see my girls. [Weren't you afraid she would hurt them? Is that why you stayed?] No, I knew she'd never touch them, she was always good to them; I didn't have to worry about them. But then she got married again, and they were both into drugs, and one night she killed him. I tell you, she was *mean*!'

This man was undoubtedly a victim of abuse by a very violent woman, but his case differs in important ways from the experiences of many battered women who are unable to 'walk' and never go back. Wives may be physically restrained from leaving or have to leave when the abuser is not around; they usually take their children with them; they may not have transportation, employment or other source of income; and they usually fear that their abusers will find them and either harm them more or force them to return. This battered husband knew that he could strike back or leave whenever he was ready: he had a job, a car, money of his own, and no fear of being followed and forcibly returned. The decision was his to make. His psychological and physical scars remain, but he is totally free from his abusive spouse.

Social learning theory leads to the conclusion that husband abuse is mainly psychological rather than physical, because physical abuse by wives is much less likely to be rewarded, given the usual differential in physical prowess plus the cultural approval of male violence. When abuse by wives is physical, the kinds of assistance battered husbands need are more limited than the needs of battered wives, but they are available and the men must take the initiative and search out the kinds of help they need. The preponderance of scientific evidence leads to the conclusion that the vast majority of victims of spousal violence are females, whether wives or lovers. *Most importantly*, in the years *since 1977 when the image of the 'battered husband syndrome' was publicized, there has not been a single report of scientific research on a sample of battered husbands.*

In sum, there undoubtedly are many violent wives and some battered husbands, but the proportion of systematically abused husbands compared to abused wives is relatively small, and certainly the phenomenon does not amount to a 'syndrome' as popularized.

Discussion

This paper attempted to set the record straight on the subject of the 'battered husband syndrome'. It was apparent from the start that the mass media gave extremely wide distribution to one small tidbit of social science research, but the general public, being unable to discriminate between rigorously designed and conducted social scientific research and sensationalism, largely accepted some claims as 'scientific fact'. It should be clear that the original claims were based on data that were seriously biased and misinterpreted and baseless conjecture was introduced as fact. Other scholars' works were used selectively so that any finding or conclusion that would weaken the case being built was omitted.

Claims based on a national survey are also flawed and contradictory. That study attempted to objectively measure *all* types of conflict in the family with a forced-choice instrument containing scale items that are not mutually exclusive, and to measure only acts that were used for the purpose of conflict resolution (theoretically excluding non-purposeful violent acts of 'expressive' violence). The study had breadth but little depth: the scale was incapable of measuring some violent acts, their subjective meanings to the actors, and end results of violent acts. Some very violent people may have been excluded due to the survey design (intact couple families only) and among those who refused to participate. Reports do not distinguish between attempts and completed acts, and data on 'husbands' and 'wives' are aggregated, rather than couple data, which is inadequate for concurrent validity estimates.

To its credit, the social science community responded vigorously to attack and counteract the damage from the claims and assertions of a few. Hopefully, the final word has been said about a battered husband 'syndrome', and more research will add greater depth to our understanding of violence between intimates. Researchers would do well to heed the advice of Dobash and Dobash (1979) who insist that marital violence can only be understood by taking into consideration events surrounding violent episodes and the social, historical, institutional processes, and cultural beliefs and ideals of the environment in which they occur.

Notes

1 See, for example, R.E. Dobash and R.P. Dobash, 'The importance of historical and contemporary context in understanding marital violence', paper presented at the annual meeting of the American Sociology Association, 1976; S.E. Eisenberg and P.L. Micklow, 'The assaulted wife: "catch 22" revisited', *Women's Rights Law Reporter*, March 1977, pp. 161–83; J. Flynn, P. Anderson, B. Coleman, M. Finn, C. Moeller, H. Nodel, R. Novara, C. Turner and H. Weiss, *Spouse Assault: Its Dimensions and Characteristics in Kalamazoo County, Michigan*, School of Social Work, Western Michigan University, 1975; D. Martin, *Battered Wives*, San Francisco, Glide, 1976; M.D. Pagelow, 'Preliminary report on battered women', paper presented at the Second International Symposium on Victimology, 1976; M.A. Straus, 'Sexual inequality, cultural norms, and wife beating' in E.C. Viano (ed.), *Victims and Society*, Washington D.C., Visage Press, 1976, pp. 543–9; M.A. Straus, 'Wife beating: how common and why?', *Victimology*, vol. 2, no. 3/4, 1978, pp. 443–58.

2 R. Langley and R.C. Levy, *Wife Beating: The Silent Crisis*, New York, E.P. Dutton, 1977, p. 187; *Time Magazine*, 'The battered husbands', 20 March 1978, p. 69.

3 M.A. Straus, R. Gelles and S. Steinmetz, *Behind Closed Doors: Violence in the American Family*, New York, Doubleday, 1980.

4 S. Steinmetz, 'Wifebeating, husbandbeating – a comparison of the use of physical violence between spouses to resolve marital fights', in M. Roy (ed.), *Battered Women*, New York, Van Nostrand Reinhold, 1977, pp. 63–72; S. Steinmetz, 'The battered husband syndrome', *Victimology*, vol. 2, no. 3/4, 1978, pp. 499–509; S. Steinmetz, 'Women and violence: victims and perpetrators', *American Journal of Psychotherapy*, vol. 34, no. 3, 1980, pp. 334–50.

5 Steinmetz, op. cit., 1978.

6 Ibid., p. 499. Steinmetz, op. cit., 1977, p. 64

7 *Time Magazine*, op. cit., p. 69.

8 Ibid.

9 *San Gabriel Valley Tribune*, 'Not only wives: study shows husbands battered too', 29 January 1978, p. 5.

10 *Los Angeles Times*, 'Who struck Jane . . . or John?', 12 February 1978, p. 20.

11 *Chicago Daily News*, 'Husband is more battered spouse', 31 August 1977, p. 3.

12 *Chicago Sun Times*, 'Some statistics in the battle of the sexes', 5 February 1978, p. 3.

13 G. Storch, 'Claim of 12 million battered husbands takes a beating', *Miami Herald*, 23 April, 1978, p. 16.

14 Newspaper clipping provided and translated by Asta Magni Lykkjen, Oslo, Norway, 21 August 1978.

15 Discussed during a private conversation with Pirkko Lahti, Helsinki, Finland, 7 August 1978.

16 Steinmetz, op. cit., 1978, p. 499.

17 L. Leghorn, 'Grass roots services for battered women: a model for long-term change', in *Battered Women: Issues of Public Policy*, Washington D.C., U.S. Commission on Civil Rights, 1978, pp. 138–42 and pp. 444–62.

18 M.D. Pagelow, 'Testimony' in *Domestic Violence*, Hearings before the Subcommittee on Select Education of the Committee on Education and Labor, House of Representatives, Ninety-Fifth Congress, Second Session, Washington, D.C., U.S. Government Printing Office, 1978, pp. 268–71.

19 K.J. Tierney, 'The battered women movement and the creation of the wife beating problem', *Social Problems*, vol. 29, no. 3, 1982, pp. 207-20.

20 M.D. Pagelow, 'Victimization in the home: an overview of current research and community services with some suggestions on filling unmet needs', in *Domestic Violence*, Hearings before the Subcommittee on Select Education of the Committee on Education and Labor, House of Representatives, Ninety-Fifth Congress, Second Session, Washington, D.C., U.S. Government Printing Office, 1978, pp. 272–91.

21 M.D. Fields and R.M. Kirchner, 'Battered women are still in need: a reply to Steinmetz', *Victimology*, vol. 3, no. 1/2, 1978, pp. 216–22.

22 S. Steinmetz, *The Cycle of Violence: Assertive, Aggressive and Abusive Family Interaction*, New York, Praeger, 1977.

23 Steinmetz, 'Wifebeating, husbandbeating. . . ' , op. cit., 1977, p. 33.

24 Perhaps another method was employed but the writer has been unable to deduce it any other way from available printed sources.

25 Steinmetz, 'Wifebeating, husbandbeating. . . ' , op. cit., 1977, p. 7. In summary, the estimation of 250,000 battered husbands may have been arrived at in the following manner: extrapolating results from her own New Castle County study, comparing these figures with police reports of serious family assaults in the same year, obtaining an incidence rate based on county population, estimating the rate of under-reporting, and then generalizing this rate to the national population of 47 million couples.

26 Steinmetz, op. cit., 1978, p. 502.

27 M.D. Pagelow, 'Social learning theory and sex roles: violence begins in the home', paper presented at the annual meeting of the Society for the Study of Social Problems, 1978.

28 Fields and Kirchner, op. cit., p. 216.

29 S. Steinmetz, *The Cycle of Violence* . . . , op. cit., 1977, p. 89.
30 Ibid.
31 Steinmetz, op. cit., 1978, p. 502.
32 Steinmetz, *The Cycle of Violence* . . . , op. cit., 1977, p. 89.
33 Steinmetz, op. cit., 1978, p. 502.
34 Ibid., p. 501.
35 Ibid., p. 503.
36 Pagelow, 'Social learning theory and sex roles . . . ' , op. cit., 1978.
37 S. Steinmetz, 'Violence between family members', *Marriage and Family Review*, vol. 1, no. 3, 1978, pp. 1-16.
38 Steinmetz, 'Wifebeating, husbandbeating. . . ' , op. cit., 1977, p. 69; Steinmetz, *The Cycle of Violence*. . . , op. cit., 1977, p. 90; Steinmetz, 'The battered husband syndrome', op. cit., 1978, p. 505.
39 E. Pleck, J.H. Pleck, M. Grossman and P.B. Bart, 'The battered data syndrome: a comment on Steinmetz's article', *Victimology*, vol. 2, no. 3/4, 1978, pp. 680-3.
40 Fields and Kirchner, op. cit.
41 Ibid., p. 53.
42 Steinmetz, 'The battered husband syndrome', op. cit., 1978, p. 499.
43 Pleck *et al.*, op. cit., p. 682.
44 M.E. Wolfgang, *Patterns in Criminal Homicide*, Philadelphia, University of Pennsylvania, 1958.
45 Steinmetz, 'Wifebeating, husbandbeating. . . ' , op. cit., 1977, p. 69; Steinmetz, *The Cycle of Violence*. . . , op. cit., 1977, p. 90; Steinmetz, 'The battered husband syndrome', op. cit., 1978, p. 505.
46 For a more extensive discussion of spousal homicide, see the author's forthcoming book, *Family Violence*, to be published by Praeger Special Studies in 1984.
47 T.J. Flanagan and M. McLeod (eds), *Sourcebook of Criminal Justice Statistics - 1982*, U.S. Department of Justice, Bureau of Justice Statistics, Washington, D.C., U.S. Government Printing Office, 1983.
48 Pleck *et al.*, op. cit., p. 682.
49 Wolfgang, op. cit., 1958, p. 214.
50 Ibid., p. 252.
51 Ibid., p. 252.
52 Fields and Kirchner, op. cit., p. 219.
53 M.E. Wolfgang, 'Victim-precipitated criminal homicide' in M. Wolfgang (ed.), *Studies in Homicide*, New York, Harper and Row, 1967, p. 82.
52 M.E. Wolfgang, 'A sociological analysis of criminal homicide' in M. Wolfgang (ed.), *Studies in Homicide*, New York, Harper and Row, 1967, p. 23.
53 Straus, op. cit., 1978, p. 449.
56 Straus *et al.*, op. cit.
57 Ibid., pp. 24-6.
58 K.J. Ferraro, 'Definitional problems in wife battering', paper presented at the annual meeting of the Pacific Sociological Association, 1979.
59 Straus *et al.*, op. cit.
60 C. Safilios-Rothschild, Excerpts from her presentation at the Ninth World Congress of Sociology, Uppsala, Sweden, 1978.
61 R.E. Dobash and R.P. Dobash, *Violence Against Wives: A Case Against the Patriarchy*, New York, Free Press, 1979.

62 Straus *et al.*, op. cit., p. 254.
63 Straus *et al.*, op. cit.
64 Straus, op. cit., 1978.
65 Ibid., p. 446.
66 Ibid., p. 447; Straus *et al.*, op. cit., pp. 27–8.
67 Dobash and Dobash, op. cit., 1979; J.B. Fleming, *Stopping Wife Abuse: A Guide to the Emotional, Psychological and Legal Implications for the Abused Woman and Those Helping Her*, Garden City, Anchor Press, 1979; M.D. Pagelow, *Woman-Battering: Victims and Their Experiences*, Beverly Hills, Sage, 1981; Pleck *et al.*, op. cit.; L.E. Walker, *The Battered Woman*, New York, Harper Colophon, 1979.
68 Straus *et al.*, op. cit., p. 36.
69 Ibid., p. 41.
70 R.J. Gelles, *The Violent Home: A Study of Physical Aggression Between Husbands and Wives*, Beverly Hill, Sage, 1974; Steinmetz, 'Wifebeating, husbandbeating. . . ' , op. cit., 1977; M.A. Straus, 'Leveling, civility and violence in the family', *Journal of Marriage and the Family*, vol. 36, February 1974, pp. 13–29.
71 Straus *et al.*, op. cit., p. 41.
72 J. O'Reilly, 'Wife beating: the silent crime', *Time Magazine*, 5 September 1983, pp. 23–4 and 26.
73 Straus, op. cit., 1976; Straus, op. cit., 1978; M.A. Straus, 'Social stress and marital violence in a national sample of American families', *Annals New York Academy of Sciences*, no. 347, 1980, pp. 229–50; M.A. Straus, 'Ordinary violence versus child abuse and wife beating: what do they have in common?', paper presented at the National Conference for Family Violence Researchers, 1981. This article has since been published in D. Finkelhor, R.J. Gelles, G.T. Hotaling and M.A. Straus (eds), *The Dark Side of Families*, Beverly Hills, Sage, 1983, pp. 17–28.
74 Straus *et al.*, op. cit.
75 Straus, op. cit., 1978, pp. 448–9.
76 R.E. Dobash and R.P. Dobash, 'Wives: the "appropriate" victims of marital violence', *Victimology*, vol. 2, no. 3/4, 1978, pp. 426–42; Fields and Kirchner, op. cit.; Pagelow, 'Victimization in the home. . . ', op. cit., 1978; Pagelow, 'Social learning theory and sex roles. . . ' , op. cit., 1978; Pleck *et al.*, op. cit.
77 S. Abrams, 'The battered husband bandwagon', *Seven Days*, 1978, p. 20; E.S. Adler, 'The underside of married life: power, influence and violence', paper presented at the annual meeting of the American Sociological Association, 1977; E.R. Barnett, C.B. Pittman, C.K. Ragan and M.K. Salus, *Family Violence: Intervention Strategies*, U.S. Department of Health and Human Services, Washington, D.C., U.S. Government Printing Office, 1980; R.A. Berk, S.F. Berk, D.R. Loseke and D. Rauma, 'Mutual combat and other family myths' in D. Finkelhor, R.J. Gelles, G.J. Hotaling, M.A. Straus (eds), *The Dark Side of Families*, Beverly Hills, Sage, 1983; I.H. Frieze, D. Bar-Tal, J.S. Carroll (eds), *New Approaches to Social Problems*, San Francisco, Josey-Bass, 1979, pp. 79–108; N. Jaffe, 'Assaults on women: rape and wife beatings', Public Affairs Pamphlet no. 579, New York Public Affairs Committee 1980; J.A. Marquardt and C. Cox, 'Violence against wives: expected effects of Utah's spouse abuse act', *Journal of Contemporary*

Law, vol. 5, Spring 1979, pp. 277–92; B. Star, 'Patterns in family violence', *Social Casework*, vol. 61, no. 6, 1980, pp. 339–46.

78 R. Dobash, 'Battered women in defense of self defense', *Spare Rib*, June 1980, pp. 52–4; N. Fiora-Gormally, 'Battered wives who kill. Double standard out of court, single standard in?', *Law and Human Behaviour*, vol. 2, no. 2, 1978, pp. 133–65; T.L. Fromson, 'The case for legal remedies for abused woman', *New York University Review of Law and Social Change*, vol. 6, no. 2, 1977, pp. 135–74; T. Lewin, 'When victims kill', *National Law Journal*, vol. 2, no. 7, 1979, pp. 2–4, 11; Martin, op. cit.; M.H. Mitchell, 'Does wife abuse justify homicide?', *Wayne Law Review*, vol. 24, no. 5, 1978, pp. 1705–31; N. Wolfe, 'Victim provocation: the battered wife and legal definition of self-defense', *Sociological Symposium*, vol. 25, Winter 1979, pp. 98–118.

79 D.J. Mulvihill and M.M. Tumin, *Crimes of Violence*, a staff report submitted to the National Commission on the Causes and Prevention of Violence, vols 11, 12, 13, Washington, D.C., U.S. Government Printing Office, 1969, pp. 210–15.

80 C. Schudson, telephone interview.

81 Minnesota Department of Corrections, *Report to the Legislature*, St Paul, 1979.

82 Ibid., p. 58.

83 C.R. Watkins, *Victims, Aggressors and the Family Secret: An Exploration into Family Violence*, St Paul, Minnesota Department of Public Welfare, 1982.

84 Steinmetz, 'Wifebeating, husbandbeating. . . ' , op. cit., 1977.

85 Pagelow, 'Social learning theory and sex roles. . . ' , op. cit., 1978.

86 Steinmetz, 'Wifebeating, husbandbeating. . . ' , op. cit., 1977, p. 65.

87 Fields and Kirchner, op. cit.; G. Levinger, 'Physical abuse among applicants for divorce', in S. Steinmetz and M.A. Straus (eds), *Violence in the Family*, New York, Harper and Row, pp. 85–8; J.E. O'Brien, 'Violence in divorce prone families', *Journal of Marriage and the Family*, November 1971, pp. 692–8.

88 Dobash abd Dobash, op. cit., 1978.

89 Ibid., pp. 435–6.

90 Mulvihill and Tumin, op. cit.

91 Perhaps some of the higher rate of American women's aggression against male victims is a reflection of the easy availability of firearms in the United States, which tends to lessen size, weight and muscle differentials. By contrast, guns are much more difficult to obtain in Scotland and Great Britain, and they are not to be found in approximately one out of every two homes as they are in the United States.

92 Dobash and Dobash, op. cit., 1978, p. 436.

93 Walker, op. cit.

94 Russell, op. cit.

95 Ibid., p. 89.

96 Ibid., pp. 96–7.

97 I.H. Frieze, 'Causes and consequences of marital rape', paper presented at the annual meeting of the American Psychological Association, 1980.

98 Ibid., p. 10.

99 Dobash and Dobash, op. cit., 1979; Pagelow, op. cit., 1981; Straus *et al.*, op. cit.

100 M.D. Fields, 'Does this vow include wife beating?', *Human Rights*, vol. 7, no. 20, 1978, pp. 40–5; Fiora-Gormally, op. cit.; Lewin, op. cit.; M.D. Pagelow, 'Does the law protect the rights of battered women? Some research notes', paper presented at the annual meeting of the Law and Society Association and the ISA Research Committee on the Sociology of Law, 1980; Pagelow, op. cit., 1981.

101 K. Gepfert, 'Mother shot dead in front of 2 children', *Los Angeles Times*, 24 May 1979, pp. 1, 12; 'Reporter to be arraigned in stabbing death of wife', *Los Angeles Times*, 28 May 1979.

102 Straus *et al.*, op. cit., p. 35.

103 Ibid., p. 25.

104 M.E. Szinovacz, 'Using couple data as a methodological tool: the case of marital violence', *Journal of Marriage and the Family*, vol. 45, no. 3, 1983, p. 641.

105 Straus *et al.*, op. cit.

106 Dobash and Dobash, op. cit., 1979.

107 Szinovacz, op. cit., p. 632.

108 J. Bohemeier and P. Monroe, 'Continued reliance on one respondent in family decision-making studies: a content analysis', *Journal of Marriage and the Family*, vol. 45, no. 3, 1983, pp. 645–52.

109 Straus *et al.*, op. cit.

110 Szinovacz, op. cit., p. 642.

111 Ibid., p. 643.

112 Ibid., p. 642.

113 E.S. Adler, 'The underside of married life: power, influence and violence', in L.H. Bowker (ed.), *Women and Crime in America*, New York, Macmillan, 1981, pp. 300–19.

114 Ibid., p. 313.

115 Ibid.

116 Russell, op. cit.

117 Frieze, op. cit., 1980.

118 Pagelow, op. cit., 1984.

119 Although some who proposed the idea of widespread husband-battering included in their list of potential victims men who are physically handicapped or incapacitated, there were two wives in the writer's study who were beaten and abused by husbands confined to wheelchairs and suffering from degenerative, incurable diseases. To most people this may seem preposterous, yet the children who came with their mothers to a shelter provided full verbal accounts of lives of terror and dictatorial domination by two fathers who, apparently, were tyrants. The psychological abuse these families suffered apparently made them so fearful of being locked in rooms, whipped with belts, and so forth, that they failed to see the relative physical weakness of their abusers. The notion of helpless old men being battered by much younger wives was also raised and this undoubtedly does occur, but in the writer's study there was one eighty-one-year-old man who psychologically terrorized and physically abused his sixty-five-year-old wife. There seem to be unusual cases on both sides of the debate.

120 S.W. Rawlings, *Perspectives on American Husbands and Wives*, U.S. Department of Commerce, Bureau of the Census, Washington, D.C., U.S. Government Printing Office, 1978, p. 4.

121 Minnesota Department of Corrections, op. cit., p. 58.
122 Pagelow, op. cit., 1981.
123 Minnesota Department of Corrections, op. cit., p. 60.

DATE DUE